\

April Was Here

Leaving My Mark

By

April O'Brien

Dedication

This book is dedicated to all young survivors, and to my sisters and brothers, I love you all. In loving memory of my children, Katrina Michelle and Michael Anthony, I miss you so. To Kevin, how do I thank you for saving my life? Kindness is your one defining characteristic.

Screaming on the inside

My name is April, I am fifteen years old, and I am up a huge tree. I am clinging precariously to a branch that is hanging about 15 feet off the ground. I am screaming frantically and crying uncontrollably, because I am witnessing my little sister Shelly being ripped apart by a ferocious grizzly bear.

I am hanging onto a branch just out of the bear's reach, screaming Shelley's name as I try hopelessly to reach for her. I can almost grab her hand at one point, but not quite. Her cries and screams tear at my heart as she keeps reaching for me. She is only six years old, and there is nothing I can do to help her.

I am hoping for someone to help us, but there is no one. I keep screaming as the bear continues ripping my sister apart. I yank branches off the tree and throw them down at the bear, but it is like throwing toothpicks at him. His attention is not on me, but on one of the things I love. The feeling of helplessness is overwhelming. Shelley screams my name, and then all goes silent. The growling and grunting of the bear and my incessant screaming are all that's left.

Her parents were old beyond their years because of the hard life they had lived. My mom wanted out; to a place she had seen in magazines or heard about from other people her age. She had no one to tell her she had worth or potential, because my grandparents had never been taught that themselves.

My mom grew up in a hard place where poverty doesn't breed hope. She was young and beautiful, but a lost seventeen-year-old thinking her ability to attract men was her way out. She married a good looking young boy, himself only nineteen, hoping he was the answer to her problems, but running from your problems doesn't always work; not without knowing what you're running from, or where you're running to. Of course, her life didn't get any better or even change very much. Marriage wasn't the cure-all she had thought it would be. Of course, no one could tell her anything, and that would be something she had to learn for herself.

The realization came too late, because she had me at seventeen, so now she was really stuck. Like quicksand, the harder you struggle to get free, the deeper you go.

What is that saying? "The rich get richer, while the poor have babies!" Well, my family was proving that saying to be true, because at the same time my mom was pregnant with me, her mother, my grandmother, was having another baby of her own. Yes! After raising three children almost to adulthood, my grandmother had my aunt Kari Jo when she was forty-seven years old, just five months before my mom had me. "The poor have babies."

Now, my grandma was a *real* grandma. She was pudgy, toothless, and white headed. She only had four different dresses that all looked pretty much alike. She sure could cook, though; she made the best fried chicken or fried catfish with cream pie. Every meal was served with homemade jelly, fresh sliced tomatoes - and love. I remember the smells of her cooking so well.

For some reason, I don't know exactly why, but my grandmother breastfed me right along beside her new baby. I bonded with my grandmother, and I guess for a while I sort of had two moms and a sister because Kari Jo and I were so close in age.

I was always with my grandparents and Kari Jo, so it was like we were sisters. For a very short time, I had my dad, who was just a teenager, and my grandpa in my life, too.

My dad was young and wild, and he wasn't really around much, even back then. My grandfather was a sad person because he was very ill. As long as I can remember, he didn't have any teeth and had to walk using crutches. He had worked for the mines back when they sustained the area, but he had fallen down a fifty-foot mine shaft, which had permanently injured him. Grandpa ended up having one foot that just hung there and didn't function.

Of course, back then, and especially there, no one was liable for anything like they are today. No one took care of him or gave him disability. I think he got Social Security of about two hundred fifty dollars a month, and that was it. Any additional income he had at all was from horse trading; that's not actually trading horses, but everything else you could think of, such as guns, boat motors, trailers, washers, or anything else you could trade, fix or sell. Besides trading, he was an excellent fisherman and gardener, and he hunted squirrel, rabbit and deer.

My grandpa drove an old pick up. He called it his "pick-em-up-truck." It had a clutch, and he used his crutch just like a leg. He used it to push the clutch down on the truck, push the boat off the bank of the river, or reach up and shake cherries down from a tree. He was very resourceful, but he had to be; he had no choice. I remember how he could even use his crutch to shoot his rifle. Grandpa would balance the gun on it or use it to sight in on something. He did all of it as well as any man that had two functioning arms and legs could. Grandpa was a very interesting man. He had ridden a motorcycle in one of those metal balls at the carnival back when he was younger. Even though he could also curse up a storm, it never bothered me because I loved my grandma and grandpa very much.

Thank God my grandparents were there, because my mom was still a child herself and didn't want to be tied to me. They had a toddler of their own, so it was no big deal that I was there all of the time. My poor grandparents, by the time they were in their mid-forties, they both had gray hair, no teeth, and were old beyond their years, dirt poor and with two little babies to take care of.

Soon, my mom was going to change all of that. She was on her way to having another baby, making it three. Yep! At nineteen, she had my little brother David. After she had David, she kept me at home with her a lot more so I could help out. I remember when I was only three, she told me to go and get her a diaper for the baby. We, of course, didn't use disposable diapers back then. I went to the other room and got her a diaper. I brought it out, eager to please, proudly handing her the diaper. She looked at the diaper and then slapped me across the face. She said, "Go get me another diaper. This one has a hole in it. This should be used for a dish rag!" I walked back to the other room, my enthusiasm gone and my ear hurting, but my heart was hurting much worse than my ear. I got another diaper and returned it to my mom, who yanked it out of my hand without any kindness.

In my mother's eyes, her life was stifling, and she saw us as the ties that bind. As I would realize later, I was the first tie. The rest were incidental.

By now, my mom was twenty with two small children, but she had bigger problems than that. My dad, now twenty-two, had been imprisoned for stealing a car, taking a minor across the state line, and blowing up a gas station or something like that. Anyway, he was sent to the state penitentiary. My mom divorced my dad while he was in "Big Mac", the state pen, then we were back to just the three of us. I was always in charge of my little brother David, because my mom had a new job. She worked really hard trying to find us another daddy, one that was not in prison. Well, before I was three and David was one, she found us one! From what I remember and have been told, he was a very nice man, and oh so steady; he had a steady paycheck, and he was in the Air Force, so he had benefits, too. Best of all, she seemed happy with him, and he truly seemed to care about me and David. Things were looking up. Of course, I was still getting those diapers, only now I was changing them as well. It was a good thing. I was going to need the practice, because before long my mom and new daddy were going to have a new baby of their own.

Who knows how life might have turned out if things would have been different? We only get what is, not what could have been. Bill, the good daddy, the providing daddy, the loving daddy, was coming home from the Air Force base one night. It was a sixty-mile drive, and he was driving two of his buddy's home to their families for a three-day weekend. They had just come off a forty-eight hour guard duty stint. They stopped and had a beer on the way home. The lack of sleep, the beer and the sixty-mile drive would prove fatal. He wrecked the car and was killed instantly.

They said he fell asleep at the wheel and was thrown from the car, hitting a construction barrel. It was a military funeral with a closed casket, I remember it well. They played Taps and folded a big flag into a triangle before handing it to my mom. Soldiers shot off seven guns three times, and every time they did my mom would jump. I remember that so vividly.

I was sad, even though I did not realize the finality of what had happened. I knew I didn't see the nice daddy anymore.

So now we were three again, with one on the way. My mom didn't have any good luck. She had asthma and ended up in the hospital for the last few months of her pregnancy. While my mother was in the hospital, David and I were able to go back and live with Grandma and Grandpa; so, I was happy at least. I was with Kari Jo again, and Grandma looked after David so I could just be a kid. I was always happiest when I was with Grandma and Grandpa.

Eventually, my mother had my little brother. She named him William, after his daddy, although I would always call him Billy. She got out of the hospital and collected me and David and took us back with her and away from Grandma and Grandpa. I was needed more than ever now, because that stack of diapers was getting bigger and bigger.

Bill, our second daddy, at least left us with some provisions when he died. He had government benefits that were passed on to us. My mother got a total of about four hundred and fifty dollars a month, including medical benefits. That was a lot to her, especially back in 1960. For a little while, she stopped looking for a new daddy for us, and our family now totaled four. When Bill died, he had a small life insurance policy that my mom got. It didn't make her rich by any means. It was for a few thousand dollars, but to her it was a fortune. She took her grand amount of money and moved us to New Mexico, or Arizona, I don't remember which. I was so sad; I didn't want to leave my grandparents or Kari Jo, my great granny, or my grandpa's bird dog, 'Ritz.' They say I cut my teeth on that dog's ears! Everything I loved and everyone who loved me was in Oklahoma. We had to leave the safety of familiar surroundings and loved ones to a place where we didn't know anyone. Mom decided to go to school, which was great for her, but it left me in charge a lot. Without my grandma to help, it was rough. My mother did not love us! She didn't know how. We were her "ties that bind", an obligation. We made her feel trapped, because she was. I don't think she hated us, but she definitely resented us. We were a constant reminder of a life wasted, at least in her eyes anyway. She blamed us for her misfortune instead of enjoying us, like she could have. Mom did not have a husband to share in the discipline of now three small children. She became the sole disciplinarian, and she took this job very seriously. My mother had a lot of pent up frustration, and being the oldest, I took the brunt of her frustration. Unfortunately, this happens a lot in one-parent families where the parent feels the children are a burden instead of a blessing. The parent ends up taking their aggression out on the one reminder of their unhappiness, their children. My mom would hit me with everything you can imagine, from skillets, irons, and clothes hangers, to telephones, belts and belt buckles. Not to mention her hands and feet, or anything close when she lost control.

By now I was six years old, and things were tough, but we did live in an actual city, and we had indoor plumbing. That's when I found out a toilet was used more for washing out dirty diapers than anything else. I remember nothing pleasant from this time in my life. I yearned for Oklahoma, my grandparents, Kari Jo, and especially the lush, green countryside there. I hated the desert; I needed things around me that were alive.

My mom seemed to be fairly happy and looked to have some hope for the future. She loved going to school, because it took her away from us and this nightmare we called home. It put her with people her own age. She had her little bit of income, which allowed her to go to school. It wasn't enough to raise three children, but it paid the rent. I believe she was in business school at the time, but we were still destined not to have any stability in our lives, and then there was always my mom's luck.

I Was Loved

As a child, I remember moving often. We lived in Oklahoma, Kansas, Delaware, Missouri, Arkansas, Arizona, New Mexico, and back to Oklahoma, all before I was six. So I don't remember exactly where anything happened, like what state I went to for school or what grade I was in. Not to mention being able to remember any of my teachers' names. I do remember specific people who were our neighbors or friends of my mother. My siblings and I didn't make friends because we were never in one place long enough. That was why I loved Oklahoma so much, because it was always the same and there were always people there who knew me, loved me and wanted me there.

My mom had not stopped searching for someone to love her either. I remember a lot of different men in her life. None were ever around for long. I mean, she had three small children; that was overwhelming for most men. I do remember a few specific men. One man lived with us for a while in Arizona; he was nice, and funny. He had red curly hair, just like me. He bought me a bike that had training wheels and streamers hanging from the handlebars. I liked him very much. Mom, on the other hand, did not seem happy with him. I remember one day we were all in the kitchen together. My mom was boiling eggs, and the red headed man was holding my little brother David. We were laughing because David had said a bad word and the man was encouraging him to say it again. My mom didn't care who she took her aggressions out on, and thankfully it wasn't always us. She was yelling at the man to stop it, but he thought it was funny. Mom turned around and threw that whole pan of eggs – hot water and all – towards the red curly haired man. It hit the wall behind us, with eggs and hot water going everywhere. I remember he was nice, and I liked having him there, but mom made him leave. I remember us taking him to the bus station. I pretended to have something in my eye, because I didn't want him to know I was crying. He said he would see me again, but he didn't. I never forgot him, though, because he left us something so we would never forget him: the beginnings of a new baby sister.

Eight months later, my little sister Shelley was born. So now I am six years old, David is four, Billy is almost two, and of course there was Shelley. I just couldn't get rid of those diapers.

At this time, my mom was a whopping twenty-three, with four kids and still no husband. Things got tougher and tougher, especially on me. The older I got, the more useful I became and the more responsibility I had. If I had been in my mom's shoes, I might have resented my life, too. She was still a child herself, and children raising children almost never works out.

Soon, my mom started going out again, looking for the elusive lost love of her life. She went to bars and was out partying a lot. If we were lucky, she would dump us off on someone. Most of the time, I stayed with the kids by myself, but fate played a hand and we moved back to Oklahoma. Once again, I had my grandparents and other relatives to help. Life was so much easier there for us children.

Kari Jo and I could be kids together again. We played in the mud and climbed the big chat piles that were left over from the mining days. There are still plenty of good memories, like digging up worms and picking blackberries. We would help my grandma cook or help Grandpa seine for minnows and craw-dads or pick catalpa worms, all of which were used for fish bait. When my grandpa took us fishing, he would run a trot line (a fishing line that ran the width of the river, held up by plastic jugs, with many hooks hanging from it). We would find some of the weirdest stuff on that line, like big loggerhead turtles and gar (a type of fish that looks like a saw). We even did weird things like play with the air bladders that came out of one type of fish that would float like little balloons. We would put stuff on them and float them around. One time – and I swear this is the truth – my grandpa cut a big fish open and a mouse ran out of it. I remember the time we went camping at twin bridges, Kari Jo rolled into the water in her sleeping bag while she was sleeping. We hunted rabbit and caught forty pound catfish! I learned that happiness was not something you took for granted, so I enjoyed every minute I was there.

One day, my mom came to me and said, "We are moving back to New Mexico." My heart dropped, but I was shocked when she continued with, "Would you like to stay here with Grandma and Grandpa and go to school with Kari Jo?" I was the only one old enough to go to school at the time. I jumped for joy and eagerly said, "Yes! Of course I want to stay here." I was sad to see my brothers and sister leave, but I was so happy to stay there with my grandparents, Kari Jo, and all of the familiarity. Best of all, I had them all to myself, a real treat. So my mom packed up David, Billy and Shelley and moved to Deming, New Mexico.

I stayed in Oklahoma and went to second grade with Kari Jo. I think I was happier that year than any other year ever. No diapers to change; I could just be a kid. Even though poverty was our way of life, it never bothered me. Everyone that lived there was in the same boat. In fact (and this is the truth), our town was so poor, one day a little girl in my class came to school in her slip. She either didn't have a dress to wear or didn't know any better. More often than not, about half of the kids came to school with no shoes on. It didn't bother me, though; I was so happy then.

I remember this one little girl in our school who died from a tonsillectomy. She was hemorrhaging, and her parents were of some religion that didn't believe in blood transfusions, so she died. They had her funeral at our school. Her casket was up on the stage in the auditorium, which was also the school cafeteria. We only had one school in town, so half of it was the high school, and the other half was the grade school. I guess it was used for a lot of things. Kari Jo and I went to her funeral. It was a freak experience, besides the fact that I had only been to one funeral in my life, when I was three and the good daddy Bill died. It was an open casket funeral, and the little girl's mother freaked out. She ran up on stage and tried to pick the girl up and drag her out of the coffin. Some men had to go up there and drag the mother out of the auditorium screaming and crying. The cafeteria was a place I used to dream about. We had always wanted to eat in the cafeteria, but after that I never wanted to eat in there again.

Now that I was back with my grandparents, I was happy every morning when I woke up. The same people would be there that had been there the night before; it was wonderful. Kari Jo and I would swim in the ponds and play on the railroad tracks or with our friends. We got a nickel a week for allowance, and once a week my grandma would give us fifty cents to go to Howard Martin's market to buy a half gallon of strawberry ice cream.

Another fun thing we got to do once a week was drive out to this neat farm for fresh milk and eggs. The milk was still warm in a gallon jar with cheesecloth over it, and you would have to skim the cream off the top. There was always a litter of either puppies or kittens, sometimes both. They had a sow that was so big, she could hardly get up, and when she had a litter, there were always twenty or more little piglets. This mother pig was the size of a sofa, I swear! These were the days I would remember fondly, the times that would sustain me later. I did know love; I just knew resentment also.

A day or two after school let out, my grandpa came to me and said, "Your mom needs you to come home and help her with the kids." I knew I would have to go back with her eventually, but my hopes were that she would move back Oklahoma or I would somehow get to stay there. When he said to me, "You have to go home," I thought to myself, *I am home, why can't she come home?* It wasn't to be, at least not right now.

We loaded up my grandpa's "pick'em up truck" so he, Grandma, and Kari Jo could drive me to New Mexico. Kari and I rode in the camper. The whole way there, we lay on the bed in the overhang and cried. We made plans on when I would get to come back. We were very close and didn't want to be separated.

When we arrived at my mom's house, it was very late at night, so we woke her and the kids up when we came in. I remember walking through the house looking at everything and realizing I was a stranger there. I found a drawer open in a cupboard, and inside was a baby black bunny. Apparently, it was the kids' pet, but that wouldn't be my biggest surprise.

The kids had all grown so much in a year. Shelley was walking, and they seemed very glad to see all of us. Kari Jo and I were just wandering through the house, checking stuff out. When we opened the door to my mom's room, I found my real surprise: there was a baby girl lying on the bed. Kari Jo and I went over to it, looked at each other, and said, "I wonder whose baby this is?" Maybe she was babysitting for someone! We went into the living room and asked my mom who she was babysitting for. She said, "I'm not babysitting for anyone. That's your new baby sister, Darla. Isn't she beautiful? And by the way, April, would you go and get a diaper and change her?" I had almost forgotten what a diaper was, but it didn't take long to get back in the swing of changing them.

My grandparents and Kari Jo only stayed one day. When they left, my heart left with them. I cried every day for them, and I kept a straw Kari Jo had used for months. I didn't have a lot of time to cry, because four kids were a real handful. I was eight years old.

\

We stayed in New Mexico for the next year. By now, I was in the fourth grade. My brother David was in the first grade, and the other three were not in school yet. School had its good and bad points, but it got me out of that hellhole. Not everyone in New Mexico was poor like they were in Oklahoma, so I was an outcast. Anytime someone asked me where my daddy was, I had to say, "I don't have a daddy." Of course, back in 1964 that was not as common as it is now. Another thing was, we definitely stood out when we were all together. I had bright red hair, David had reddish brown hair, Billy had brown hair, Shelley had black hair, and Darla was a platinum blonde. People would always say stuff to my mom like, "Aren't they such beautiful children, and all so different." Or "Aren't they a conglomeration." Stuff like that. We stuck out like sore thumbs. Moving from one world to another was hard, but it taught us to fit into any situation.

Finally, my dream came true and we moved back to Oklahoma. Yeah! All of the fond memories from my childhood were from Oklahoma; no other place mattered. We were back to my grandparents, Kari Jo, family, wild asparagus, fishing, and freedom.

We got a little – and I do mean little – house in Picher, OK. Two bedrooms for six people and a dog, but I didn't care. I wouldn't have cared if it was a shed (that would come later). I spent as much time away from that house as possible and spent time with my grandparents and Kari Jo.

I have to admit, we were really cute kids. In fact, I have come to believe my mother resented us because of how much attention we drew away from her. My little brother David was so cute because of his red hair and freckles. He looked and acted like "Huckleberry Finn". He was constantly coming in with little snakes, turtles, frogs or lizards in his pockets. He was ornery, too. I remember one time he got a snapping turtle stuck on the end of his finger and my grandpa had to cut the turtle's head off before it would let go. David was always getting into trouble.

Billy, my second youngest brother, the one whose daddy had died before he was born, was quieter and easily led by David. Of course, where one went, so did the other. Billy was darker than the rest of us; his skin, hair, eyes, and his personality. He was the only one of us who had a legal and willing "other family", which was his father's family. They also lived in that area of Oklahoma. He was the only son of the son they had lost. Billy was very special to them, and they treated him so, but they didn't exclude me or David. I remember going over to his grandma's house to stay plenty of times, and they were always nice to us. David and I had been around when Bill was alive. Of course, Shelley and Darla hadn't been born then, so they didn't even know them. It was still hard on the rest of us when Billy got presents from them and we didn't. It's hard for children to understand the differences adults have between them.

Then there was Shelley. She had the black hair, but she had freckles, too. She was so cute. She was the one who was the "surprise" the nice man in Tucson had left us. Shelley was a sweetheart.

Then there was Darla. She was the newest addition to our brood. She was the one with platinum blonde hair who needed a lot of attention. Everyone called her the white tornado, and she was always calling every man in my mom's life "Daddy". We all wanted a daddy, but Darla always actively looked for one.

\

You would think I would have been closer to the girls than the boys, but our age differences made it easier for me to play with the boys than the girls.

So by the time my mom had her twenty-fifth birthday, she had made her father and mother grandparents five times. I didn't find any of this stuff out until later in my life, but I thought you may be wondering, so here goes. Remember the man in Tucson, the one with red hair like me, the one who got me the bike? Well, apparently he was my and David's real dad. He was let out of prison and came to Arizona. He would deny that Shelley was his later in life, and he swore mom was seeing some other guy when he got to Tucson. I remember him being at the house and mom throwing the pan of eggs at him.

One of the times we had moved back to Oklahoma a couple of years earlier, my mom had gone to see an attorney there. She was trying to get my dad to pay her child support. Well, apparently this lawyer took his work very personally. He put everything he had into his work, and I do mean literally. He's the one who had given my mom our little sister Darla as a gift. Now, this man already had a family and had no intention of giving them up for my mom and her brood. Ironically, my father never paid a penny in child support, but the attorney did. Before my mom had Darla, she had her tubes tied to prevent any more additions to our growing family, but she'd been just days pregnant when this happened. Darla would be the result of that torrid affair. Did you get all of that?

When my mom had gone back to Tucson and left me in Oklahoma, she went for the sole purpose of giving Darla up for adoption. That was why she'd left me there. I was the only one old enough to know what it meant when her belly got big, and she'd put Darla up for adoption. In fact, Darla had already been adopted by a couple. Mom had given birth to her but had never even seen her. The people had already flown to Tucson to pick her up. When Darla was ten days old, my mom tried to kill herself, but she failed. She ended up back in the same hospital where she'd given birth to Darla. Somehow, the doctor who had delivered her helped my mom get Darla back. All I knew was when we showed up in Tucson, I had a new little sister. I knew nothing about how all of this came about until later in my life.

Life was hard, and getting harder with more mouths to feed, except my mom didn't feed us very much. Mostly, Grandma fed us, or whoever was babysitting at the time. It was hardest on the boys, not having a man in their lives. It was hard on us girls, too, but hardest on them. It was really hard to watch men come and go in and out of our lives. My grandpa would take the place of a dad while we were around him, but he wasn't doing well.

My mom was beautiful and could get any man until they saw she had five kids; then they ran like their pants were on fire. Let's face it: she wasn't easy to live with, even if she liked you. So sad for my mom; she was young and pretty, but oh so stuck.

It seems to me if we didn't have all the diversity of different people in this world, it would be a pretty boring place, but I would have loved for my life to be a little boring. Some people have said to me, "April, you've had such an interesting life." As long as I can remember, all I've ever wanted was for life to be boring. Just give me the same mom, the same dad, the same house, the same town. It sounds pretty good to me.

When Billy used to go to his (other) grandparents' house, they would let me and David go with him sometimes. I thought they were rich, because they had carpet, television, nice furniture and indoor plumbing. Being older, I can look back now and realize they weren't rich. It's funny how our perspectives change. Of course, like I've mentioned before, I thought everyone who had indoor plumbing was rich. It's hard for people my age to believe I didn't have indoor plumbing, but a lot of people to this day still live like that back there.

Here's something I survived that I'm proud of. When I was five years old, our old blind bird dog "Ritz" (named after the cracker) and I ended up falling into an outhouse. I didn't actually fall all the way in. I fell, but I caught myself by hanging onto the edge for dear life. The dog, on the other hand, tried to help me, but being blind, he got up on the other stool (it was a double) and did fall in all the way. Eventually, my screaming and his barking brought help. Once they pulled me out, they would have to tip the outhouse over to get the dog out. My brothers and sisters still laugh at me for that, but can you imagine how tragic that would have been. "Here lies April, drowned in an outhouse." Well fortunately, or unfortunately (however you want to look at it), I survived to use another outhouse. You may be wondering why the dog was in the outhouse with me anyway? Well, we never went out there alone. I remember Kari Jo and I always had to lead my great granny out there whenever she went, because she was blind. We would play around the outhouse and wait for her, then lead her back to the house. Ritz, the dog, always went with us everywhere, outhouses and all. The time I spent with my grandparents was what kept me going.

One of the times we lived by my grandparents in Oklahoma, they took me and Kari Jo to a "hoot-n-nanny" (a hick social gathering). They also took me to quite a few "pow wows" (big Indian dances). This particular time, the hoot-n-nanny ended rather late and my grandparents thought my mom expected me home, so that's where they took me. We pulled up to my house after eleven at night. My mom's car was in the driveway and the lights were on, so my grandpa made sure I got inside before heading on home. Once I got inside, I called to my mom to let her know I was home, but I got no answer. I started wandering through the house looking for her. I went into the kids' rooms and saw they were all asleep in their beds, but I couldn't find my mom anywhere. I got scared and started thinking all sorts of things. Had someone come in and taken her? I even passed by the couch, scared she'd been killed and hidden behind it.

Grandpa and Grandma didn't have a phone, so I couldn't call them. My aunt Reta (my mom's sister) did, but she had just had a baby a week or two earlier, so I didn't know if I should call her or not. Eventually, when I couldn't find my mom anywhere, I broke down and called my aunt Reta. She came over at two in the morning with her new baby in tow, got on the phone and started calling the bars. You thought I was going to say the police, didn't you? No, she started calling the bars, and I'll be darned if she didn't find my mom at the "Four Forty Club".

Apparently, my mom thought my grandparents would just keep me with them that night. She had left all four of those kids by themselves and gone bar hopping. Actually, she had done it quite a bit before this; apparently, I had just slept through it. I remember lying in bed after my mom got home while my aunt yelled at her for twenty minutes. It

\

wouldn't be the last time I would hide in my room while someone yelled at her about her treatment of us. I got in so much trouble the next day. When my mom got mad, she would punish you in more ways than one. First, she would use physical punishment before making you do all of the housework. Then for a day or so she would give you the silent treatment. I tried very hard not to do anything wrong. On the other hand, it was just the opposite with my grandparents. My grandfather only punished me one time. One of the years I lived with them and went to school with Kari Jo, I went to a Girl Scout meeting after school without telling them. When it let out, I started walking towards home. Here comes my grandpa on his crutches. He had been looking for me for an hour. He swatted me one time across the bottom and told me never to go anywhere without telling him again. That one swat did more for me than all of the beatings my mom gave me put together my entire life. My mom's anger and violence wasn't just directed towards me. Even inanimate objects felt the blunt of her fury.

I remember one time, I walked into the kitchen and she was on the phone with her boyfriend at the time. All of a sudden, she started beating the phone on the wall with the handset. Now, this was when phones were actually wired into the wall, but heavy and hard to break. She beat that phone for five minutes. When she was done, it just hung there in pieces. We didn't have a phone for months, because she was afraid to call the phone company and let them see it.

My mom never had trouble finding good looking boyfriends, and she even talked marriage a couple of times. She was four-foot-eleven and only weighed a hundred pounds, but the anger and power in that tiny package was dynamite. Unfortunately, we were usually on the receiving end of that explosion. I got it more than the rest of them, because I was the oldest. I would come to realize later in my life that my mom resented me most of all, because I was the one who had ruined her life. I was her first, and the rest of them were just incidental. She whipped me with clothes hangers, skillets, belts and anything else handy. She's thrown an iron, a cast iron skillet and dishes at me. She would even line us up and whip all of us if she couldn't get one of us to confess to whatever, just to make sure she got the right one.

A friend of mine asked me, "April, what kept you going? What was your motivation to go on?" I don't want to make it seem like my life was *all* bad, because it wasn't. What kept me going was the knowledge that I was wanted and loved by my grandparents and Kari Jo. There were times when I had experienced so much joy in my life that I wanted more. I knew love and happiness was out there, I was always a happy child. I just had some real moments of reality along with the good. Yes, I experienced some sadness and some downright abuse, but I knew love and happiness. I suppose that was what kept me going, even though I did have some strange experiences. You know almost all comedians are very sad people who have learned to deal with their sadness through comedy. It's either become a comedian or a mass murderer. Lucky for us, most of them become comedians.

I remember there was a little college about ten miles from us, and for Christmas one year they decided to do something for the poor children in the area. So they did an adopt-a-child for Christmas thing. Different couples or families would take these children for a few days during Christmas. The college would put on a big party on Christmas night for the children. Santa Claus would be there to hand out presents to each child. I went with a young couple that didn't have any children yet, while my brothers and sisters went with other people. They were all very nice, but it was still weird spending Christmas with strangers. They took me out to eat and to the movies, things I never got to do. Anytime I got one-on-one attention from adults, it was very special for me. I had always felt like one fish in a pond of many.

We had a few strange Christmases. I remember one when Grandpa and Grandma came out to Arizona to spend Christmas with us. My grandpa took twenty silver dollars, threw them out in the back yard, and then had us go find them all. One other Christmas, Kari Jo and I saved our money for six months and bought Grandpa a carton of cigarettes (of course, this was back when they would sell cigarettes to anyone). Grandpa always rolled his own, and we thought it would be the best present ever, but the gift he gave us for Christmas that year was that he had quit smoking. We took the cigarettes back and bought him some new underwear.

One year on Christmas morning, I got a real surprise: my first and only Barbie. Now, this was in about 1966 or 1967, and the first bendable knee Barbie had just come out. I was so shocked and excited when I opened my present and it was a brand new Bendable Knee Barbie. As I pulled her out of the box, I noticed her knees were bendable all right. You could bend the knees frontwards or backwards, because they were just hanging there, attached only by a tiny bit of plastic. My sisters had opened the box the night before and tried to chew Barbie's legs off before putting her back. They were very little when this happened and probably didn't mean to destroy my Barbie. I taped up that doll's legs and played with her like that for years. I guess I had the first 'Injured

Barbie'. I should talk to Mattel. I saw a doll advertised once in a magazine that was pregnant. You could take her stomach off, take the baby out and make her skinny, so injured Barbie isn't so farfetched.

I had good Christmases, too. Anytime I was with my grandparents and Kari Jo, it was a good Christmas. I remember one Christmas we had a little silver tree with a light behind it that turned the tree different colors. It was one of the few things that were shiny and bright that I remember from my childhood. My mom had gotten it at the commissary. She got everything at the commissary, and in fact Air Force bases determined where we lived. We did everything at the base. We received medical treatment and bought groceries, clothes, and everything else we used. There was one in Tucson, AZ, and Deming, New Mexico, and everywhere else we lived.

I have to tell you about some of the babysitters we had growing up. There was this one lady who was blind in one eye and couldn't see out of the other. Really! She was a real caricature. I can't remember her name, but she ironed clothes and babysat for a living. There were always so many kids over at her house that she wouldn't have known if one of us came up missing or not. She wouldn't allow us in the house, so we all had to stay outside. Good thing the bathroom was outside. I think she was addicted to Coca Cola, because I remember her always standing in front of the ironing board with a Coke in her hand. I never saw her any other way. She had a room full of little green Coke bottles; some were empty, and some were unopened. We could go to the door and ask for water, but we had to stay outside, rain or shine. As I said, there were always so many kids over there that we took care of each other. In fact, there were always a lot of kids everywhere I went. I mean, just me, my brothers and sisters made up five. Add any more, and you were working on a brood.

We also spent a lot of time with a lady we called "Granny Tabor". She wasn't really our granny, but everyone called her that. Now, her house was always neat, even though she had ten children of her own. I was never sure how many of the children were her real grandchildren, but I did know there were a lot of kids, and she would spend her days cooking and feeding us. Granny would line us up outside and make us take a bath in a metal washtub. I don't know how clean those of us got who were at the end of the line, but she tried. She had a big, giant propane tank in her back yard that we played on like it was a jungle gym. The railroad tracks also ran through her back yard. We would put pennies on the tracks and wait for trains to crush them. Scary how we played on those tracks all the time. Now that I look back on that, all I can say again is, nature took care of its own.

I was forced as a child to fit into any situation, whether it was being the only child in a room full of adults or one of twenty children all playing on the same chat pile. It made me very versatile.

Let me tell you more about those chat piles we played on. There are big mountains of gravel called "chat"; hence the name "chat pile". Some of them were over a hundred feet tall and took up acres of land. They were left over from the mining days, and some were so big you could drive a car up to the top, as long as you drove around the side in a circle. All of the teenagers did just that because there was nothing else to do there. You could climb up to the top of one and roll down it. All of the kids in the area played on "chat piles", even though they were very dangerous. Kids have been buried under the chat when it would slide, just like an avalanche. Now most of the chat is gone, because they found out they could use it to make roads, but back then it was just useless mine leavings. Like I said, "ignorance is bliss."

The best way for me to give you a mental picture of where I grew up would be to tell you to watch the movie "Sling Blade". I believe it was filmed within fifty miles of where I grew up. The houses we lived in were very little, about six hundred square feet on average. They were all made of tar paper and asbestos siding, but it didn't matter to us because we were never inside anyway. Our world was outside where it was green, playing in the lakes, ponds, rivers, and streams. They have the best fishing in the country, in my opinion anyway.

The town I lived in was called Picher, Oklahoma, and it's now a legal ghost town. More than five hundred people still live there, and most of them still live without indoor plumbing. Isn't it strange that we're now past the turn of a new century and people in this country still live like that?

One of the only sad memories I have that's associated with my grandparents has to do with Ritz, my grandpa's dog. You know the one that fell in the outhouse with me, the one I cut my teeth on as a baby, chewing on his ear? Thankfully, I don't remember that, but we all loved that dog. My grandpa had been driving in a rain storm sixteen years earlier and saw a female dog get hit by a car. He stopped and found the dog dying in a ditch on the side of the road. During this process, she gave birth to some pups. He couldn't save them all, but he saved one: Ritz. My grandpa had taken this puppy that was just minutes old and raised him to be the dog we all grew up with and loved. When Ritz was sixteen years old, he lost his teeth and vision. My grandpa had to take him out and shoot him. I think it was the hardest thing he ever had to do, but life is hard and he did what he had to do.

Hard or not, it was still a neat place to grow up in and explore. We never had many toys, but that didn't stop us from playing. One of the houses my grandparents lived in had a metal bait tank out in the yard. My grandpa would fill it up for us to use as a swimming pool. It was cleaner than a lot of ponds I swam in and more sanitary than some baths I've had.

My life as a youngster was broken up into two parts: when I was with my grandparents, and when I wasn't. When I was gone from them, I was with my mother and my life reverted back to caregiver, babysitter and whipping post, but there was always the hope of going back home.

The Changeling

Between the time I was eleven or twelve, we were spending

more and more time living in Arizona or New Mexico than Oklahoma.
My grandparents would still come and visit us. We would go home to
Oklahoma for short periods, but my living with them for a year at a time
was over. I was much too valuable to my mom to leave behind, because
then who would take care of the kids? At times, it wouldn't just be my
brothers and sisters; she had a habit of making friends with other women
in her situation. No money, no man, and lots of kids. My mom had this
one friend named Shirley who had eight kids, so guess how many that
made for me to watch? Not counting if any more were to join us. In fact,
when the two of them got together, it was like a circus. More than once,
we would all go somewhere, which was a nightmare in itself, and
someone would say, "Where is the baby?" Then someone else would
say, "I thought you had her!" Someone else would say, "I thought you
had her!" So off we went, back to the house to find Darla still sitting on
the couch in her baby carrier, crying her eyes out. Another time, we left

Shelley on some church's steps (accidentally, of course) and had to go back to get her.

It was unbelievable trying to get us all fed or loading us up in a car. Of course today, if a police officer stopped a car and there were fifteen people in it (most of them kids), they would freak out, but we did it and survived.

Every time we moved, it was by car. Some of the trips we had were pretty wild. For one thing, we never had a decent vehicle, so there were always car problems to deal with. One trip in particular, we had an old Opal station wagon. We were moving from Oklahoma to Deming, New Mexico. Somewhere over a hot desert mountain, our car broke down. We had us five kids, my mom, a Collie, a cat, and a Chihuahua. Of course, to make matters worse, poor Billy (who had the chicken pox) kept throwing up into a big Tupperware bowl. We were at least one hundred and fifty miles from any other human life. Back in the sixties, the world was still very big, and there weren't all the people on the roads there are today. Mom couldn't leave us there in the car, so we all went walking down the highway; what a menagerie. Believe it or not, a very nice traveling salesman with a brand new car stopped. He ended up giving us a ride all the way to where we were going, about 300 miles. Poor guy, I bet he never forgot that experience; Billy throwing up the whole trip. There are nice people in the world.

Another time, we took a train somewhere. My mom couldn't afford to feed us on the train, so when it stopped she made me and David leave the train and go find a store to get bread and bologna. We almost didn't get back in time, and the train was starting to leave without us. If we wouldn't have been barefooted kids screaming after it, they would have left us there.

My mom finally got us a TV of sorts. She found one where the volume didn't work, and then found another one that had volume, but no picture. So we stacked them on top of each other – and voila! TV! Eventually, mom was able to get us a good TV, but we would only have it two weeks a month. My mom's VA checks came on the first, so every month on the first of the month we would go get the TV out of the pawn shop, and every month about the fifteenth of each month we would take it back to the pawn shop, like clockwork.

I remember once when we lived in Tucson, Arizona, I was at our neighbor's house whose daughter was a friend of mine from school. They were the neatest family, and they happened to be Mormon. I went to their church once and liked it. I hadn't been to a lot of churches in my life up until then, but I liked their church. I thought they were rich because they had a maid come in three times a week, but then I figured everybody was rich except us. I remember her name, it was Mrs. McNamara. Isn't that funny I can't remember my friend's name, but I'll never forget her maid. One day I was over there, and the maid was washing the windows and doing laundry. My friend's little brother was a year or so younger than us, and he had a crush on me. My friend and I were sitting on the sofa eating ice cream when her little brother came over to me and started putting pepper in my hair and on my ice cream. He was saying, "You have black dandruff, you have black dandruff!" I jumped up and started running from him because I didn't want pepper in my hair. I was trying to run outside through the sliding glass door. I do mean "through the sliding glass door"; I thought it was open. Mrs. McNamara had done a good job of cleaning the windows that day. When I woke up, I was outside propped up in a chair. Mrs. McNamara was wrapping a ripped up sheet around my leg and hand. There was blood everywhere. I had run straight through that glass door. In fact, I had gone so straight through it that the hole I left in the window was only about fourteen inches in diameter. I was very fortunate I had only cut my hand and legs. Never a dull moment! They called my mom, who immediately came and got me, put me in the car, and drove me out to Davis-Monthan Air Force Base. A Corpsman sewed me up with almost two hundred stitches. I still bear the scars from that experience, and I would be on crutches all summer long. I had to go back to the base hospital a year later to have plastic surgery on my hand. Apparently, the Corpsman who had sewed me up left glass in my hand. That was just one of many visits us kids made to the emergency room at the base hospital.

One time, my little sister Darla was playing on this old tilt-a-whirl we had. It was like a four-way merry go round. You sat in the seat and it had pedals, and four of us could ride it at one time. You pushed with your feet and pulled with your hands, which made it go around faster and faster. It was fun, but old, rusty and falling apart. Darla somehow got her leg caught in some piece of loose metal, and it took a hunk of meat out of her leg. I ran her in to my mother, who put us in the car and rushed her out to the base. On the way there, a police officer tried to stop us. My mom stopped long enough to tell him she was rushing my sister to the hospital and then took off. The officer got in front of us and escorted us out there. Then he waited for us and gave my mom a ticket, honest! Darla had a nasty wound on her leg, and she bears the scar of that ordeal to this day. We all have at least one scar from childhood.

My little brother David had a dirt bike. One day, he got that thing going 75 miles an hour through the desert. He hit a barbed wire fence; it took almost one hundred stitches to sew up the crease in his leg. You know the crease that runs between your leg and all those other very important parts. The doctor told my mom that if it had been any closer, he would have been a girl.

My brother Billy got bit on the mouth by a dog, and he almost took off his own toe with a shovel.

Shelley was allergic to everything. I remember the time she was bitten by some black ants, and she swelled up like a watermelon. One time a squirrel bit her, and they were going to give her a series of rabies shots in her stomach. Luckily, they were able to find the squirrel because it was missing a foot. Anyway, with five kids, there were bound to be battle scars.

We've witnessed some pretty traumatic things young children shouldn't have to see. One time, my mom was driving along with all of us in the car. We were sitting at an intersection, when right in front of us a garbage truck and a big gasoline truck collided. The guy in the garbage truck went through the windshield, and the gas truck had turned over and was spilling gas everywhere. The guy who had gone through the windshield had had his arm cut off as he did so. He was rolling around on the ground in all of this gasoline, screaming. It was horrible. My mom told us kids to keep our heads down, but of course we didn't. We were stuck there because there were cars behind us and the wreck was in front of us, so we couldn't go anywhere. The police came over to my mom and asked her if she had anything to wrap this man up in until an ambulance could get there. We always had an old Army blanket in the trunk, and she gave them that. After it was over and they had taken the man away, the police came back over to us and asked my mom if she wanted the blanket back. She said no, of course. I will always remember that.

One time, we were driving along and saw a beautiful horse get hit by a train. The impact had torn its back leg almost all the way off. My mom took all our shoelaces and made a tourniquet to put on the horse's leg, but when the police got there they shot the horse and then asked her if she wanted the shoelaces back! I swear to God.

Experiences, experiences, we had many. We also had some pretty unusual meals when we got those creative juices flowing, or was it just hunger pains or five kids all saying, "What's for dinner?" By the last few days of each month, we had some pretty creative meals. I learned to make a meal out of just about anything. We would have chocolate chip pancakes, goulash, Spanish rice, peanut butter with syrup sandwiches, and sometimes tuna with cream of mushroom soup over toast. If nothing else, it taught me how to make a meal from whatever was in the cupboards. Cooking has been as big a part of my life as diapers have.

Conviction

When I was twelve, my life changed completely: my mom, the

bar hopper, sometimes mother of five, lover to many, ex-wife of two,

found religion. "The worst sinners make the best Christians". Her friend,

the one with eight kids, took my mom to church for the first time. Our

lives changed a lot after that. Now, we won't get into any kind of

discussion on religion. My views are biased, so I won't impose them on

you. On one of those first few nights we were at church, my mom was

saved. We started going to church a lot after that. Things changed fast

and furious for us, and some of the changes were good. Mom started

showing more attention to us, and she even quit going out to bars all the

time. Church filled our lives; she made us go almost every night, and

twice on Sunday. I was changing all on my own. On top of watching my mom and our lives change drastically, I was growing up and out. I was coming into my own age of rebellion.

We joined a little church in Tucson called Del North Baptist Church. It sat right behind "Flowing Wells" Junior High and high school. Even though at that time I was still in sixth grade, I would eventually go to both.   I remember in sixth grade, two big things happened to me. One was that I started my period and went through puberty. The day I started my period, we were going to a swimming party. My mom thought it would be funny to embarrass me by announcing it to everyone there. I just sat by the pool instead of getting in it; I was horrified.

I also had another one of my most embarrassing moments that year. Each day when I walked home from school, I would have to cross a fairly busy street that had a drainage grate running across the intersection. See, in Tucson, when it rains, it floods. There are things that look like cattle crossings, only they are drainage ditches covered with grates, and they're everywhere. Well, one of my legs slipped down in-between two of the grates, and it wouldn't come out. So here I was in the middle of a busy intersection, with my leg stuck down in-between two metal bars. Luckily, no one drove over me, but I definitely stopped traffic. Many people tried to pull my leg free, but it wasn't going to come out of there without a fight. The more they pulled on my leg, the more sore and swollen my knee became. It was so embarrassing and spooky. I had blocked traffic in four directions. Finally, a police officer came, took a bucket of black grease out of his trunk, rubbed it all over my leg, and yanked with all of his might until my leg finally popped out. The nice officer drove me home in his police car, but I had a sore knee and leg for a week; never a dull moment.

\

As time went by, church filled almost every need my mom had. It supplied her with friends, money, food, clothes, and a social life. They even helped her get a real house, and it gave us all something to do after school. It did what a church should do, and I was always glad when she was happy, because it made life easier for all of us. At Christmas time, the church would send us a box of food and presents. It would even supply my mom with a man, even if he was a married man. In fact, he was the minister of the church. Some things never change. He was very good looking and had a beautiful blonde wife with two small, beautiful blond children. He appeared to have the perfect life, but appearances can be deceiving.

Now, I can't make judgments, or even statements, about things I didn't see with my own eyes, but I do know the minister and his wife divorced. It was a big scandal at the church, and his wife had been a very big part of that church. She taught the Sunday school class, and their children were the prince and princess of the church. This rocked the church to its core. I know he and my mother liked each other and they went places together. He would come over to our house a lot, and I liked him. He was a very nice man, but the church was all aflutter. Since my mom had become very involved at the church and it was her whole life, they didn't act flagrantly, but I was old enough to hear people talking. I knew what they were like away from church. I don't even know for sure that the divorce wasn't already inevitable, but none of that would matter for long.

This young, good looking preacher had other hobbies. He loved to skydive, and he would go every weekend. Well, one weekend his chute didn't open. It devastated my mom and the church. Does this mean God really is a God of wrath, or was it just really bad luck? Come to think of it, none of the men in my mom's life had very good luck: prison, death, ruined lives, and now this. If it wasn't *her* bad luck, it was still bad luck.

After her good looking preacher died, my mom threw herself into the church even more. She went back to college, and we hardly ever saw her. The church got a new preacher, and things settled down. We lived in Tucson for the next couple of years, and I ended up going to Flowing Wells Junior High School. We would go back to Oklahoma only for visits, or my grandparents would come out to visit us.

The summer I was thirteen, Kari Jo and my grandparents came to Tucson to visit us. Of course, they came in their old "pick'em up truck" with a camper on it. Tucson, Arizona, has some real beauty around it. It sits at the base of the Catalina Mountains, and on the outskirts there is a little mountain called Mount Lemon. You can drive straight up the mountain to snow covered greenery. Afterwards, within forty-five minutes you can drive back down and be in one hundred degree temperatures again. Grandpa decided to take us all on a day trip up there. We all piled into my grandpa's truck. All six of us kids got in the camper, while Grandpa, Grandma, and Mom rode in the front. We had a blast, but of course any time I could be with them, I was happy. Once we got to the top, we kids jumped out. We could tell Mom and Grandpa were frustrated and miserable. Grandma had started freaking out on the way up there, begging my grandpa to let her out of the truck, and she was still crying and really frightened. We stayed up there and played for a few hours while Grandma calmed down some, but she did not want to go back down that mountain. When it was time to go, she actually begged my grandpa to leave her there, but of course we couldn't do that. Kari Jo and I put her in the camper with us. We held her hand while she lay on the bed, but she still cried all the whole way home.

It was so hard for me to see the strongest woman in my life act like this, but other things were happening to her, too. One day she asked my mom to hand her a towel, only she didn't say "Myrna", she said, "Reta, hand me that towel."

My mom looked at her funny and said, "I'm not Reta, Mom."

My grandma looked at her and said, "You are too Reta!"

My mom looked at her quizzically and said, "I'm not Reta, Mom."

Grandma looked confused and said, "Well, who are you then?"

My mom again gave her an even stranger look and said, "I'm Myrna, Mom. What's wrong with you?"

My grandma just looked at her for more than a minute or so, with no recognition. Finally, Grandma said, "Well, of course, Myrna. I don't know what I was thinking."

We all looked at each other with confusion and finally went on about our business. It was like she had a bout with Alzheimer's, but she was only 57. We noticed she was having more and more headaches, too.

The summer I was fourteen, my mom came to me to tell me we were going to move back to Oklahoma. We were going to stay at the lake with Grandma and Grandpa. Of course I wanted to go, I lived to be with them. The only thing was, my mom wanted to leave on the first of the month because the rent was going up on the house or something, but I was just about to complete a full year at one school. It would be the first time in my whole life I had actually gone to the same school with the same people. I was now supposed to move across the football field with the same people to start high school. It may seem simple to you, but to me it was a milestone. I needed some stability in my life, and for the first time I had friends, not just brothers and sisters. I had over a week of school left, which would include a dance and graduation from eight to ninth grade. All of this was supposed to happen the same time my mom wanted to leave for Oklahoma. I desperately wanted to do these things, so I begged and pleaded with my mom for us to stay or work something out. To my surprise, she agreed. Mom was best friends with a woman named Gladys. She was from our church and was also married to the principal of Flowing Wells High School. They had a son and a daughter my age whom we spent time with. Now, *they* were definitely rich, because they had a swimming pool, a music room with a baby grand piano and white carpet. I remember one day when we were over there, Gladys was cutting the ends off celery and carrots as she prepared a salad for dinner.

My mom spoke up and said, "You aren't going to throw that away, are you?"

Gladys looked at my mom and said, "Yes."

My mom said, "I could feed my kids for a week from what you're throwing away."

I don't know why I told you that, except it's stuck in my mind ever since.

Anyway, somehow they worked it out so I could stay there with Gladys and Vic McNealy. I could complete my year at school, and then I would travel to Oklahoma by bus ten days later. The McNealy's may have even paid for the bus ticket; they were very nice people.

So my mom took the kids to Oklahoma, and I moved in with the McNealy's. It was a surreal experience. I was afraid to touch anything, but they made me feel at home and they seemed to use everything. It was a culture shock to me. I got to go swimming every day, and I ate very well; it was fun. Except for one day when I ran into the house to use the restroom and opened the door without knocking. To my shock and embarrassment, there was Mr. McNealy sitting on the toilet.

I just stood there going, "Hu-hu-um, I am so sorry."

It was awkward to run into him after that. I mean, he was the principal of my high school!

One night, their two kids talked me into pitching a tent in the back yard by the pool so we could sleep out there. While we were setting up the tent, a boy I knew from school was walking by. The McNealys' yard had a tall chain link fence surrounding it, so you could easily see through it. The boy stopped and started talking to me.

"Are you going to sleep out here?" he asked. I told him yes. "Can I come back after dark and see you?"

I thought about it for a while. I had never had a boy show interest in me before. It seemed neat and daring.

I said, "OK, make sure it's after these kids are asleep."

I mean, I figured we would just talk through the fence or something. I didn't see anything really wrong with it. I didn't even know what sex was. So, it was purely innocent on my part.

Sure enough, about eleven o'clock I heard him softly whispering, "April? April?"

So, I slowly maneuvered my way out of the tent and met him at the fence. He was a year or two older than I was, and he was quite bold. He climbed over the fence, even though it was eight feet tall.

I was telling him, "No, no!", but he was already over.

He led me behind the pool house so we wouldn't wake the kids and quickly turned into a very knowledgeable sixteen-year-old. It was my first experience at being felt up, and my "No"s got louder and louder. The next thing I knew, Lisa, one of the children, had crawled out of the tent and was yelling my name. All of a sudden, the back porch light came on. I jumped up and ran back to the tent, while he hauled butt over the fence. He wasn't as quiet this time, and out came Vic McNealy.

He yelled after him, "Who's there?"

By now, I was back with the kids in the tent and acted like I didn't know what was going on. Needless to say, we slept in the house that night, and every night after that. In fact, those kids probably never got to sleep outside again because of that incident. To this day, I've never admitted to that, so if either of the McNealys read this, I am so sorry.

Well, I graduated and went to the school dance. I don't remember what I wore or if it was fun or not, but I know it was exciting. I loved watching people and being watched. I loved "experiencing", but only the good stuff, mind you; I'm not a masochist. My life would be so full of change, much more than average. I would need this experience later.

Anyway, after I graduated, went to the school dance, and lived in a whole different world for a couple of weeks, I got on a greyhound bus bound for Oklahoma. It was a different experience all on its own. It was just a bus trip until we pulled into Oklahoma City for a layover.

When the bus pulled into the station, it was right around lunch time and there were quite a few buses in this partially enclosed bus area. The fumes were overwhelming and may be what caused what I was about to witness. As we were leaving the bus, the man in front of me collapsed just as he stepped off the last step. When he fell, he hit his head on the cement, busting it wide open. The man immediately went into convulsions, and blood was going everywhere. Many of the passengers started forming a circle around him, and I was forced into the center of this mass of people who wanted to see what was happening. A woman knelt down on the ground next to the man and tried to keep him from choking on his tongue while covering the gash in his head with her hand to stop the bleeding.

All of a sudden, the lady looked up at the crowd of people and yelled, "Give him some air!"

She stood up and pushed me back with her bloody hand. I looked down to see blood covering my chest. I freaked out and started screaming as I tried to pull my shirt off. Everyone around me started moving backwards. A man came over, took me by the arm, and quickly escorted me into the bus station. The nice man gave me a clean new shirt that said "Greyhound maintenance crew". I never knew what happened to my shirt, and I don't know what happened to the man who fell. When I came back out of the terminal to get on the next bus, there was a guy washing the sidewalk off with a hose, and the man who had been bleeding was gone. All I do know is that when I arrived in Miami, Oklahoma, I had on a Greyhound maintenance shirt and I hadn't had a boring trip. In fact, I would never forget it, and I had a story to tell everyone.

When I got off the bus, my mom and Kari Jo were there to meet me. I loved seeing Kari Jo, because I knew I was home. So I jumped from dances, swimming pools and grand pianos to a barefoot, river swimming, peach picking girl. That would turn out to be the best summer I ever had.

The Lake

Summer of 69

My grandparents had moved about thirty miles from where we used to live, to a little cabin community at "The Grand Lake of the Cherokees." It was like a little summer place, but it was on a big private farm. There were cattle everywhere; they would come up to the lake every night and every morning. It never mattered where we lived, as long as I was with Grandpa and Grandma. It's a good thing I'm not picky, because my grandparents were living in a little thirty-foot trailer, and my mom and the kids were staying in a metal storage shed. I swear to God, a ten-by-ten foot tin storage shed, but all they did was sleep in it. It had mattresses on the floor and clothes in the corner. The rest of the time, they were down at my grandparents' trailer. The adults were almost always sitting outside by the trailer, and all of the kids were always in the lake. The only time any of us were inside was to cook or go to the bathroom. We couldn't drink the water that came out of the tap because it was sulfur water and stunk like rotten eggs. So we would go down and carry fresh water from the pump house, at least once a day. It drew from a natural spring and was the best and coldest water I've ever tasted. Of course, every cabin would use it because of the sulfur.

My mom and the kids had been there for ten days or better by the time I got there and had settled into this existence. Luckily, there was no room for me in that tin shed. I didn't want to be there anyway; I just wanted to be with Kari Jo. There wasn't enough room for me in their trailer either, and it was too hot to sleep in there anyway. So my grandpa put me and Kari Jo in sleeping bags in the back of the pickup truck. That was where we would sleep for three months. I didn't care; I was happy to be there. There was this BIG bull named Bullet. More than once, I would wake up to him putting his nose over the bed of the truck and licking my face. The first time it happened, he scared me so bad I screamed. After that, if I woke up and he wasn't somewhere right around there, I would worry about him. That was the summer I grew up.

Now, when I was fourteen, I was built like I was twenty. I definitely could fill out my mother's bathing suit, and there were *boys* at the lake. Kari Jo and I both grew up that summer; it was the summer of a lifetime. We had friends our age, and the other kids did as well. We had so much fun and practically lived in that lake. We played hide and go seek, swimming up under the docks. They were built out of wood, and there were air pockets up under there. We would swim up under there and breathe in these air pockets in-between the joists of the docks. I remember one of the times I was hiding under one of the docks. I had braced my foot against one of the boards to push off, when suddenly a snake went right across my foot. It gives me the shivers whenever I think of that moment. I probably wouldn't even get in that lake today, but that summer I was invincible, young, pretty and free.

Some of the cabins sat right on the lake, and some sat farther up on the other side of the dirt road, but none of them had a bad view. Today, the little place where we stayed that summer is a big resort. I hope they have better running water.

Kari Jo and I did everything you could imagine. We smoked grapevine and our first cigarettes. One of the boys from the cabins had stolen it from his mother. They were "Lark" cigarettes; weird that I would remember that. We met our first boyfriends that summer. Mine was Billy Mosley. His parents had a cabin there where they went every summer. Kari Jo's boyfriend was Billy's best friend, Greg Horn. Greg also had parents who had a seasonal cabin up there. We made out and got our first feel of a boy. We even experimented a little (very little); we were actually good girls. We made a friend up there named Diane Alderson, who was much more advanced than we were, and she was a real learning experience. She gave us some true romance magazines and always wore a black bikini. Diane was a year or two older than us and was much more knowledgeable about sex and life than we were. Diane introduced us to music, boys and all kinds of things. Most of the time, Kari and I would swim or fish all day. We still loved to go berry picking and finding all kinds of weird fruit trees.

When my grandpa was young, he did some kind of weird fishing. It has a name, but I can't think of it; I want to say "noodeling", but I'm not sure that's what it was called. He would swim down in the rivers and let a fifty pound catfish bite on his hand and bring them up that way; I swear it is true. There were giant catfish heads (skulls) hanging from

\

trees there. It was like a trophy thing, and they were as big as human heads. Back in my grandpa's day, there are stories of catfish that weighed over a hundred pounds. I have seen one as big as sixty pounds, but now most of those big fish have been fished out.

One night, Kari Jo and I took my grandpa's walkie-talkies out to the truck with us. We gave one to the boys, and we kept one. After everyone was asleep, we talked to them and planned to meet them somewhere. We had to hold them under the sleeping bag because the crackling noise was so loud, but we thought we were being so sneaky, so off we went into the night to meet Billy and Greg. It didn't take five minutes before Grandpa pulled up behind us in his pickup truck.

He threw open the door and said, "Girls, get in, now!"

My grandpa never had to hit me to make me sorry for what I had done wrong. Just seeing the hurt in his eyes was enough to break my heart. He made us tell him where the boys and other walkie-talkies were. Grandpa went and retrieved the walkie-talkies, then let Billy and Greg know their fun was over for the night. Needless to say, we didn't try that again, but we always seemed to find other trouble to get into.

Grandpa didn't tell my mom about that incident. In fact, I didn't have to deal with my mom hardly at all that whole summer. I just made sure that wherever she was, I was not. This was a good thing, because the older I got, the more we didn't get along. In fact, every time we came face to face, there was a confrontation.

One day a bunch of us older kids, Kari Jo, me, Greg, Billy, Diane, and even my little brother David found a bunch of big inner tubes. We tied them together and went on an adventure around the lake. Of course, we couldn't go all the way around because it had more than 160 miles of shoreline, but we tried. We drifted way far from our area and found a big hole in the side of the bank which was only accessible from the water. The boys helped us girls into this hole, which actually was a cave. We figured someone had been living there, because we even found an old clawed footed bathtub. There were candles and other things that told us someone had stayed in there for a while. How they had gotten a bathtub in there was beyond me. We had so much fun, it took us all day to get back home. After everything we had seen Grandpa catch on that trot line, I can't believe we still spent a whole summer in that water, but we did.

One night, a bunch of us were sitting up high on the bank of the lake, when all of a sudden a big house boat came around the corner. It was covered with lights, there was music playing and people were dancing. It was like something out of a movie, only I had seen very few movies at that time. I couldn't even imagine such opulence out there on that lake. A couple of the older boys dove into the lake and swam out to the boat. Eventually, people from the boat began to swim out to where we were. It was so neat. We spent many of those long, hot summer nights just sitting around talking and learning from each other, growing up. It was the summer of 1970.

One day, my brother David talked us into getting in trouble. He got this girl he liked to swim out behind one of the boat docks with him while we all hid in the bushes. He talked her into taking off her bathing suit top. Once he had accomplished this, he grabbed it and threw it out to us, and we took off with it. We eventually gave it back to her, but the damage was done. She went home and told her father, and he came down and told my grandfather. We all got in trouble for that one.

Like I've said before, my little brother David has always looked and acted just like Huckleberry Finn. There wasn't one day when he didn't show up with some sort of live creature in one of his pockets. That was the summer David got the snapping turtle stuck on the end of his finger and Grandpa had to cut its head off to get it off. We were in the water so much that my feet turned yellow and stayed that way for months. We used to swim down to the bottom of the lake and grab handfuls of mud, then come to the surface and throw it at each other. One time when we were doing that, David and I came up just inches apart, and he pushed that handful of mud right in my face. It got into my eye, and my mom had to take me to a doctor to get my eye cleaned out. I had to wear a patch for a week. That wasn't the only time David caused me to wear a patch on my eye. One time, we were wandering around in the bushes somewhere and found an old windmill. He was adamant about getting this thing to turn, so he climbed to the top of it while I stayed down at the bottom. Well, he finally got it to move, but when he did, a piece of rust got in my eye. Again, I would have to go to the doctor to get my eye cleaned out, and again I would wear a patch on my eye.

I had to make one more trip to the doctor that summer. One day all of us were swimming, but when I came out of the lake blood was squirting out of my knee. It was squirting in spurts as my heart beat. It was the freakiest thing. There was no injury, it was just spurting blood. No matter what the adults did, it wouldn't stop, so my mom had to take me to town, and a doctor cauterized it. He didn't even know why it had done that. Always something with me, I swear.

As the summer passed and August loomed in the near future, things started changing. My mom's brother David and her sister Reta and their families all came to the lake. My uncle David brought a camper, and my aunt Reta had a tent. This also included my aunt Reta's husband, Uncle John, and their two daughters, Kari Lavern and Melissa. My uncle David was there with his wife, Aunt Jo Caroline, and their three children, Linda, Danny and Jackie. So the group of kids got larger, as did the meals. In total, there were eighteen of us: Grandpa, Grandma, Mom, Reta, David, Jo Caroline, John, me, Kari Jo, Kari Lavern, David, Billy, Shelley, Darla, Melissa, Linda Caroline, Jackie and Danny. We had fun and got to know each other. It was a very special time, and now that I look back on it, that was to be the last time we would all be together.

I knew something was wrong with Grandma, because strange things were happening and I caught the adults talking a lot without us kids around. Kari Jo and I were the oldest and were included more than any of the other kids, but they didn't tell us there was a reason for us being all together. I saw things in my Grandma I knew weren't normal, but I loved her so much. I never thought it may be anything really wrong. I noticed sometimes she would repeat herself or ask the same question that had just been answered. More than once, I would come running up to her while she was sitting on the big stump outside of the trailer, ready to give her a hug, and my mom would stop me and say, "Grandma doesn't feel good right now, so leave her alone."

In the meantime, all of us kids had fun playing together. My cousins Linda Caroline and Kari Lavern were almost my and Kari Jo's age, so the four of us bonded and had a blast. My Uncle David's kids were from Tennessee, and they had the cutest accents. In fact, it was so cute that I was always telling them to "say something else." They would call Grandma and Grandpa "Grandmother Rigg" or "Grandfather Rigg". It was so cute. They were so prim and proper.

My Uncle David had come a long way from his meager beginnings. He had become a pilot in the military and had his own plane, a little Cessna. My Aunt Jo Caroline had driven her and the children up from Tennessee, while my uncle David had flown his plane in. He worked for the DuPont Company, and my aunt Jo worked for the Tennessee Valley Water Authority. Uncle John and Aunt Reta had good jobs, and they were definitely the most successful of all of us and were doing pretty well on their own. Uncle John was a CPA and had his own small accounting business.

The day came when the adults sat me and Kari Jo down and told us Grandma was sick. They told us she had a brain tumor and was going into the Oklahoma University hospital in Oklahoma City. Grandma was scheduled for surgery in just a couple of days. Kari Jo and I were told we would be allowed to come along, but we had no idea how serious this was. I mean, as kids, we figured the adults were fixing whatever was wrong, so how could this be a bad thing? We were going to go to Oklahoma City with the adults, and we would stay in a motel, something else I'd never done before.

Most of the other kids came along, except my brothers and sisters. I don't know who watched them, but I don't remember seeing them there. My aunt and uncle's children did go, but they couldn't come to the hospital because they were too young. You had to be fourteen to go up to the room where Grandma was.

The trip to Oklahoma City was an adventure in itself. We ate out at restaurants and got motel rooms, and just going to the hospital was strange to us. We had been very sheltered from anything that costs money, so we were in wonder of it all. In fact, my uncle David even took me and Kari Jo up in his airplane. It was just one wonder after another. How could the best summer of my life eventually end up being the worst?

I didn't have any idea just how scary this was until the day of the surgery. I was up in Grandma's room with my mother when they came in and readied Grandma for surgery. She was on the gurney waiting to be wheeled out, when she sat up and grabbed my mom's hand and said, "Myrna, I'm scared! I don't want to do this!"

My mom took her hand, while I took the other. Mom told her, "It'll be OK, I promise. This will make things better."

I told Grandma I loved her and that it would be OK, but even I was beginning to realize how serious this was. I had never seen her so scared or vulnerable as when they wheeled her away with that little cap on her head.

She again reached for us and said, "I'm so scared, Myrna!"

My mom blew her a kiss and again reassured her it would be OK, but as soon as they had her out of sight, my mom broke down and cried. I knew then this was very serious. When the she-wolf shows weakness, it puts fear in the pack!

The surgery would take over nine hours; I mean, this was back in 1970. Brain surgery was still experimental. Kari Jo and I wandered the hospital and had somehow come up with a pack of cigarettes from somewhere. We ended up sitting in the cafeteria, where back in 1970 not only were you able to smoke inside, you were able to smoke inside a hospital; weird, huh? So Kari Jo and I were sitting in the cafeteria, and I lit up. I was smoking and talking up a storm to Kari, when all of a sudden her jaw dropped to the floor and her eyes grew to the size of saucers. I asked her what the matter was, but she didn't say a word, so I just took another drag off my cigarette. The next thing I knew, I was on the floor. My mom had walked up behind me, and Kari had just frozen. She didn't even tell me to look out or anything. My mom hit me so hard across the face, it knocked me to the floor. She grabbed the cigarettes, yanked me by the arm, and dragged me back upstairs to the waiting room. Thanks, Kari! I was dizzy for an hour. My mom and I only had one form of communication: her hand connecting with some part of my body. Not saying I didn't deserve some form of punishment, but come on. I felt like I had been broadsided with a brick. My mom gave the cigarettes to my uncle David and told him her tale of my indiscretion. The strangest thing happened after that. At some point later in the day, he pulled me aside, gave me back the cigarettes and told me not to let her catch me again. Now, I'm not saying what he did was right, but it was the first time I had been treated like an adult. I loved him for it. I'm not sure he would do the same today.

Finally, late into the night, a nurse told us my grandma was in recovery and we could see her one at a time. We were told at that time the surgeons had removed a tumor the size of a lemon out of her brain. The adults started taking turns to go in and see her first. I went in to see her last, and I was terrified as I walked into that big room. Every person in there was hooked up to tubes and needles. This was intensive care, and it was horrible. There were two nurses holding a patient up, patting her on the back, asking her to cough.

I walked up to them and said, "I'm looking for Pearl Rigg, can you tell me where she is?"

They looked at me funny, and one of them said, "Well, honey, this is Pearl Rigg!"

I looked at this person they were holding and didn't even recognize her. There was no resemblance to my grandma. I had just seen my grandma ten hours ago. She had white hair and a twinkle in her eye; this person was bald and drooling and had no recognition of me or anything around her.

I looked at the two women and said, "You're lying! This isn't Pearl Rigg!"

They said that yes, it was indeed Pearl Rigg. I just grabbed my heart and started crying. I ran out of the room, past my relatives.

I looked at them through streaming tears and yelled, "What did they do to Grandma?"

I was in shock. I had just realized I'd lost my grandma, my mother, my lifeline. Her body was there, but I didn't even recognize that. I don't even remember the rest of that trip. I didn't go back and see her again. I couldn't be consoled, because I'd just been dealt my first dose of reality and loss. I would lose my grandma, and it would be the greatest loss of my life. I was different after that; I had been disappointed before, but never devastated. My grandma had not gone through a long period of disease or had an open wound or any other obvious sign that her life was ending. It was such a sudden shock to me, and no one seems to understand my relationship with my grandma.

We went back to the lake, but my heart didn't go with me. Plans were made for us to return to Arizona, and summer was over, but I didn't want to go. Kari and I lay awake at night and made plans for me to run away and somehow stay with her. We went through every scenario, but of course it wasn't to be. I ended up going back to Tucson with my mother, brothers, and sisters.

Summer's over, back to real life.

We ended up moving into a trailer, where my attitude and relationship with my mother worsened. I wasn't happy to be there, and my mom and I fought all the time. I didn't know what was happening back home, but I did know they put my grandmother into a nursing home.

Starting high school was both sad and happy. I had friends for the first time I knew from the year earlier. Getting a schedule and different classes was fun. Flowing Wells High School at that time was one of the best schools in the country. It had won the Bellamy Award twice and was state of the art back then.

We had an indoor swimming pool and were offered electives such as bowling, archery, golf, and things of that nature. I took it all.

It was 1970, and black light posters and hippies were in full bloom. Bell bottoms and halter tops were the choice of fashion, but as usual my mom would go for none of that. Being the oldest of five poor children didn't allow me to "keep up with the Joneses", per se. Heck, I remember what a financial ordeal it was when I had to buy a gym suit. It is so much a part of the whole high school thing to be accepted. Money may not solve all the problems, but if it's used right, it can solve many of them. Money had never mattered to me, because where I came from, everyone was in the same boat. Now in Tucson, to me it did matter to be different. Even without all the trappings, I was usually liked by all who knew me, including boys. I was being approached by boys for the first time on a regular basis, but I couldn't really have a social life. I couldn't afford to do what other kids could do. My mom actually allowing me to do any of what they did would have been a miracle.

I would never bring anyone to my house – EVER! I mean, when you walked in, there were kids and toys everywhere, nothing to be proud of. In fact, I was ashamed of where I lived. You could drive down any street we'd ever lived on and be able to tell our house every time. We stuck out like a sore thumb, because our yard was never cared for. In fact, we trashed every yard we ever had. The boys would dig holes and leave broken toys everywhere. I never had a room of my own to take people to, so I never took them to my house. Besides, almost anytime I walked in the door, my mother would find something to be mad at me for. It was almost guaranteed she would yell at me or hit me in front of people, which was the worst.

I don't really have any memories of me and my mother just sitting down and talking civil, except the day my mind clicked about Shelley. I had never really wondered about where we came from or who our father was; all I knew was that we didn't have one. I knew David and I came from the same man, because we both had red curly hair and freckles and Martin was our last name. My mom, Shelley, Darla and Billy's last name was Hughes. So I knew that difference, but for some reason I had always thought Shelley was Billy's dad's, too, because she had dark hair like Billy and her last name was Hughes. I always knew there was something different about Darla. I had just never asked about that. All I knew was she had Darla the year I was with Grandpa and Grandma, and she was the only one with platinum blonde hair.

One day, something popped into my mind about Bill, Billy's dad, and Billy's dad dying before he was born. It was like a light came on in my mind. Without thinking, I looked at my mom and said, "Wait a minute, if Bill died before Billy was born, then who is Shelley's father?" My mom just stood there and looked at me. As I said, there was no privacy in my house, so my mom took me out to the car. She sat me down and started telling me about our fathers and where we all came from. It was an enlightening experience. It was also the only time I remember my mom and me actually talking without yelling at each other. That's when she told me about my dad and him going to prison and coming back and her having Shelley. Then she told me about going to the lawyer in Oklahoma, trying to get child support from my dad, but getting pregnant by her lawyer. She told me about giving Darla up for adoption and all that went along with that, then how my dad had run off with his brother's wife and gotten her pregnant, but then she went back to her husband and raised the child as their own. So the fact is, my cousin was really my sister. Go back and re-read it. Yes, my cousin is my sister. I wasn't in shock or anything; it just put everything in order for me. It allowed my mind the freedom to understand much of what I had suspected all along, and I was at the age where I wondered so much about my father. In fact, I used to see red-haired men on the street and wonder, *Is he my father?* I fantasized about what he would be like and wanted very much to know him.

Things between me and my mom were getting worse every day. She was always yelling at me for everything. Even though we were getting older and able to take care of ourselves, it seemed like we were more of a burden to her. Nothing I wore, ate, said, or did was without retribution from her. She was determined that I could do nothing right. I did like church, because there I was accepted. I could do things with the church I couldn't do with my school friends. The church had activities, or they would pay for a poor kid to attend something like summer camp or bowling trips. That was also something my mother would accept. If I did anything with someone from church, she didn't object, not like when I wanted to do something with someone from school. I know some of you are thinking she was right and smart to be that way. You may be right to a point, but she did it for the wrong reasons. My mom did it to control and dominate; she did not do it out of love.

One time, they had a contest at church. Whoever could bring the most kids to vacation bible school over those two weeks would get to take a ride in a helicopter over Tucson, then have lunch at the ice cream shop. There would be one winner from the boys, and one winner from the girls. Well, with the help of my brothers and sisters and friends, I got over 136 kids to come to at least one session of vacation bible school. I actually won the contest, and it was the neatest thing. I got the crown, a ride in the helicopter, lunch and a day away from my house. It was a wonderful experience. Unfortunately, the relationship I had with my mother was deteriorating, and I hated to go home.

\

We lived across the street from a family that had three boys, ranging in age from older than me to younger than me. Two of them were on the high school football team, and very popular. I didn't hang out with them or anything; I just knew them by living across the street from them. They would always say hi and were nice to me. One day, I was standing in the kitchen handing out cookies to the kids. My mom was standing next to me, yelling at me about something trivial, just screaming in my face, and I knew better than to fight back with my mom, ever! I always just stood there and took it. I knew I wouldn't win the fight, and I was scared of her. For some reason, this one day I just couldn't take anymore. All of a sudden, I took the bag of cookies and wadded up the bag, crumbling the cookies inside. I threw it on the floor, then turned and walked out of the house. We lived on a "culdy sack"; you know, roads that come off a bigger road and look like a light bulb. You drive in, and then there's a circle at the end where you have to turn and go back out the same way you came in. Well, I walked up the main road to about the third culdy sack, and there was a big group of guys just standing there. Most of them were on the high school football team, and my two neighbors were among them. I had been walking with my head down, and I was crying. By the time I looked up, there I was right on them.

Tony Lott, my neighbor, said, "Hi, April, what's going on?" He could see I was crying and asked what was wrong.

I tried wiping my eyes so I wouldn't look too stupid in front of ten of the best looking, most popular guys at my school. I hid my embarrassment with a nervous laugh.

"Oh, my mom and I just had a fight."

Tony asked me what we had fought over. I told him I didn't even know. He said, "Oh, you'll be all right. It's normal to fight with your parents."

Now, these were big guys, and I was five feet tall, so Tony put his elbow on my shoulder like an arm rest while he was talking to me, and he was trying to get me to laugh.

All of a sudden, my mom's car screeched to a halt right next to us. I could see in the car, and she had brought my brothers and sisters with her. She jumped out of the car with a big leather belt in her hand and ran up to me and Tony.

Mom stuck that belt in his face and said, "Get your fucking hands off my daughter, right now!"

Tony, shocked, immediately lifted his arms over his head and said, "Hey, I wasn't doing anything to her!"

She shook the belt in his face and screamed obscenities at him. The other guys were just standing there in shock as my mom turned to me and started beating me with that belt. She was slamming it against any part of me it would hit. When one of the guys tried to stop her, she turned on him and he backed off. My mom resumed beating me, while the whole time she was screaming for me to get in the car. I tried to open the door, but it was locked. My two little brothers were in the back seat, but they were huddled in the far corner of the car, trying to get as far away from that wrath as possible. I kept trying to open the door, but my mom just kept beating me. Finally, David got up the nerve to jump up and unlock the door, and then he jumped right back to his place of hiding. He had good reason for fearing her. I huddled in the back passenger seat as she sped off to our house, the tires squealing as we left.

My mom beat me all the way home, reaching over the seat to hit me –
and if my brothers were in the way, then too bad. Once we got home, she
continued to hit me with the belt all the way into the house. I was both
verbally and physically abused by her once we got inside. Honestly, the
verbal abuse was always the worst. Mom was like an unleashed tornado
when she lost her temper, which was almost every day.

All of a sudden, there was a knock at the door. My mom stopped
what she was doing, gave me a dirty look and answered the door. It was
Tony Lott's mother from across the street, and she pushed her way into
our house. I ran to my bedroom, not knowing what else to do; a survival
instinct, I guess. After a minute or two, I could hear yelling and
screaming coming from the living room.

Mrs. Lott said, "If I ever hear of you treating another one of your
children like that, I will have you arrested!"

My mom screamed at her that it was none of her business what
she did with her children. It was horrible, but I will never forget that
women for caring. Back then, the laws were very different than they are
today.

After Mrs. Lott left, my mom came in my room to yell at me
some more for causing all the trouble. She didn't hit me again that day,
but I was so embarrassed. I didn't want to go to school because I had
bruises all over me, but most of all the whole football team had been a
witness to this. I was so scared that I even contemplated ditching, but I
went on to school to face the music. Once I got there, I was shocked at
what happened. Instead of people whispering behind my back, they came
up to me and started saying things like, "You poor thing" and "Oh my
God. Your mom is crazy!" These were popular people, ones who had

never even given me the time of day before. It was weird, like I'd become their martyr. From then on, these kids started saying hi to me at school and actually talking to me! I just now realized I was interesting and people were interested in asking me questions and listening to my answers. I remember whole lunch periods where ten or twelve people would sit around me and ask me weird questions and be fascinated by my answers. All kinds of stuff, like all the places I had lived and things I had seen or done. Talking to people about my life turned into my outlet. The realization I've just had is: "That's why I write!" I need to tell people the things I've seen and lived through. It's what keeps me going. I needed someone to know, I needed someone to be interested and care, even if they couldn't do anything to fix it. Surely, someone I talk to won't make a mistake I've made or will better understand why people are like they are. Maybe my experiences will even make someone more tolerant of others than they were before. When you meet someone, you never know what their life has been like or why they're different from you. There must be a reason for all this life experience I've been forced to learn.

Sorry, my mind wanders; back to 1970. My mom and I were like worst enemies, instead of mother and daughter. We fought all the time. We had such different views and interests. We had had no early bonding, because I'd bonded with my grandmother. My mom had no respect for me, nor I for her. We became enemies, and our psychological and emotional problems were many, and growing.

The weird thing about my mother was that she had found a place for herself by helping others; not us, but others. She was practically the minister of the church. She went on visitations and did everything with the church, or her school. She had been going to college off and on from as far back as I can remember. All I know is she was never home. One time, my mom took in this girl, about my age, from a reform school so she could try to rehabilitate her (like we didn't have enough problems with the five of us). Her name was Maria Jo Story, and boy was she wild. Sadly, she had been in foster care or reform schools all her life. Just what I needed, someone I could look up to.

For some reason, my mom put me and "Jo", as we called her, in a room together. Kari Jo was there, but I don't remember why. I think they were there visiting or living there. Maybe this was before the summer when Grandma had her surgery. I do know the first thing that happened after Maria Jo moved in with us was she talked sweet Kari Jo into helping her steel a bunch of forty-fives from a record shop, with a baby buggy of all things. They had someone's baby in a buggy, went in to the record store, and hid the records down in the buggy under the baby. I don't know how she had Kari Jo involved in that, but she got into all kinds of trouble. Kari Jo wasn't one to get into trouble. Maria Jo was a troubled girl, but they let her come back to our house.

We were in a room together, without my sisters, so she had plenty of opportunity to influence me. I was very susceptible to influence; anyone who showed interest in me could influence me.

Jo told me one day she was going to sneak out of the house that night to meet her boyfriend and wanted me to go with her. I said no at first, because I knew my mother's wrath – and anything that would invoke it – and I wanted nothing to do with. Like I said, I was susceptible to influence, so eventually she talked me into it.

I was scared the whole day while we planned this big event. We went to great lengths to pull this off. During the day, she talked me into a lot of things. We took two apples, set them on the pillow of each bed, and put hairpieces on each one. After that, we made the beds up to look like we were in them, just in case my mom should open the door to look in. After everyone went to bed, Jo's boyfriend and one of his friends appeared at my window. In Tucson it's so hot, we never shut our windows, and there were no screens on the windows anyway, so it was easy to get out.

These guys were at least three or four years older than I was, maybe even older than that. Once we were outside, I knew I'd made a mistake, because I was scared. Jo and her friends talked me into helping them steal my mom's car. It was a sixty-six Chevy, and you didn't need a key to start it. We quietly pushed the car out of the driveway and a little ways down the street. When we felt the coast was clear, we got in and off we went. The first thing they did was stop and buy beer. I had never drank beer before, so it tasted gross to me. I just let the others drink it, and boy did they.

Right from the start, I knew this guy wanted more from me than I was willing to do. Still being a virgin, I was determined to hang on to it as long as I could. Now, Jo's boyfriend and his friend were pretty drunk. The guy in the back seat with me had roaming hands, but he finally figured out he wasn't going to get anywhere with me. I can't remember why, but the guy in the back with me and Jo's boyfriend started fighting with each other across the front seat. Jo stopped the car, got out and just started walking up a nearby alley. I ran up to her while both guys grabbed their quart bottles of beer and followed. We'd walked a little ways when we came across a horse in a pen that was backed up to the alley.

I'm an animal lover, and always have been, but my passion is horses. I LOVE horses and have always wanted one. As soon as I saw this horse, I was able to get it to come up to the fence. I was so happy it let me pet it and love on it.

One of the guys (can't remember which) came walking up saying, "Nice horse, nice horse."

To this day I don't understand why, but he lifted up his quart size beer bottle and smacked the horse over the head with it. I screamed and started running, yelling at the top of my lungs.

Jo and her friends ran after me. One of them grabbed me and put his hand over my mouth. He was telling me to be quiet, or I would wake up the whole neighborhood and we would get arrested. I finally calmed down enough to stop fighting him. When we finally got back out to the end of the alley, I was still crying. I told them all I wanted to go home RIGHT NOW! I couldn't believe I was with these bad people.

We went back to the car, and they told me they would take me home. I just wanted to get away from all of them. After getting in the car, someone noticed it was almost out of gas. We found the only open gas station in the area, probably the only one for miles. Remember, this was back in 1970, so there were no self-serve stations yet. Once we pulled up to a pump, the attendant came out and tried to put gas in the car. Unbeknownst to us, the gas cap needed a key. The attendant came up to the window, asking for the key to the gas tank. Jo looked back at me, and I just shrugged my shoulders; I didn't know you needed a key to open the gas tank. We had to tell the attendant we forgot the key and we'd have to go get it. We drove off and stopped up the road. Almost in unison, we said, "Now what?" We didn't have enough gas to get the car home. One of the guys got out and pried off the gas cap with something he found in the trunk, and then we drove back to that same gas station.

In the meantime, the gas station attendant had already decided something wasn't kosher and had called the police. We gave him two dollars and just sat, oblivious to what was about to transpire. All of a sudden, the police pulled up behind us. In a flash, all four doors opened and we took off running in four different directions. To this day, I don't know how I did this, but I got away and ran three miles home.

I climbed back in the window the same way I had gotten out. My clothes smelled like beer, so I quickly took them off and threw them in the bottom of the closet. I grabbed the apple and stuffing out of the bed, threw them in the closet, got my nightgown on and jumped into bed. I was breathing so hard, I thought I was going to pass out. As soon as I was under the covers, the doorbell rang and the dog started barking. My heart was thumping so hard, I was sure my mom could hear it in the other room.

I heard the doorbell again, and then I heard my mom open the door. I could catch most of what they were saying. The police officer asked my mom if she owned a sixty-six Chevy and did she have a Maria Jo Story living there. My mom said yes to both questions. I heard the officer ask her if she knew her car was missing. My mom said, "WHAT?" No, she didn't know her car was missing, what did he mean? The police officer told her they believed Miss Story had stolen her car, and she was now in custody. They believed her daughter had been with her. My mom said, "My daughter is in bed!" The officer said Maria had told him her daughter April was with her. My mom offered to show him I was there and surely couldn't be involved.

My heart was pounding so hard, I thought it would burst. I still couldn't control my breathing. I heard my mom coming toward my bedroom. I just hunkered down and did the best I could at calming myself down. She opened the door and turned on the light.

I looked up, as sleepily as I could, and said, "What's the matter?"

My mom turned to the officer and said, "I told you my daughter is in bed."

She looked back at me, then quickly looked around the room, then walked over to Maria's bed and lifted the blankets up, exposing the wigged apple. The police officer was standing in the bedroom door, looking at me. My mom checked under the bed for Jo, like she'd really find her under there somewhere.

She gave me a puzzled look and asked, "Where is Jo?"

I looked at her standing there with the wigged apple in her hand and said, "I don't know. She was here when I went to bed."

Both the police officer and my mom began to interrogate me, asking me if I'd been with her or knew anything about this. I looked at both of them and boldly lied.

I said, "No. I don't have any idea what's going on!"

My mom looked at me. "You better not have anything to do with this, April, and I mean it!"

They apparently believed me, because they finally left the room, but I still felt like I wanted to pass out. I jumped up and quickly pushed all the things I'd haphazardly thrown into the closet out of sight. Slowly, I crept up to my bedroom door and listened, trying to hear anything. I was shaking so badly, my knees were knocking together. I heard the police officer tell my mom how to get her car back and that the only damage was that the gas cap had been pried off. My mom came back in my room and told me she was going with the police officer to get her car and that I'd have to stay with the kids. I told her that wasn't a problem.

I kept asking her what happened, and she said, "Maria Jo is in big trouble, and thank God you weren't with her!"

Needless to say, I never saw Maria Jo Story again after that. I never found out what happened to her, but to this day my mom doesn't know I was involved in that. Not something I'm proud of, but it did happen.

The Home

Honestly, that was the only bad thing I'd done up to that point in my life, and my mom didn't even know I'd done it. She would definitely find plenty of other things to dislike about me, though. My mom didn't like my hair, my clothes, or my friends (what few I had). I didn't do anything to her satisfaction, like cleaning the house, or if the kids did something wrong, it was always my fault. If she didn't like what I made for dinner, I would get in trouble. It just didn't matter what I did, she would find fault with it.

At the time, I thought of myself as a pretty good kid. I didn't talk back, I didn't wear controversial clothes like the other kids, I didn't go out, I cleaned the house without too much argument, I would babysit the kids, I never messed with drugs, and I was a virgin. Overall, I didn't think I was so bad and didn't understand where the conflict came from. Maybe it was because I was coming into my own, and it was like having another woman in the house. As I grew up, Instead of enjoying me as a friend or companion, I was becoming a competitor, at least in her eyes.

My mom and I fought so much. I was becoming a person separate from one of her children, and our relationship wasn't based on love, so it was doomed. I say we fought, but in reality she yelled or hit me while I cowered and kept my mouth shut. If I tried to stand up to her, there would be hell to pay and I'd end up paying the price for it. It was wearing on me, and eventually I was getting tired of taking it. I stood up for myself once or twice, but I lived to regret it. Our conflicts manifested themselves into arguments, like the day we had one of the most life-changing fights ever, for me anyway.

My mom had driven by and saw me walking home from school, holding a boy's hand. I wasn't a slut or anything, I was only fourteen and still a virgin (just don't want you to forget that). I'd only been felt up one time, by Billy Mosley (oh yeah, by the guy at the McNealys' pool, too); OK, maybe I was a slut.

Anyway, I came into the house, went into the bedroom and changed clothes. My mom walked into the bathroom where I was standing. I saw the sweater I'd been wearing in her hand. She walked up to me and slapped me, then shoved the sweater into my face.

My mom screamed at me, "You've been smoking! Smell this sweater! It stinks like cigarettes!"

Then she just let loose on me with all her might; she slapped me and hit me for what seemed like forever.

My mom kept screaming, "I saw you with THAT BOY! You're a slut!" over and over.

When she was finally through, she jumped in her car and left. The ironic thing about that day was, I hadn't even been smoking. I'd smoked cigarettes before, but not that day; I'd just been standing around a bunch of kids at the bus stop who had been.

I started cleaning the house and dreading my mother's return. When she got back home, I was expecting to get it again, but she came in all smiles and said, "How would you like to go live somewhere else?" I asked her what she meant, if we were moving again. She said, "No. I'm wondering if you want to go live with your aunt Martha in Texas."

Now, Aunt Martha wasn't really my aunt; she'd been the church secretary when Dick Buck was alive, and we all called her Aunt Martha. After the tragic death of Pastor Buck, she'd gone to be the secretary for another preacher in Corpus Christi, Texas.

My mom said, "You could live with her and go to school. Martha works for the man who runs it, you can go there."

I was mad at my mother, so the thought of getting away from her and my stifling life sounded great to me. Needless to say, I jumped at the opportunity.

"Yes, I'll go live with Aunt Martha in Texas. When am I leaving?"

She told me we would fly to Texas and would be leaving tomorrow. I was in total shock! I was going to get away from my mother, my responsibilities of my younger siblings, and I was going to fly on an airplane. Maybe I would even have a room of my own. I couldn't believe my luck. I remembered Aunt Martha being a very sweet lady. I wouldn't get to say goodbye to anyone at school, but I needed to get away from the battles with my mother, so I was excited.

When I went to bed that night, I was thinking all kinds of things, and no more fighting with my mom. I even started missing my little monster siblings; who would take care of them when I was gone? The thought of a new life, in a new place, away from my mother, was overwhelming. I didn't sleep all night, but the next morning I got another treat. My mother almost never bought me new clothes, but she took me out and bought me three new dresses. She even let me pick them out, and I was in seventh heaven. It was a great morning as I packed my suitcase.

That evening, my mom and I left Tucson on an airplane; it was so exciting. Once we got to Dallas, we had to take a twenty-five seat commuter jet on to Corpus Christi. It was a real adventure for me. My mom and I didn't fight one time, even though the trip took all day.

When we landed, Aunt Martha was waiting for us. I remember she had a little Volkswagen Carmengia. She was still as nice as I remembered, but I was a little ambivalent. I didn't know her that well, and by now I was having a little anxiety about being so far from anyone or anything familiar. I still mustered up some excitement as we drove through town, trying to take everything in.

The first thing I remember about Corpus Christi after getting off the plane was the humidity and cold. It was September 16, 1970. Corpus Christi had just been through hurricane Cecilia less than a week earlier, and it had done quite a bit of damage. As we were on our way out of town, I wondered just how far out she lived.

After fifteen minutes of driving out into the boonies, I asked, "How far we were going?"

Martha said, "Well, I thought we'd go by the school first."

For some reason, that got me worried. Just where was this school? Apparently, it wasn't in town.

Finally, another half an hour later, we pulled off the main road and up to this big red brick building. The front of it had a steeple on top, and it said on a big sign, "The Peoples Church". Right below that, it said, "The Rebecca Home For Girls" I knew right away I was in trouble.

We all got out of the car and went inside through these big white double doors that led us into a big foyer. It had red carpet, and there were doors coming off all three sides of the foyer. The doors that were straight ahead were big white double doors, just like the ones we'd just come through. Then there were regular sized doors that went off both the other sides, two doors on each side. Above the big double doors facing the front was written "Ye who enter, enters the house of the Lord." I was getting very leery; was I going to be going to a church school?

I looked at my mom and said, "Mom, I don't think I want to do this."

She said, "You haven't even seen it yet," but I was getting the gist of it.

A tall woman and man came out of one of the side doors that said "Office" on it. They walked over to us and introduced themselves as "Granny and Poppa".

The woman shook both my mom and Aunt Martha's hands, then she looked over at me and said, "Well, April, let's introduce you to the girls."

The lady named Granny opened one of the big swinging doors that faced us. I was amazed at the size of the room it opened into. From the foyer, you entered facing an altar of a church way down at the end of a huge room. It had a podium with a cross on it that sat up on a stage under an even larger cross. There were doors with numbers on them, running up and down both sides of this huge room. Up by the podium and stage area, the room had red carpet. There was an aisle that led all the way from these big double doors up to the altar. Right in front of the altar and podium, down three steps, was a choir bay. It had rows of seats on both sides that were red also, and they sat one row above each other like stadium seating. The seats faced the aisle that ran down the middle of the room. It was like a double-sided choir bay, each side had a little wooden fence around it.

Up on the stage area, I noticed about twenty girls sitting in a circle in front of the altar. There was a woman sitting in a chair in the middle of them, and she was holding an open Bible on her lap. All the girls had nightgowns and robes on; some of them had rollers in their hair. They stood up and came at me all at once. They started hugging me and saying how much they loved me and that God loved me. I looked at my mom with begging eyes and knew I didn't want to be here.

Suddenly, my mom and all of my problems didn't seem so bad; all I could think of was that I wasn't going to school here. Each girl introduced herself to me; they were all smiling so hard, it looked like a room full of Cheshire cats. I wasn't even listening to their names, because I'd already decided I wasn't going to go to school there.

This one particular girl walked over to introduce herself, but the woman called Granny stepped up and said, "Carol, this is April, and she'll be your new roommate! You want to come with us and show her the new room?"

My mind stopped dead in its tracks and went berserk at the same time. It was then I realized they wanted me to stay here at this church, not with Aunt Martha, as I'd thought.

My mind reeled as I looked at my mom. "Mom, no! I don't want to stay here! I can't stay here, Mom!"

I had said it in front of everyone, but I couldn't help it. All faces turned towards my mom.

"Stay the night, April, give it a chance. I'll come back tomorrow with Martha and see how you are."

I was protesting very loudly, more with my eyes and body language than verbally.

The big man called Poppa walked toward me and took me firmly by the arm. He led me, and the procession following behind me, to one of the many white doors that ran down the inside of the building. It was closest to the way we'd entered. The best way to explain this building is to tell you to think of an H. When you walked in, you were at the bottom of an H, and the room ended in the middle of the H, except the sides kept going, just like an H. Doors ran all the way up both sides of the H. The big wall with the cross on it (at the end of the altar & behind the pulpit) made the room seem like it ended there, but behind that wall were utility rooms, such as laundry, and more of the numbered rooms.

The front area we first walked into faced the altar with the huge cross clearly visible on the wall and had rows of folding chairs facing the choir and stage. That part of the room had a tile floor. It was a church, except it had bedroom doors running up and down the entire length of this huge room. So other than the doors, it looked just like a big, red church! Chairs, carpet, and accessories were all red, except for the big tiled area we first stepped into that had the folding chairs facing the stage.

Anyway, Poppa had a really good hold on my arm; in fact, he was hurting me. Poppa was a big man, too, powerful, and not just physically; he had a very formidable presence to him. So I was led to one of these doors, and he opened it. The room had three beds, a set of bunk beds against one wall, and one single bed against the other. There were two dressers, one in-between each bed, and they were all made up with green bedspreads. The one window in the room had a curtain that matched the bedspread. It wasn't an ugly room, but there was no carpet, just bare cement floors. Besides that, it was a bit dank in there, too. Poppa proceeded to tell us how "with God's help" they'd just survived Hurricane Cecilia and the Devil was trying to stop them from doing God's work.

The building had just been completed less than a month earlier and had just been dedicated before the hurricane hit. Water had ruined the brand new carpet in all of the side rooms. Then Poppa proceeded to tell us how they had all almost died in the hurricane, but God had protected them. I had just come from Tucson, Arizona, to a place that was damp and cold. Besides, I was cold with fright; I was just plain cold, I wanted out of there.

My mom, Martha, Poppa, Granny, me and my roommate, Carol, all gathered in this little room. Poppa shut the door and sat me down on the edge of one of the beds.

He turned to my mom and said, "You two, go on and let her stay here, she'll be fine."

I looked at my mom and said, "No, Mom, I don't want to stay here. Please! I want to go with you and Aunt Martha. Then I'll come back here with you tomorrow."

Poppa stood up and guided my mom and Aunt Martha towards the door. He repeated himself, "Go, leave her here, she'll be fine. Let us get her settled in."

I stood up and said, "No, Mom, please let me go with you! I don't want to stay here. I'll be good, I promise, please!"

She looked at me and said, "No, April. I think you should stay here tonight. It won't kill you to stay here and check it out. I'll be back tomorrow."

Poppa stepped between us and told them to leave. He went with them and shut the door behind him.

So there I was. Granny and a woman named Elaine were still in there with me, as was the girl who was lucky enough to already occupy that room, Carol.

I started to cry when Granny stood up, looked at me and said, "You can shut up that blubbering right now. It will get you nothing but trouble."

Of course, that just made me cry even harder. I tried to push past her as I yelled for my mom. Granny immediately pushed me down on the bed and pointed her finger at me.

"You're going nowhere but to bed, and don't get any ideas to the contrary."

At that moment, I was so scared, mad, devastated and frustrated, but it was about to get worse. All of a sudden, Poppa walked back into the room with my suitcase. He handed it to Granny, then went back out the door. She sat my suitcase on the bed across from me and opened it. She started pulling stuff out and throwing it on the floor. I tried to stand up and protest, but the other woman, Elaine, pushed me back down on the bed. Then she, too, started helping Granny go through my clothes. I grabbed one of the new dresses my mom had just bought me and questioned why they were throwing my stuff on the floor.

Granny looked at me with fire in her eyes and said, "These are the clothes of a tramp. You won't need them here, because we won't allow you to be a tramp anymore!"

She grabbed the dress out of my hand and slapped me across the face, knocking me back across the bed. I was a fourteen-year-old virgin. I didn't even know what a tramp was.

Granny threw my hairbrush at me, followed by two pair of underwear and a nightgown. Everything else was in a pile in the middle of the floor. She picked up one of the two pair of bikini underwear I'd talked my mom into buying for me that morning.

Granny held them to my face and screamed through her teeth at me, "Only a harlot would wear these so boys could see her naked!" She slapped me again. "It won't take long, girly, and we'll get all these horrible, sinful, thoughts out of your head. You'll see. God will cleanse your mind."

At that moment, I was having the most sinful thoughts I'd ever had. I wanted to kill my mother for leaving me there, and I wanted to kill this six foot tall woman who was treating me just like my mother, hitting me and screaming in my face about how bad I was. Was I born under a bad sign or what?

Granny threw my suitcase on the floor next to my pile of stuff and started shoving everything back in it. She picked up my makeup bag, opened it and started ranting and raving about how it was a sin to paint your face just to attract men. It was a whore thing to do. All I had in there was lip gloss and a tube of mascara; I wonder what she would have done if I'd had blush or eyeliner! Granny locked the suitcase and told me to get in the bathroom and get that trash off my face. I mean, she was serious about the makeup now!

She said, "You look like a whore! We do not paint ourselves here."

I mean, holy smoke, all my mom would allow me to wear was mascara and lip gloss, and even that was a fight. The other girls at school wore paint (so to speak). I mean, this was during the Flower Power era, love-ins, and all that implies. Charles Manson wasn't even convicted yet.

I got up, crying and holding my sore cheek as I went into the bathroom. I immediately started looking for a way out of there. This was a scary woman, and a scary situation. The bathroom, in fact the entire building, was created very efficiently. Every two rooms would share one bathroom in the middle. There was a door on each side of a big mirror and two hand sinks. Then there was a door in the middle, across from the mirrored wall that had one stool and a tub and shower combination. The school had about forty rooms, and they all had bedding for three. So that's sleeping space for well over one hundred and fifty girls, even though I never saw more than about twenty of them. My mind was only concentrating on how to get one girl out of this mess: me.

As I washed my face, I noticed I was being watched. Granny wouldn't let me shut the door. I just kept telling myself, *Tomorrow, I'm going to tell my mom Granny hit me and took my stuff. Surely, she won't leave me here after hearing that.*

Once I'd washed some of the devil off me, Granny threw my nightgown at me and told me to put it on. I was embarrassed and wanted some privacy.

"Oh, you'll get naked for a boy, so don't give me that innocent act." I reluctantly put my nightgown on. She snapped her fingers, and pointed to the clothes I'd just taken off. "You won't be needing those either," she said. Granny then took me by the arm and led me to the bed that would be mine. "It's twenty minutes till lights out. You'd better listen to Carol and learn quickly, or there will be consequences." She then looked at Carol and said, "You're in charge now, Carol. Teach her quickly, or you'll suffer the ramifications of not doing your job. Do you understand?"

"Yes, Granny," replied Carol.

Then Granny and Elaine left the room, slamming the door behind them. Now I was alone with Carol.

I couldn't stop crying, and I was practically hysterical. I was not going to stay there; my mom would not leave me there after I told her what they did. *I am not going to stay here, and that's all there is to it! That woman Granny is crazy!*

I got up, walked to the window and pulled back the curtains. Carol jumped up, took the curtains out of my hands. She put them back the way they were, being careful to remove each crease with gentle strokes. She looked at me with fear in her eyes.

"You can't touch the curtains or the window EVER!"

I looked at her and thought to myself, *Great, she's as crazy as the rest of them, just what I need.* She looked scared, though.

"They patrol the outside, and if they see you even move the curtains, you'll get a whipping! There's a metallic tape on all of the windows; it's an alarm system."

"You can't be serious!" I told her.

She shook her head vigorously to the contrary. I realized at that moment this was some sort of prison I'd entered.

"Well, I'm not going to stay in this piece of shit prison! I'm getting out of here tomorrow!" I told her.

Carol's mouth dropped to the floor. "You can't say things like that. You'll get a beating. You can never cuss in here. You can't even use slang, like 'gosh' or 'golly', because they're forms of exasperation. Especially cussing, or using God's name in vain! You'll be beaten!"

I said, "Well, then I won't say it in front of them, but I am getting out of here!"

She looked at me, almost crying. "No! You don't understand! They can hear everything you say!" She pointed above the door, and there was a built-in speaker in the wall. "All of the rooms are monitored from the office, so you must be careful! I'm only allowed to tell you this once. We can never get caught talking about how to get out, or alarms, or anything like that after this."

My heart sank, as if it could sink any lower. I really was in a prison. I lay down on the bed and cried so hard, I couldn't breathe through my nose anymore. While I was lying on the bed crying, Carol was telling me other things I needed to know to survive at the home.

She started off by telling me that as soon as I found Jesus, all my problems would be solved, and she was just like me when she first arrived here, and it would all be OK.

I was thinking the whole time, *Yeah! It'll be OK because I'll be gone from here tomorrow.*

Carol continued telling me stuff I couldn't believe. I couldn't part my hair down the middle because it was worldly. No listening to music, except the religious music everyone sang together. No fried foods, no cussing, no talking about running away, no male attire (shorts or pants), no adornment of the body (tattoos, makeup, jewelry), anything like that. Nothing but dresses to the middle of the knee, no longer, no shorter, because that was worldly! We couldn't consume anything with refined sugar, carbonated beverages, or pork. No newspapers, television, or radio. Never miss or be late for Bible study, broadcast, or church. If you were, for sure you'd get a beating then.

Carol went on and on, until all of a sudden someone came banging on the door yelling, "Lights out!"

Carol jumped out of bed and ran to the light switch by the door, flipping it off. She quickly ran and jumped back in bed.

"Absolutely NO talking after lights out, so goodnight, April."

I cried all night long. When morning came, I couldn't even open my eyes, because they were so swollen from crying. I didn't know if it was light outside or not. The heavy rubber backed curtains weren't letting in any light, so Carol got up and turned the light on.

All of a sudden, someone came by banging on the door again. This time, they were yelling, "Time to get up, breakfast in thirty minutes."

Then the knocks proceeded on down the hall, doing the same thing to all the doors.

I got up and went into the bathroom to wash my face. There were two other girls in there from the room next door, so I went back and lay down on the bed. Our door opened, and there stood Granny. She threw a pink polyester dress at me and told me to put it on.

"We'll find you some other dresses later," she said. "You girls get dressed, breakfast is in fifteen minutes.

I told Carol I didn't want breakfast; I just wanted to stay there in the room until my mom got there.

She looked at me and said, "You don't have a choice. If you miss breakfast, then you miss roll call and you get a beating. You have to go."

So I got up and put this ugly dress on that was too big for me. At this point, I looked just the way I felt.

Carol told me we had to make our beds or we'd get a beating, so she helped me make my bed to their specifications. There could be no wrinkles, it had be tucked in right, or (you guessed it) you would get a beating. After we made my bed, Carol checked the room once more before we exited.

She said, "They do room inspections while we're at Bible study."

Great, inspections and Bible study; I didn't think it could get any worse. I just kept telling myself that as soon as my mom got there, I was telling her about all this stuff and I was leaving. I was not going to stay there in that prison. I reluctantly followed Carol out of the bedroom and back into the big room, the church. I was hoping my mother would come soon, because I couldn't wait to get out of there.

\

The big room had all tiles on the floor from where you entered at the front of the room, up to where the red carpet started. After that, all of the red carpeted area was the church. If you stood on the red carpet and looked towards the entrance and tiled area, you saw big metal tables that folded down from the walls. You could also see big silver doors that slid up to reveal a kitchen and serving counter. When we came out, there were about twenty-five girls standing in line against the wall my bedroom door opened from. As I walked out, all the girls started smiling and hugging me again. Every one of them was telling me God would help me and that it would be OK. All of a sudden, the sliding doors on the wall started opening and I could see into the kitchen. Granny, Elaine and a girl I didn't know were behind the serving line. The man called Poppa came into the room. He counted us all, then told us to bow our heads for prayer. After he prayed, everyone except me said "Amen."

The line finally started moving, with me and Carol bringing up the end. Once I got to the serving counter, I was given a bowl of oatmeal, a piece of toast and a glass of milk. I carried it to a table and sat down next to Carol. All at once, every one of the girls came up to me and started telling me I was their sister now and God had sent me to them, and I would see the light. Each one of them told me they had been "just like me" when they got there, but God had saved them and would do the same for me. I just thought to myself the only light I wanted to see was the Arizona sun. I told them my mom was coming soon and I wouldn't be staying, but I thanked them anyway. I got a lot of real sorrowful looks and a lot of "I will pray for you"s in return.

I couldn't eat for more than one reason; we were having oatmeal, my least favorite food. Plus, the milk smelled like something dead.

When I asked one of the girls what was wrong with the milk, she said, "Oh, its goat's milk, but you'll get used to it."

I thought, *No, I won't.* It tasted worse than the water at the lake.

She proudly announced that they milked the goats themselves. It's a good thing I wasn't rude or mean, or I would have told them all what I was thinking right then. That milk truly was the worst smelling stuff, and I just didn't feel good. I asked them where the sugar or butter was. They told me we couldn't eat any sugar unless it was unrefined, and there was only butter on special occasions.

I thought to myself, *This is getting better and better.*

They did say that sometimes they got honey for their toast, but again only on special occasions. I had to finish every bite of what I'd taken, or guess what? Yep. I would get a whipping.

I told them, "I can't eat this stuff, or I'll throw up, I mean it."

They all looked at each other and whispered between themselves, then they offered to eat and drink my stuff for me so I wouldn't get in trouble, which I gladly let them do. I told myself I would eat later, after I got out of there.

After breakfast, we had to go to Bible study, and then to broadcast. What is broadcast, you ask? Well, I was finding out a lot about this place, very quickly. I learned that this "Girls Home" was masterminded and owned by a very powerful man named Lester Roloff. He was brilliant and used his brains to build an empire.

This girls home was run by Poppa and Granny, but it was one of many endeavors this man owned. He also owned a radio station, old folks home, boys home, home for alcoholics, and he even had an adoption agency. Since he was a minister, each endeavor helped the other one. At the old folks home in Rio Grande Valley, there were orchards of fresh citrus fruits, like tangerines, oranges, grapefruit, and lemons, which were then shipped to all of his other homes to feed everyone.

The boys home was located off the coast of southern Texas, and it was called "The Lighthouse". There, fish was caught and shipped to all the other homes.

The girls home also helped supply food to the other homes by growing acres of watermelon alongside a huge vegetable garden. They raised and milked goats, and even had a few cows. Chickens were also raised and slaughtered. All this stuff was sent around to the other homes, so all his ventures supported each other.

Brother Roloff (as I came to know him) owned an airplane and piloted it himself. He would preach a sermon twice every day from his radio station in Corpus Christi. It was broadcast worldwide, and I found out the girls would sing religious songs on his "broadcast" every day. In fact, I was told sometimes he would even come out to the home and do his show from there.

He had a large corporate headquarters in Corpus Christi, Texas. "The office" was where a whole work force of people would just sit and open envelopes. Each envelope either had cash or checks which were separated into two piles, and they would do this all day long. He employed over fifty people at that office, and his organizations brought in millions of dollars a year. This was back in 1970, and that was a lot of money for the time. He also preached every Sunday from the "Home", and those services were open to the public. That was why the tables were retractable, because every Sunday they were folded up into the wall, and then that area was set up for the public. The girls were kept up front in the little boxed areas close to the pastor's altar and weren't allowed to make contact with the public. Other than that, it was like any other Sunday church service. As he preached fire and brimstone, they passed the collection plate.

As I said, this was a very brilliant man, and I am in no way saying his heart or intent wasn't in the right place, but he didn't live at the home. He wasn't very accessible to us girls, and if he had known exactly what was going on and condoned it, then I didn't want to know him. He ran all the homes with private donations, because he wanted to have nothing to do with the state, or government in general.

There were four particular girls at the home who were privileged. They went to town each day and sang as a quartet on Brother Roloff's shows. The girls traveled with him in his plane all over the country, where they would sing and give testimony. The group was called "The Honey Bee Quartet". No matter if he was in town or out, everyone was required to listen to his two broadcasts every day. That was what broadcast was, and during broadcast no one could speak; we had to sit there and listen for forty-five minutes. I just wanted it over and for my mom to come back.

After broadcast, we had to go to Bible study, which was an hour long. The girls had to memorize one chapter of the Bible each week; not a verse, but a chapter. I was wanting out of there so bad, I couldn't sit still.

Finally, that was over and we had one free hour before lunch. As soon as we were free from the regimen, all the girls ran over to me. They were asking me questions and telling me they loved me and were praying for me. My mom still wasn't there when we went to lunch.

Lunch was interesting. We again lined up and went through this ritual. We were given a piece of fruit and a cheese sandwich; I was hungry by then, so I ate. I asked the girls where I could get a glass for some water. They told me we were never allowed to drink anything with our meals.

I looked at them and said, "What? We had that smelly milk with breakfast."

They told me milk was only given when they got oatmeal. If I wanted a drink, I had to wait until I was through eating, and then I could go to the water fountain on the wall. I asked them why. They said Brother Roloff believed that if you drank while eating, it disrupted your natural digestive system. I just couldn't believe this place.

Finally, my mom arrived there after lunch. As soon as I saw her, my heart lifted and I went running to her.

Before I could get to her, Granny stepped in-between us and said, "April, we want to talk to your mom for a little while before you visit."

I looked past Granny at my mom, using every pleading expression I could muster that said, *Get me out of here*, but she went into the office with Granny, Poppa, and Aunt Martha. All I could do was wait out in the main room with the rest of the girls.

So far, I had counted about 35 people in this whole big building. Including me, there were 28 girls, but I found out there were trailers out at the back of this big farm. That was where the pregnant girls lived. There were seven or eight of them, plus the two women who lived with them. They only came up to the big building for weekend church and things like that. They had their own kitchens and did their own Bible study.

After almost an hour of waiting, they all came out of the office and Mom was crying. Poppa, Granny, that trustee lady Elaine, and my mom took me into the room I had just spent the night in. They sat me on the bed and proceeded to tell me that, for the time being, this was the best place for me, and I WOULD be staying here. I stood up and started begging her in front of all of them, telling her all I'd heard from these girls. I told her I'd be good and never give her another problem. I started crying, and I didn't care who was there.

I was begging her, "Mom, please don't leave me here! Please! You can't leave me here!"

Poppa said, "April, you are staying, and we will not listen to anymore. Begging will not change this. It's happening, so you better accept it." He picked up my hair brush and tried to hand it to me. He said, "Dry your eyes, brush your hair, and get ready for church!"

I stood up, got right in his face, and looked at him with hate in my eyes and said, "I am NOT staying here, and you can't make me!"

Without any warning, he hit me in the face with my hairbrush, right across the mouth. He looked at me with a look I'll never forget and said, "You ARE staying, and if you ever threaten to run away, I will give you a beating you'll never forget. We're thirty miles from anyone, remember that! Now get ready for church!"

I looked at my mom while I was rubbing my swelling mouth, but she wouldn't look at me; she just turned away from me.

I can't even begin to tell you what I was feeling at that moment. I was numb, crushed, and devastated. All I was sure of was that my mom was giving me to these crazy people. She was punishing me for something I didn't do. If I did do something, all she had to do was tell me, and I would fix it. I needed to talk to her, but there was no way they were going to leave me alone with her; I saw that.

While my mind was off in oblivion, Granny picked up my hair brush and quickly brushed my hair. She said, "There, that's better. You'll learn to love it in time."

I didn't even argue, because I was having brain cloud. My mom was really going to leave me here.

They led me out of the room and back into the church, where they sat me down with the other girls. I don't remember much after that. I do remember Granny taking a picture of me and my mother before she left. I do remember that when she did leave, I tried to run after her, begging her again not to leave me there, but Granny grabbed me and drug me back inside the building.

As soon as my mom was out of sight, Granny slapped me across the face and said, "Shut your crying up right now, or you will get a beating. You are here, and you will learn the rules and abide by every one of them. We will change you; there's nothing you can do about anything, so get used to it."

Now that my mom was gone, I was truly alone. Oh, I had people around me, at all times. In fact, I wasn't allowed to be physically alone at all. I know I walked around with a Kleenex in my face for at least two weeks. I cried all the time. I went to sleep crying, and I swear to God I woke up crying every morning. It was horrible, and I was so miserable. I kept thinking this was as bad as it gets, but they kept proving me wrong. I didn't know it then, but I wouldn't see my mom or my siblings again for almost two years.

Repentance

They kept me pretty busy with regiment and duty. I had a lot to learn, and quickly, because if you made a mistake, it meant a whipping. Poppa used a twenty-two inch board with holes in it to whip us, at least for the first few months I was there. After that, he had a two-inch wide piece of leather, which was saddle sewn down the sides, and it had a piece of metal in the middle of it. I kid you not: the reason for the change was that the board kept breaking.

If you did something really bad, you went immediately to the office to have a private board meeting with Poppa. If you just got points against you, then you went to a public board meeting. Points were given for anything you did wrong, like you'd get one point for leaving hair in the garbage can, or you'd get two points for getting a C as a grade in school. If your bed didn't pass inspection, you got three points. There were all kinds of ways to get points. Room inspections were done at least once a day, usually while we were at school. Many times, we could see Granny and Elaine doing surprise inspections while we were in Bible study.

If you got caught trying to escape, talking bad about the home, hiding something you shouldn't have in your room, or you tried to sneak a letter out, you got immediate retribution from Poppa.

There were two board meetings a week, on Saturday night and Tuesday night. If you accumulated five points from one board meeting to another, then you got a whipping. All of us girls would go out into the church area, where they would call your name. Usually, Granny was the one to read the list. If your name was called, then you waited in line so Granny, Poppa and Elaine would take turns whipping us. You had to bend over the altar, then lift up your dress in front of everyone there (including Granny and Poppa's 14-year-old son). Their son and daughter (who was in the Honey Bee quartet) lived there with them. They all had a big apartment up at the front of the building. Man, would they whip us; they were serious about this whipping stuff. They would hit us so hard, they would wear themselves out and have to take turns. As I said before, I've seen many boards broken on the behinds of many young girls. If you showed any kind of emotion, yelled or tried to pull away, then you'd get it harder. The worst was being called towards the end of the list, because you had to anticipate longer.

The board meetings were more embarrassing than an office visit, but much less painful. Believe me; you never wanted to get called to the office, for any reason.

I remember one night, right after I'd arrived there, a new girl named Paula Lyons had been heard over the intercom planning to run. Paula was a tough girl, half-white and half-black, which in 1970 was already a hard thing to deal with. Paula had so many more problems than just that. I believe she'd always been in some kind of trouble. She had dyed red hair that was short and wiry. It gave her a wild and somewhat scary appearance. She was a big girl and pregnant, but not very far along. Paula was actually just a very sad and lonely person, but if she liked you, she could be very kind once you got to know her.

Our room was up at the front of the building, by the dining area and office. After lights out this one night, we awoke to someone screaming. We got out of bed and tried to look under the door to see what was happening. I could tell it was coming from the office, and I recognized Paula's scream; they were beating her. It lasted at least fifteen or twenty excruciating minutes. After it was over, I watched from under the door while Poppa, Granny, and Elaine carried Paula to her room. I know I wasn't the only person who heard it or watched from under the door. We all knew what happened to her, and I knew none of us would ever forget that place.

When I first got to the home, there were 28 girls plus the pregnant girls, and we got at least one new girl every few days. I didn't know it then, but I was at the beginning of what would become a very large operation. The "HOME", as we were told to refer to it, was huge. I don't know how many acres Brother Roloff actually owned, but it had to be thousands. What he didn't own wasn't worth owning, and nothing was built on it anyway. You could look for miles in either direction and not see a thing except for the "Home", and it was an incredible, huge, working farm.

There were a few girls there who probably needed to be somewhere, but most of them were pretty much like me, just from an unstable home life. They'd really done nothing wrong. There were no girls there over eighteen, and the youngest was twelve.

A couple of them had had a hell of a life already. I remember this one girl who had been forced by her father to go into the garage, along with her brother and sisters, and watch as he tied their mother to a chair, poured gasoline on her, and set her on fire. He forced them to watch her burn to death. Another girl had stabbed her father to death with a knife in a corn field for raping her repeatedly. She was only twelve, and very sweet.

The rules I had to learn were endless. In fact, it would be easier and less time consuming to tell you what we "were" allowed to do, instead of what was taboo. All the girls had to wear dresses to the middle of the knee, no longer, and definitely no shorter. No shorts, pants, or any "male attire" of any kind. We had to wear matching dresses at church or any other time the public was there. It was easier to keep track of us that way. We were each issued three uniforms, and they were made of polyester. One was blue, one yellow, one pink, and we were told prior to the event which color to wear. The reason we were kept in uniform was that the difference was "worldly", and being different wasn't tolerated. If you were different, then you were worldly and that was a word I heard a lot there.

We weren't allowed to have pork, fried foods, carbonated beverages, or anything with refined sugar in it, like candy or cake. We weren't allowed to listen to radio or television, or read newspapers, books or magazines. All our mail was censored in and out. If they caught you saying ANYTHING like "Get me out of here!" or "Please bring me home!", you would get a beating. And if you said anything bad about the home to someone on the outside or got caught trying to tell anyone what they were doing to you there, you would get an especially bad beating. Half the time, you would get a letter that was all blacked out except for a couple of words, and then you would get a beating just for what someone else wrote to you.

On top of beatings, they used privileges to punish you, too. In a place where you have no control over anything, it's easy to do, because they make everything that doesn't hurt a privilege. So all they have to do is make you miss dessert, which we had only on Friday nights. It was usually cottage cheese with some canned peaches on it, but twice a year a company donated five gallon barrels of ice cream, and they'd let us each have some. So if you missed that night, you had six months to think about it. These people were cruel, domineering authority figures who were there for only one reason and that was to act as prison guards and transform us to a set specification. They were power hungry, and yet sometimes they could sound very emotional and sincere.

When I got to the home on September 16, 1970, there were 28 girls, but during my stay the number grew to over 350. I saw hundreds of girls come and the lucky ones go. So when I talk about some of these things, like board meetings, I remember the first ones. There were many for me, because I always learned the hard way in the beginning. Many of the board meetings (where we got our whippings) would have a line of two hundred or better girls at any one time! That was when Granny,

Poppa, and Elaine would get tired and take turns. It was a horrible way to live.

Now Brother Roloff, Poppa and Granny, may have started out with good intentions (whatever!), but it eventually grew so big that things got out of control. No one should have total control over someone else's life and brain like that. I know there's someone out there right now saying, "Well, they were trying to help you!" Believe me; you wouldn't say that if you were going through it yourself. We were brainwashed and not given a choice of what to eat, drink or think. We were there for one reason, to conform. There was no choice; you either did it, or else.

Back to our "can't do list. We weren't allowed to use any slang whatsoever, like "gosh," "golly," or "gee whiz." You couldn't even say, "Man, that's a big elephant!", because that was a form of exasperation and it was a sin. It was the same as saying "shit," "piss," or "ass." If you ever took the Lord's name in vain, I think they would have killed you. We couldn't part our hair down the middle, because in the early seventies the hippies were parting their hair down the middle, so it was worldly. We weren't allowed to have gum or candy of any kind. At Christmas, we could accept edible gifts, but only if there was enough for every person. If there wasn't, then it stayed in the office with Granny and Elaine. Even if you got caught singing or humming a worldly song (in their eyes), you got a whipping.

"Idle hands are the devil's workshop," they would say, and they made sure we didn't have idle hands. This was a big farm; like I said before, where they raised cows, goats, chickens, and vegetables, so there was plenty to be done. There were even a couple of dogs and cats out in the barn area.

When you pulled into the 'Home', you came off the highway onto a paved driveway that turned into a huge paved parking area. The parking area was in front of the big, red brick building that had white trim and pillars out in the front, giving it a colonial look. Because everything was so flat, we could see the highway from the front of the building, but just barely. Behind the big church-dormitory combo and office building was a big red two story barn. Then behind that, were more out buildings and chicken coops. The barn sat a good quarter-mile or better behind the dorm, and to the right. There was pavement all the way around the building, and it looked very out of place way out in the middle of nowhere.

If you went to the back of the building and stood looking towards the barn, you would see two dirt roads that went on forever. I don't know where they led; they just ran straight away from the building on either side. The barn sat on the right of the "right" dirt road. In the middle of the two roads, directly behind the big building, there was a fenced area that had all of the goats in it.

I know it was just over a mile to walk around the goat pen, because we had to do it at least once every day. If you got into trouble at school, then it was laps around the goat pen.

On the "left" side of the dirt road and the goat's pen were about five house trailers. Apparently, all the girls had lived in trailers before the new building was finished, which was completed only a month or so before I arrived. When I got there, they had just gone through that hurricane and a few of the trailers had been destroyed by it. The pregnant girls and their trustees still lived in the ones that were left standing. There

\

was a huge, ten acre watermelon field over to the right of the big building. That was the layout of this big farm

We only wore our uniforms when the public was involved. At all other times, the dresses we wore were donated. In fact, donations were sent out to the home almost every day. There was everything from clothes, food, animals, and money, to tractors and busses. Some of the dresses they forced us to wear were too much; they definitely didn't want us looking attractive (to anyone).

Remember, they had to come to the middle of the knee; anything else was unacceptable. They would put a pile of dresses in the middle of a room and then let us go through and grab what we wanted. As more and more girls came, there were more and more of us who had to find dresses to wear. It would always turn into a pulling match; it was horrible.

The day after my mom deserted me, I had to go to my first day of school. We went through our regimen of oatmeal with goat's milk, and then on to broadcast and Bible study. Next, we had to go outside and line up on the right side of the building, because that road led to the barn, then we were all marched (in a perfectly straight line) up the dirt road. In fact, every time we moved from then on, we were required to move together in some form of unit. The barn looked small from a distance, but the closer you got, the more amazed you were at how big it actually was. It was definitely a huge old building, and about a half-mile from the dorm. I've always been very aware of my surroundings, so I was taking in everything (like how to get out of there, mostly).

Back by the barn area, there was quite a bit of activity. I saw two other men and Poppa, all dressed alike, in zip up coveralls, cowboy hats and boots. They all had shovels in their hands and were standing together, just talking. Those men who helped Poppa never came up to the dormitory area; I only saw them when we were back by the barn.

There were at least two or three large out buildings back there, as well as some cattle and dogs. There was also a large chicken coop, with the endless clucking coming from inside.

All of us girls were lined up in front of a set of wooden stairs that went straight up the side of this tall barn building. We were instructed to march straight up those stairs to a door, by a woman I hadn't seen before. We went inside the top floor of this barn, which was a big hayloft. It had an A frame design, so the middle of the room was regular sized, but the room got smaller down at the edges (hence, A frame). Along these edges were slats of wood that divided it into cubicles, and they were about two and a half feet wide. Each divided section had a desk top and a chair. In other words, you couldn't see the person sitting next to you, but the teacher could see all of us. The middle of the room was empty except for a desk at one end, and at the other end the wall was full of papers and books. It was hot, and not well lit. It was called "The Heavenly Hayloft". Under us was the main body of the barn where the cattle and hay were kept. It was an actual, functioning barn.

I was stopped by the woman who led us into this room. She asked me a couple of questions, then assigned me a cubical. We all ranged in ages and grades, so we did correspondence school, working on different things at the same time. You could not see or interact with each other, but the teacher would walk up and down behind us all day to keep an eye on us. She would go from girl to girl and help them with their work. There were no interactive activities during school, except when we walked around the goat's pen or went to lunch. You could be alone and quiet for six and a half hours every day, so it made for some very long days. Being secluded made it hard to learn all the rules, because you couldn't talk to each other. We had to wait until our free time, because that was when we were allowed to mingle, which was normally between school and dinner.

Poppa was about forty-five years old, six-foot-four, and a very handsome man. He had an air about him, a very strong presence (especially if you met him with a board in his hand). He always wore zip up overalls, boots, and his cowboy hat, which gave him an even taller appearance. No other men were ever allowed anywhere around us. In fact, even the male workers never eyeballed us or made any attempt to speak to any of us. There, strange men were taboo, and anything that had to do with sex was taboo. Men were associated with sex, so we were kept very separate from any of them.

I learned from the first that the beliefs of this organization were that everything we'd ever done, insinuated, or thought about had turned us into very bad sinners and had something to do with sex. Every time they got a chance, they were yelling down at us from the podium that we'd either done it, seen it done, wanted to do it, or had just thought about it, and that made us sinners. We had to cleanse ourselves and forget those things that made us bad, and we were preached to every night by someone. Whenever there was an "altar call", we were expected to step up there, where we would cry and beg for forgiveness. This was expected of us if you wanted to conform, or even if you didn't, you had to do it. Now don't get me wrong, I have nothing against anyone who truly repents or someone finding peace because they have faith. I just don't think it should be forced on anyone.

At first, my mind reeled with ways to get out of this place. Home had never seemed so good. Eventually, though, I resigned myself to being there and trying to get out the easiest way: through the front doors I had come through originally. I saw so many girls get beaten for trying to run, and none of them had ever made it. The beatings were a great deterrent.

Granny, Poppa, their daughter and son all lived in a big apartment that came off the foyer, at the entrance of the big building. Their apartment doors were the other two doors that came off the other side of the foyer, across from the office as you first came in. So none of us ever knew what went on up there. I don't remember where their son went to school; not with us, I do know that. I just know he wasn't around us on a private basis (that never happened), but he did go to all church functions and board meetings.

The pregnant girls were hardly ever around us. They were kept back in the trailers, except for church on Sunday. Sometimes we would see them walking around the goats' pen, but they were never really around us much. They were like the worst of the worst, because they were walking reminders of sin. They stayed at the home until they went to have their babies, and then we never saw them again.

I remember this one day, a good looking young man drove up in a little sports car. He went inside and had a horrible fight with Poppa. He was screaming that he wanted to see his girlfriend and he wanted his baby, but Poppa physically threw him out. The poor kid left crying, "You can't do this to me!", but they did. His girlfriend stayed at the home until she had her baby.

\

When I first got there, there were empty rooms everywhere. And in the rooms that were occupied, there were never more than two girls, but it was filling up quickly, at the rate of one to two new girls every week. By the time I had been there a couple of months, there were sixty girls or so.

It was nice not being the new girl for very long, because new girls got watched more. They got in trouble more, too, because they were being listened to over the intercom, always under suspicion, and being scrutinized just as I once was.

We were bombarded with put downs and negativity constantly; things like "You're sluts, sinners, and harlots." We were told our thoughts were evil and sinful. They would scream at us from the pulpit that we had the devil in us and it was their job to get him out, and they were persistent, too.

There wasn't much one-on-one contact between us and the adults. Everything we did was done as a group. No one wanted to get called up to the office for any reason. That kind of personal attention wasn't wanted by any of us.

They Know What's Best

Whoever "they" are?

One night after church, when I had been there for about four

months, I got called to the office. I was terrified and walked very slowly

up to the office door. When I walked in, Granny and Elaine were in there

waiting for me.

I knew something bad was coming, but my mind blew when

Granny looked at me and said, "April, your grandmother is dead." I

freaked out and called her a liar. She said, "Why would I lie about

something like that?"

My mind was reeling; my grandma was gone, my real mother.

The woman who had breastfed me and loved me was gone.

I fell back in a chair, looked at Granny, and asked, "When is her

funeral?"

She looked at me and said, "Well, April. We didn't think you were ready to hear about this, so we waited to tell you,"

I said, "Waited how long?"

She said, "She died right after you got here."

Not only was my grandmother gone, they had waited four months to tell me. My heart just broke. I had never lost anyone who meant that much to me, and I was going to get no sympathy from them. Granny told me I would be under watch and not to try to run, then she told me to go back to my room. I turned and left the office. I just stood outside the office and cried. I couldn't believe my grandma was gone. My mind conjured up terrible visions of her already rotting in her grave. I couldn't believe I couldn't even go to her funeral or talk to my grandpa, and what about Kari Jo?

The last time I had seen my grandma was in the hospital in Oklahoma City. I knew then I had lost her, but my child mind didn't realize the finality of death, at least until it became a reality. I couldn't imagine never seeing her again. Who would love me now? No one could understand what I had lost or how much a part of my life had died that day, or how empty my life would be without her. I felt like my mother had died and I had just been left to a mean aunt. I still miss her to this day.

The fact that they waited to tell me, I had no one there to grieve her loss with, no one who loved or knew her; it left me unable to find any closure on that subject. It put me into a state of submission, and I did everything I could from that day on to conform and get out of the home alive. Even though at that time, I truly believed in my heart I would die in that home.

Within two weeks, I would be dealt another emotional blow. The year before we went to the lake, I had started my first job. I worked part-time at a poodle parlor. I did everything from cleaning dog poop up from the yard to feeding all the dogs, and I eventually got to help groom. When the summer was over, the woman who owned the poodle farm let me have a full-blooded toy poodle puppy. I picked a little silver male and named him Romeo. My dream was to eventually get a Juliet. I loved that little dog. He was one of the only things in my life that was all mine. My grandpa had fallen in love with him, too. That whole summer at the lake, he had taught him tricks and loved to play with him. He was the cutest little dog.

I received a letter from my mother just weeks after I was told about my grandma. It said Romeo had gotten out of the yard, hit by a car and killed. I took this news very hard. I was feeling the total lack of control in my life, and it was starting to feel like the things I loved in my life were dropping dead around me. I felt like I was dying.

At the home, they always tried to make death seem like a privilege. In every sermon, they preached that death was what we were all waiting for so we could be with the Lord. We were either waiting for the second coming or wishing the hell we were living in would end quickly.

There was no one there who understood my sorrow and loss. I mean, it was my grandma, and now my puppy. Every time I tried to talk to anyone about it, they would say she was in a better place. I thought a better place would have been back home in Oklahoma, waiting for me, but what did I know? I was just a virgin, harlot, and slut!

By the time I'd been there six months, I had this place down pat. If you go along, you get along. You go along with Bible study every day, church service at least once each day, and broadcast twice a day. It was impossible not to be affected by all of this. The question was, what was sincere, and what was total brainwashing? I can't to this day answer that question myself. I know I couldn't stand Granny and all of them looking down their noses at me, watching me all the time, and always putting me down.

I told you before that every night at church service, they had altar call. No matter who was preaching at you, they were telling you your heart was full of sin and you must come down and ask for forgiveness. Sometimes every girl in the place would end up down there sobbing buckets of tears; it was a very emotional thing to watch. They take everything from you and leave you only one alternative: to conform to their beliefs.

They would stand up above us at the pulpit and say we were sinners and full of the devil and the only way to get rid of him was to come down there and beg for forgiveness and truly change. So I, like everyone else, ended up down on my knees crying, asking for someone to help me. I wanted to change, I wanted to conform. What I really wanted was not to be watched or beaten or yelled at anymore. I just wanted to go home.

I think the most unfair thing they did to us was not allow it to be real. We were bullied, pushed, and threatened into submission. If you don't agree, it's because you weren't there. Religious belief and faith cannot and should not be crammed down anyone's throat.

\

The Bible I was forced to memorize talked about a loving God, a forgiving God, and a God who protected; this God they preached to us was used as a weapon against us. He was a vengeful god, a God of wrath, a God to be feared, a God that would strike me dead for breaking a manmade rule.

That kind of brainwashing has affected my religious beliefs ever since. At the time it was real for me, but only because it had to be. I had to survive, and to survive I had to conform to what they expected me to be. So eventually, I became one of the best girls there. I became a trustee. I became one of the girls trusted to be put with a new girl and be responsible for her.

Like every good, conforming girl, I was up at the podium every week giving my testimony. Telling the world just how bad of a person I was before God and the home made me what I'd become.

Please don't get me wrong; like I said, I have nothing against true change, conversion, or any religious beliefs. I admire people who take a stand for what they believe in. As long as they don't judge other people for not believing as they do or refuse to comprehend that there are many other beliefs than their own. I'm speaking purely of my own experiences. What I'm saying is they didn't give me the option of knowing what was real, from doing what was expected of me.

There's one verse in the Bible that says it all: "By your fruits ye shall be known." If a Christian wants to influence people around them with their beliefs, then let their lives and deeds speak for them. If it's real, then other people will want what they have. It works much better than force.

Atoning For Our Sins

$\mathbf{W}$e sang as a group at every church service and had choir

practice every day. As the home grew with more and more girls, the choir got bigger and bigger. As I said earlier, Brother Roloff was a very smart and resourceful man. He got the Bluebird Bus Company to donate a brand new school bus to the home. It was painted blue and had "The Rebecca Home for Girls" printed on the side. He came up with the idea to go on the road and take some of us with him, because he had already been doing this on a smaller basis with the "Honey Bee Quartet". At first, only those of us who were "trusted" got to go. We went on weekend trips all over Texas. We would all sing and give our testimony at a different church every night, and then Brother Roloff would give a sermon. The host church would take up a collection for us, and then we would be taken by twos into church members homes for the night.

People from that particular congregation would line up to fill out a document that told them what we were NOT allowed to have or do. Also, they had to understand we were to be watched at all times. If they agreed, then they took responsibility for us for the night. It was a strange experience, as each home we stayed in was different, and getting out of the home for any reason was a blessing. People were in awe of us for some reason. They would freak out when we said something like, "No. We aren't allowed to drink soda," or "We can't eat pork chops," because the paper they signed didn't have room on it for all the restrictions that were put on us. I remember some of them even trying to get us to eat something or do something we weren't supposed to. I never swayed, because I believed that if I took a drink of a carbonated beverage, I just may die the next day.

We were always paired up with someone who was trusted more than we were. If you tried to run or told anyone anything you weren't supposed to, the girl with you would tell on you. If you got caught trying to run (and it happened), you would get a beating and you would never get to leave the home again. So if you were smart, you just enjoyed every moment of being in the real world, you watched, learned, and listened. Being brought from our controlled environment and put into real world situations did cause us all kinds of dilemmas. I mean, they were expecting the impossible when they expected us to live up to their unreal expectations. Like, a man at dinner would say, "Do you want a piece of chocolate pie for desert?" And we would say, "We can't have pie or chocolate." He would say, "Well, that's ridiculous. You're going to have some pie, surely a piece of pie won't hurt you."

There were neat experiences, too. One couple took us to the Galleria Mall in Houston, TX. They bought us each a stuffed animal, which Granny actually let us keep. I got a monkey that would hug your neck. Later, we started traveling out of Texas to other states, and the tours were expanded to two weeks at a time.

One time, we got to stay with this nice woman who had the neatest two story log cabin, and it was hidden in the backwoods of Kentucky. It thought it was the coolest thing. Everything in this beautiful cabin was made of untouched tree limbs. The rails that ran up the stairs and the railing that ran around the whole upstairs were made of twisted and crooked branches. They weren't cut, straight, pieces of wood; they were actual full tree limbs that had been shellacked to give it this sheen. It was so incredible, I will never forget it. We roasted marshmallows and popped popcorn in her fireplace. It was wonderful. I've always had a fascination with neat things made of wood, especially if they're smooth to the touch, but knurly to the eye. I wonder what that says about my psyche.

Within six months of starting our tour, it was going so well that Granny, Poppa and all the girls started going, too; of course, with the exception of those who had tried to run, had gotten into really bad trouble, or were new to the home. We would be gone for a week or two at a time instead of a day or two. It got so big and we were growing so fast that eventually we had to get another bus.

Eventually, more than one hundred of us would go together in these two big buses. We even went to Dallas, TX, where we made a bunch of albums in a recording studio of all us girls singing as a choir, and of course all we sang were religious songs.

\

After I'd been at the home for a year, we had three buses and more than one hundred fifty girls traveling together. That was when we had a few girls run, or try to, and it was getting hard to keep the control they commanded over us. You never thought of running; not really. I don't know of one girl who ever ran that wasn't caught and severely punished for it. Once, it took us three weeks to travel to other states all the way up the entire east coast. Our choir would stop every night at different churches to sing. Besides singing as a choir, we all had to get up and give testimony in front of the entire congregation each night. It was all very entertaining, and churches were fighting to get us.

I think every person in America should be locked up for one week, cut off from everything. It would teach them the value of the freedom they take advantage of and for granted. It would make us all nicer to each other, and we'd be much more careful of who we gave it away to. You know that old saying? You don't know what you've got until it's gone? Well, it's true. Ignorance truly is bliss.

On one of these trips, when we had one hundred and twenty girls and two buses, we were running late trying to get to a church that evening. We were coming into Charleston, SC. It was a very beautiful, slightly mountainous area. One bus was following the other, and all us girls were trying to get ready for the service while the bus was moving, because we were running late. Since there was limited privacy, someone would hold up a towel so you could put on your uniform behind it, which was tricky on a moving bus.

It was already cramped, because one of the churches we had been to had donated six one hundred pound bags of raw sugar. These were big burlap bags, and they were taking up the whole last row of the bus. We couldn't eat anything with refined sugar in it, so this was like gold to us. Also, we each had a suitcase up over our heads on the luggage rack. Except at that moment, most of the suitcases were down on the floor in the aisles, because we were all trying to get dressed.

The next thing I know, I'm flying through the air. Girls, suitcases, clothes and giant bags of sugar all looked like missiles being thrown about. Everyone was screaming. The bus had gone right off over a cliff, nose first to the bottom of a ravine. The next thing I remember is being on top of about 50 people, with big bags of sugar and suitcases on top of me. I didn't know it yet, but we had gone straight over and straight down, about forty-five feet. The bus landed standing straight up and down, resting on its nose. I was at the top of the heap in the back of the bus, so I climbed over dozens of girls and out one of the windows and fell to the ground. Girls were coming out of every window with bloody noses and holding injured limbs or rubbing their heads. Believe it or not, the worst injures were two broken limbs and a lot of bumps and bruises. It was amazing. Especially Poppa, Granny and the bus driver; they had all been up front when it happened and were now at the bottom of this pile of humans.

After accessing the damage and each other, we all climbed the hill back up to the road. After we sorted out who was hurt and who was OK, we were gathered into a big circle and made to sit on the ground. The other bus came back after seeing us go off the road. Everyone piled onto the only bus. We stood in the aisles and rode the other ten or twenty miles into town together. Almost one hundred and twenty people were all on a bus meant for sixty.

We got to the church and did our thing. Brother Roloff milked it for everything it was worth. The rest of the tour, every service was about how God had saved us all from death. Going on tour was never boring.

Versatile, that's me.

We were growing fast, and so were the donations. They were starting construction on a new dormitory that would sit next to the first one. Every bedroom in the original dorm was so over capacity that girls were sleeping on the floors. Remember I said when I first got to the home we had empty beds in every room, and many completely empty rooms? Only, we were still getting new girls almost every week.

One of the good things about the home was the friendships I made there. I had never lived in any one place for any length of time, so I had never really made friends before. In the home, you lived together, ate together and suffered together. It was a real bonding experience. Even though girls did come and go, they mostly came and stayed. The home was a hard place to get out of.

One of the girls I became good friends with was a girl we all called "Bird Legs". Her real name was Brenda Craven, but we all called her "Bird Legs". She had the skinniest legs of anyone there, and she was as sweet as they come. She was my bathroom mate, because our bedrooms opened into the same bathroom. So if you were sneaky, you could go into each other's rooms without going out into the big room. It was a risk, though, because like everything else, if you got caught, you got a beating. Brenda had come from a troubled home, like almost everyone else there. She had one sister and one brother. Her mom had remarried, so she had a stepdad, and her little brother was a result of that union.

After you had been at the home for more than six months, you could receive a visitor (if you had a good record), but most of the girls were from all over the country, so most of us never had visitors. Brenda was lucky to be from the Houston area, which was within driving distance of the home. Her family came down to visit her, which was her stepfather, mother, her sister Allison (12), and her brother Shane (6).

Now, how they talked Granny and Poppa into this, I don't know, but they let Allison and Shane stay in the dorm with us while her parents stayed out back in one of the trailers.

At the time (this was before I had been there a year), Brenda and I both had an empty bed in each of our rooms. So Allison stayed in my room, and Shane stayed in Brenda's. I remember that night, Shane got up and peed in the bathtub in his sleep. He was adorable, but Allison was my favorite. She had hair that hung way down past her waist. She wore little wire rimmed glasses and was so sweet and polite. We had so much fun that night. Any break up in our monotonous daily routine was a treat. Being denied small daily (normal) experiences will make you appreciate any break in a stifled life.

The next day, after our slumber party (to us, any variation in our regimen was a party), Brenda's parents asked Granny and Poppa if they could take Brenda to the beach with them. It was highly irregular, and actually, they hated it whenever any parents showed up, because they had to act differently in front of them. They had to worry about what the girl would tell the outsider. Surprisingly, they said they would allow it as long as a trusted girl could go along. Of course Brenda picked me, so off we went to the beach.

It was always a weird but wonderful experience to leave the home, especially like this, with no one around to monitor us. Brenda and I were such good friends, and we got along so well; it was going to be a good day. Corpus Christi, Texas, sits right on the Gulf of Mexico. We couldn't see it from the home, but it was there, and you could smell it and feel it in the air.

Every opportunity at freedom from the home was awe-inspiring, and we couldn't get enough of it. Brenda and I had so much fun playing at the beach. Even though we weren't allowed to put on a swim suit and go swimming, we had fun just the same. On the other hand, we ate stuff we weren't supposed to eat. It was fun picking up seashells and crabs with Brenda's brother and sister, Allison and Shane. We even tried building a sand castle.

Brenda's parents seemed nice enough. I mean, we were only with them for about five hours that day. Her stepfather was nice, but he did swear a lot, and we were definitely not used to that. Her mom was nice, and it was very obvious they both doted over Shane. They didn't dote over the girls like that. You could just tell their feelings were different towards him than they were towards the girls.

Brenda's parents even bought two big bags of hard candy to take back to the home. There was enough for everybody, and Granny let all the girls have a piece. Everyone treated us like we were special for doing that. After that fun afternoon, Brenda and I became inseparable; we were the best of friends. From then on, we sat together at church, choir, Bible study, or any free time we had; we always spent it hanging out together.

A few weeks later, we were informed they were going to allow fourteen girls to go down to the old folks' home in the Rio Grande Valley for two weeks to pick grapefruit, tangerines and oranges. All the girls had to sign up on a list, and Brenda and I both got picked to go. We were so excited we were going to be away from the home again. So, fifteen of us, including Elaine (Granny's right hand), went to this unbelievably beautiful place. It was an old mansion that sat in the middle of this wonderful citrus orchard. At one time or another, it had been renovated to act as a multi-person facility for about thirty elderly people. It was like being in a big mansion full of grandmas. I was in seventh heaven.

We had to pick seven semi trucks full of oranges, grapefruit, tangerines and lemons. The work was hard, but it was worth it because we had so much fun there. There was a big swimming pool which at one time had been very beautiful, but now it was full of what looked like very dirty pond water. The caretakers told us that if we worked hard the whole week, they would clean the pool out and fill it up so we could go swimming when we were through. So we worked very hard out in the orchards. Slowly, we could see they had done more and more to make the pool usable. Something to look forward to is very important to all of us; if we don't have something to look forward to, then we have nothing.

Again, I am reminded of that saying, "Everything is big in Texas." Well, they aren't kidding. At night, we would sit and watch the biggest frogs in the world take over the place. It was just like a spooky movie. These were huge bullfrogs, and they croaked all night. It was mesmerizing to watch them. I bet some of them weighed at least 10 lbs. ot more. The oranges we picked were as big as grapefruit, the tangerines were as big as oranges and the grapefruit were like melons. It was unbelievable.

The elderly people loved having us there, and we loved being there. It was a real treat, because we got to eat real food, too. Any variation in our diet was a welcomed change.

On the last day we were there, the caretakers had kept their word and we got to go swimming. They had tried their best to clean the pool, but it was still a little green and slimy. We wouldn't have cared if it had been a mud puddle. We stayed in it ALL day long and had a BLAST. They even let us wear cut-offs they pulled out of somewhere. It was like we were doing something dangerous; not swimming in the pond, but wearing the cut-offs! There was a bunch of controversy over it between Elaine and the head of the old folks' home, but they won, and so did we.

As with everything in my life, nothing is just (normal). There is always an added bonus (memorable life experience) whenever I am involved. I don't know if I make it happen or I am more aware of it, or if I am cursed or blessed. I do know that I'm not making this stuff up, so you decide. Anyway, one of the girls almost drowned and almost drowned me, literally. Brenda and I talked her into going around the inside edge of the pool with us, by hanging on and using her hands to get to the deep end. She didn't know how to swim, and I didn't understand not knowing how to swim. I thought we were all born with the ability, because I couldn't remember when I started swimming. So here I was diving and swimming all around her, while she was slowly and timidly scooting around the edge with white knuckled fingers. The next thing I knew, she was on top of my head, trying to claw my eyes out and use me as a ladder to the top of the water. At one point, she was actually standing on my head as her weight pushed me under. I did quite a bit of my own kicking and pulling of hair, until I finally got out of her frenzied grasp. I swam away from her and back to the edge of the pool. Brenda and I finally grabbed her by the hair and dragged her back to the edge with us. She was crying, spitting, coughing, and shaking, as was I. Needless to say, she didn't swim down at the deep end with us anymore that day, and we didn't try to talk anyone else into doing it either. I was shaking so bad, I thought for sure she was going to drown me. I never again tried to talk anyone into going into deep water again unless they could swim. Everyone should know how to swim. I mean, our planet is made up of more water than land.

Brenda and I had fun the whole time we were there. I could have stayed there forever, green, lush, wet, alive and full of loving grandmas; it was heaven to me. None of us wanted to go back, but we had to.

After we got back to our routines and board meetings, Brother Roloff sent one of the semi trucks we had loaded to the home. They dumped out the entire truckload of citrus into two big piles on the side of the dormitory. Then they let us loose on them. We ate off those piles of oranges, grapefruits, tangerines and lemons for three weeks. Every day during the summer, we had free time for an hour or two at a time. We would go out there and eat ourselves sick; to us, even a lemon was like candy.

When everything you eat or drink is either allotted to you or used as a weapon against you, then everything edible becomes like money. If you were caught hoarding, stealing, or anything even close to that, it was a sin in their eyes and you were punished for sinning.

When August rolled around, our ten acre watermelon patch was ready to pick. So for two weeks, we picked and loaded (semi trucks) full of watermelons. Now, that's hard work. Remember, "Everything is big in Texas", and that goes for watermelons, too. Most of them weighed more than we did, and it must have been at least one hundred degrees each day, and 120% humidity. Our reward after we picked them was we got to eat a bunch of them, so for two weeks we all got sick on watermelon.

In fact, in one way or another we were still expected to help supply all of our own food. When the boys' home supplied us with fish during the summer, we would have an annual fish fry. Poppa would set up these big cast iron kettles outside and deep fry the fish. Now, we weren't allowed fried foods, so I don't know how they got around that, but it was a treat to everyone. Since I had grown up on fried fish, it was definitely a real treat for me.

The home also slacked up on their rule about the "sugar thing" twice a year. I told you about the ice cream company that donated ice cream twice a year. Well, it was really a bummer if you missed dessert that night. It's funny how deprivation can make things look so much more desirable than they probably are, especially where food is concerned.

The one thing they made us do for our supper that none of us will ever forget was the chickens. We had over a thousand chickens at any one time. They would make us stand in a line outside of the barn. Each girl had to go in the chicken coop, wait for one of the helpers to grab a chicken by the feet (with a long metal hook thing), then they would hand you the chicken, which you also had to hold by its feet. Then we had to take it to this man who had an axe standing by a big wooden tree stump. You would have to lay the chicken on the stump and watch while he would whack its head off. Then he would throw it on the ground, where you would have to watch it jump around, bleeding from the neck. I swear, it would still cluck and bawk, even without a head; it was horrible. As soon as you could, you had to grab the supposedly dead chicken by the feet and carry it outside. You would then get into another line and wait your turn to dunk your chicken in boiling hot water. After that, you took it over to this big drum thing that was covered with black rubber knobs that spun around and around. This poor, boiled carcass of a chicken had to be held against the drum until the feathers were beaten off it. We would then carry our chicken to a table, where we had to finish plucking it by hand. Then you would take it over to Granny and Elaine, who would cut it at the bottom so you could take it to another table to gut it. Last but not least, you had to dunk it one more time in another pot of water. At the end of the line, all we had to do was give our chicken to the girls who bagged them and put them into a big walk-in freezer. Then you would start all over again.

It was horrible. Some of the girls got physically ill when we had to do chickens. There were always the few who acted like they liked it; they even played jump rope with the intestines. Most of us hated it. At least I had killed and dressed fish and rabbits before, so it wasn't as traumatic to me, but some of those girls were actually ill from the experience. I remember a couple of girls tried to hide under their beds to get out of it, but they got caught and beaten, and they still had to do chickens.

Every Sunday was when they served baked chicken at the home. That was the day when the public could eat lunch at the home, for a price, like a restaurant. Sunday was a different day for us, because the public was involved and we had to dress up in and our wear uniforms. It was also a rule that we had to wait to eat until all of the people from town were through. We only ate twice on Sundays and didn't have broadcast that morning, because the church service was the broadcast. Brother Roloff did the broadcast every Sunday from the home. We would sing and give testimony. It was quite a show. I remember many Sundays when there was standing room only, and this place was thirty miles from town.

Brenda Craven

This chapter changed many lives.

It must have been around Halloween when Brenda first found out something was wrong at home. She already knew her mother and stepfather had split up, and her parents were fighting a fierce custody battle over Shane. All of this had happened since their visit to the home. Brenda knew her mom was scared of her stepfather, but she had no idea just how bad the fighting over Shane had become.

Around Halloween, Brenda learned her mother had gone to Allison's school for a parent-teacher meeting. She had seen Allison there and had spoken to her. Her mother had told Allison to go home, get her clarinet and go to her lesson, and she would see her at home after her parent-teacher meeting. Allison rode her bike home, and her mother had her meeting. After the meeting, Brenda's mother went home just to find that Allison's bike was lying in the front yard. She wondered why Allison was still at home and not at her lesson. She entered the house and called for Allison, but there was no answer. Brenda's mother figured Allison had gone on foot for whatever reason.

She was more confused when she went into the living room to see Allison's purse and its contents strewn all over the sofa. Still, there was no sign of Allison. Her mother knew Allison wouldn't have left without her purse, and her house key was among the contents. A feeling of dread came over Brenda's mother as she started calling Allison's friends and clarinet teacher. No one had seen her, so she called the police.

By the time Brenda was told of this, Allison had been missing for two or three days. Another one of Granny's "you're not ready to know" rules, but Brenda's mother had insisted her daughter be told. As would be expected, Brenda freaked out. Granny was right; no one was ready to hear that their only sister was missing and you were three hundred miles away and couldn't do anything about it. It changed Brenda. She became despondent and sullen. She cried all of the time and wanted to go home, and I didn't blame her. We were all very sad, because we had all just seen and really liked Allison. We all loved Brenda, and it was hard to watch her suffer.

Days went by with no news. Brenda's mother sent her a flier with Allison's picture on it. It asked anyone who had seen her to call the Houston Police. It was so sad. It was making Brenda do things she would not ordinarily do. I even saw her talk back to Granny. It was like she didn't care anymore.

It was three weeks before Brenda got the news she somehow knew was coming. Some kids and their dog were playing in a field in Pearland, TX (a suburb of Houston), and they had found Allison, or part of her anyway. She had been decapitated and mutilated. The story I was told at the time went like this. Brenda and Allison's stepfather, the guy I had gone to the beach with, had hired these two guys to kidnap Allison to use her as leverage to get Shane from Brenda's mother. Something had gone wrong, and they had killed her and then tried to hide her body. Later in my life, I swear I saw the same poster of Allison I had seen in 1971, on a forensic science show about a serial killer who struck the Houston area back in the early seventies.

Allison Craven 1960 -1971

48 hours "The killing fields" on I.D.

. All I did know then was that she was dead, and it had been a horrible death and more than Brenda could take.

After Brenda was told about Allison, she wouldn't be consoled. She lay on her bed and cried. They told her they were not letting her go to her sister's funeral.

I was so worried about her that I went to Granny and told her, "I'm worried about Brenda."

I got very little compassion from Granny. She told me Brenda would have to find solace in God and that God may have done this to bring Brenda closer to him.

Brenda was put under watch, because they were afraid she would run, or try to. Unfortunately, their concern was for her not to run, not how she felt or how she was dealing with the loss. They didn't watch her close enough.

All day, I went into her room and tried to get her to talk to me. All she would do was cry. She didn't get off her bed all day. Right before broadcast that evening, I again went in and tried to get her up. She told me to go on, that she would be out soon. I got her a dress to put on, and then I went out to broadcast. I sat down, and broadcast started. The seat next to me was still empty.

I said to Elaine, "Brenda is still not out here. Can I go get her?"

She said, "No. You stay where you are. No one misses broadcast. If she isn't out here before it's over, I will go and deal with her, and she won't like it. She better get out here!"

I sat there and couldn't concentrate. I could see both of our bedroom doors, and I couldn't take my eyes off them. She didn't come out. It was the longest 45 minutes of my life. As soon as they said the word "Amen," I bolted out of my seat to my bedroom door. I ran through my room to the bathroom door. I opened it to go through to her room. I froze. Brenda was on the bathroom floor, lying in a pool of blood. She had cut her wrists. I started screaming. I kept screaming until one of the girls showed up.

I screamed at her, "Go get Granny!", but Granny was already on her way.

Granny came in and pushed past me, with Elaine right behind her. Granny got down on the floor and put Brenda's head in her lap. She told me to hand her some towels, so I did. She wrapped them around Brenda's wrists. Brenda started moving her head and moaning. Granny started slapping her across the face, hard. She opened her eyes a little bit.

Granny started screaming in her face, "You little fool, just what did you think that this would accomplish? If you want to kill yourself, don't cut your wrists like this." She gestured, cutting across Brenda's arm. "If you want to do it right, then cut them like this, you little fool," then she motioned on Brenda's arm in an up and down motion.

She told Elaine to help her get Brenda up. They started to carry her out of the room and looked at me and the other girls who were standing there and told us, "Get this mess cleaned up."

So we did. I couldn't believe she was still alive. I had to clean up the blood, and there was a lot of it. They took her to the office and bandaged her arms. A half an hour later, they brought her back to her room and put her in bed. They wouldn't even take her to the doctor.

I wanted so badly to go to her, but it was after lights out and I knew they would be listening to her intercom, and I didn't know what to say to her anyway. She was hurting from a lot more than the cuts on her arms. She cried all night long, as did I.

The first thing next morning, I went in her room. She was awake but looked terrible and was still crying. We weren't allowed to have any glasses or dishes in our rooms, but we were allowed to have hair spray and deodorant. So we made drinking glasses out of the lids, and I took her some water. Brenda didn't want to get up, but I had only seen two girls "ever" stay in bed, and they were both very ill. So she eventually got up, and she lived; "miserably", but she lived.

I wish I could find her now.

Brenda Craven, lived in Pearland, TX, and at the "Rebecca home for girl's" in 1970-71 Nickname (bird legs)

She was never the same Brenda after that. They buried her little sister without her there, and despite all their efforts to keep her there, Brenda went home a month or two later anyway. I never heard from her after that, although I've thought of her so often. "Bird legs"…I have a picture of her jumping off the diving board, into the pool at the old folks' home. Somehow, I ended up with a few pictures from the home.

The home was a strange place. We were still denied any outside stimuli, like television, radio, any printed material or anything that was a distraction. Poppa and the rest still worked on us to conform to their beliefs. Nothing less was tolerated and we were still only allowed very little free time. By 1972, there were over three hundred girls there, and they couldn't keep us busy twenty-four hours a day. We had to become very creative. Although we always had to be careful we didn't break some rule, regulation or sin, we did have some good times while I was there. We started a "talent night". You could sing, "Religious music, of course," and some of the girls would form groups and do skits or plays.

I was in a group with four other girls. We went to Granny with our idea, and beyond our belief, she said, "Yes." So, we found (somewhere around there) some old suits and put on "mans attire". The other four girls who were with me drew mustaches on their faces and put their hair up under hats. They also wore suits and ties. I dressed like a girl and stood in the middle, with two of them on each side of me. We then "lip synced" to the song by the Blackwood Brothers Quartet, "Daddy Sang Bass, Mama Sang Tenor." It was so cute. In fact, it was so cute that Poppa and Granny had us do it for Brother Roloff. He had us do it after church one night for the public, and then he had us do it on tour for a while. It really was cute. We were pretty good, too.

\

I even have other fairly good memories of my time at the home, like the time we were standing in line at the bottom of the stairs, going up to the heavenly hayloft for school. A cow walked up to us, and some of us started backing up the stairs to get away from it. It started following us up these narrow wooden stairs. Somehow, it got to the top and wouldn't go back down. It took Poppa and two other men and a crane to get it down. They had to use a winch, and it took two hours. We all got in trouble for that, even though it really wasn't our fault. It was funny to have a break like that.

Another day when we were waiting in line to go up to school in the hayloft, we saw an animal coming down the dirt road towards us. As it got closer to us, we could tell it was a dog. From a distance, it looked like it was drunk. It was wandering from one side of the road to the other. The closer it got, the weirder it looked and acted. When it got close enough for us to really see it, we could also hear it. It was making a low, constant growling noise, and it looked mean.

One of the girls went over to the chicken coop and got Poppa. When he came over to where we were, he looked down the road at the dog. He then turned and ran to the barn. As the dog got closer, we could see he was foaming at the mouth and really looked wild. He was still staggering back and forth as he walked, and he was getting pretty close to us. We all started to get out of line and move away from it. Poppa was running back with a shovel in his hand. Without saying anything, he ran up to the dog and smashed it over the head with the shovel. It didn't get up. We all started screaming. One of the girls threw up. Poppa told us to get away from the dog, he said it had rabies. He and one of the workers carried it away. That was a weird experience; I couldn't sleep for a week after that.

Another incident from the home I will never forget involved this girl there who was only twelve. She had heard some of the girls talk about bleaching their hair (before they came to the home, of course). One day, she went into the laundry room and tried to "bleach" her hair with CLOROX! She had poured it right on her head. It was horrible; she was screaming for an hour as Granny and Elaine held her head under water. It took all of her hair off, and she got actual blisters from it. I doubt she could ever grow hair after that, and they didn't take her to a doctor either. In fact, I don't remember any of us ever seeing a doctor while we were at the home.

The pregnant girls went somewhere else to have their babies, I think. I don't believe they went to a hospital. I'm almost sure they didn't. I know we never saw them again after they delivered, ever.

Christmas was a strange time at the home. Surprisingly, we were allowed to celebrate Christmas. We had a Christmas tree up in the conference room at the front of the building. We were even allowed to receive presents (kind of). We had to tell our families what they could send. If it was food, there had to be enough for all, or it stayed in the office with Granny, Elaine and those people. We had to tell our families not to wrap anything, but instead send paper with the gifts.

During the month of December, the presents that came in were scrutinized and wrapped. The ones we weren't allowed to have had been put into a pile to be donated to some other organization or destroyed if they were inappropriate. On Christmas night after church, we got to open our presents. If you didn't have anyone to send you a present, then they'd wrap up any extra presents other girls had received and divide them up among the girls who received nothing. No one got *anything* for Christmas. I don't know how much stuff came into that home that we never saw or got, but I bet it was tons.

I don't remember much about my first Christmas there, except I was homesick. I had just been there a couple of months. I know my first Christmas was a lot different than the second. By then, there were almost three hundred girls there, and when I first arrived there weren't even thirty. So, it was much different than the first.

Sometimes I would lie in bed and wonder if my mom thought of me. I truly didn't think I would ever get out of there. I used to wonder if I died in there, would they bury me there at the home? Clearly, something a fifteen-year-old shouldn't be worrying about.

Brother Roloff put out a newspaper thing monthly. He often featured pictures and stories about some of the girls, and even the boys from the lighthouse. His favorite thing to do was show before and after pictures of the worst cases; the worse the picture or story was, the better. I still have one of those bulletins. You know, pictures like this one guy whose mug shot they used, where he was all dirty and had long hair and a beard, and then next to it would be a picture of him clean shaven and in a suit. The difference really was incredible. I wonder how many of those "changed" lives stayed that way.

Brother Roloff eventually got into trouble with the state. Girls had gotten out, and some had told stories. So, the state wanted to have some control over the home, and it got so bad that Brother Roloff ended up in jail. He wouldn't budge, though, because he took no money from the state. He eventually got out, and the state never had any say over the

\

home or how it was run. Brother Roloff put a picture of himself behind bars in the little paper he put out and milked it for all it was worth. He told how he was being persecuted by the state and how the devil was behind it. The devil was trying to keep him from spreading the word. The jail thing was a windfall for his corporation. It even helped us get the donations for a new dormitory, right next to the old one. This one didn't have a kitchen or anything; it was just bedrooms. I still have one of those pictures of him in jail, too.

Brother Roloff was a very ingenious man, and he sometimes seemed to have good intentions. He truly did want to help people; I just believe it got to be such a large operation, he couldn't keep control of it all. He had good ideas for the end result, but the process was too dramatic. What's that old saying? "The road to hell is paved with the best of intentions."

You just can't treat growing, individual people with methodical regimen and rules alone. There has to be some one-on-one attention given along with it, or it becomes just a prison to reform.

For true conviction to take place, it has to come because you want it to, not because you're forced into it. They were bound and determined to change us as a group, not as individuals. We were all to be the same, or not be at all. We were all treated like criminals, until we conformed to their will.

I don't even completely disagree with a spanking, if it's deserved, but beatings, slapping us, and especially belittling us or humiliating us were all wrong. When you tell a child, or even an adult, they're bad or scream at them in front of many people about how they're worthless or terrible, you're stealing their self-esteem, and that should be a crime.

That's where we get most of the criminals in this country, and almost all of the dysfunctional families and individuals we have now; from the lack of self-esteem or self-worth. If we don't learn to care about ourselves, then we can't learn to care for others; therefore, we can't function as productive members of society. Instead, we become burdens on that same society, which has to go around fixing all the damage done by harsh words, physical abuse and neglect. If we could learn to care about ourselves, then we would want to make our lives better, which in turn would make the lives of the people around us better. If you've lost your self-esteem, then you aren't working with yourself; you're working against yourself. We don't like anything we don't respect; it's like a form of cancer, and you eat at yourself for your imperfections. If you have self-esteem and self-worth, then your imperfections aren't so obvious to you. We'd be much easier on ourselves and others, and we wouldn't have so much aggression towards each other. That's my opinion, anyway.

I think they could have been kinder to us, but instead everything was so negative, mistakes weren't allowed, and punishment was swift and harsh. Two years out of 15 was quite a big percentage of my life at that time. Did I tell you they had quicksand around the property? Well, they told us they did. I never ventured far enough from the dorm to find out for myself, but they sure told us it was out there; anything to control and detour us.

I guess I haven't mentioned my mom since I got to the home, have I? I'd only talked to her once on the phone. If you got a phone call, Granny and Elaine sat there in the office and listened to you. I did get a few letters from my mom, as she did from me, but of course they were censored in and out. So what can I say about her? She wasn't a part of my life that entire time. She just left me there, in their hands, good or bad; it apparently didn't matter which.

By the time my third Christmas at the home came around, I was a trustee and almost sixteen. I had been at the home for almost two years by then. My mom sent me a tape recorder and a package of three one-hour blank tapes for Christmas. She thought I could send tapes instead of writing letters. I didn't think Granny would let me keep it, but she'd already seen it and allowed me to have it. Besides, I was a trustee now; I was watched with a less critical eye. I was one of the "old girls" to most of the girls. I had been there from the beginning. Almost everyone who was there when I got there was already gone.

When the brand new dorm was finally finished, I was one of the girls who got a room in it. The rooms were pretty, and getting to stay in a whole different building was a real privilege. Of course, we weren't alone; Elaine was over there with us, but it was still a status symbol to get to stay over there; "you had to have earned the privilege." There were only two girls to a room at first, and ultimately there were four. The new dorm was full even before it was finished, and we were filling up fast. A new girl arrived every two or three days now, and many more came than went.

I started making tapes to send to my mom. I would walk around all day with this tape recorder and talk to my mom, then I took it to Granny to mail. We all had to do some sort of job, and I worked in the office at the time, so I helped her and Elaine do the mail each day. It was a big process; there were almost three hundred girls there by then, and every letter going out and coming in had to be read and censored. All of us who were trustees took turns doing mail in the office. The place was getting so big that it was impossible for it to be the same as it was in the beginning. More girls meant more of everything, and that was a lot of hard work. In the beginning, either Granny or Poppa was involved in every aspect of your day and night. Eventually, as the load got heavier, they couldn't keep up with 300 girls a day, so it became a little more "lax". Like all of life does, the home was changing.

So, when I took Granny the tape to send to my mom, she listened to the first one while she was doing mail, but when I took her the second one, she said, "I don't have time to listen to those tapes, just wrap it and send it." After I saw her put the third one through without listening to it, I got brave and made one with a few "outright begs" for my freedom to my mom. I had never been able even to insinuate to her, in letter or on the phone, my desire (my need) to leave this place. I didn't say anything derogatory about the home; I just begged my mother to let me come home. Of course, if Granny or Elaine had listened to it, just the indication of me wanting to leave was enough to get me a whipping and force me to start over from the beginning. I would be watched and feared. The only way I had made it this far was by being exactly what they wanted me to be, and I didn't deviate from that. That would show my "horrible, sinful inner self." I mean, I had never suffered a broken bone there or a serious physical injury, but I had been slapped in the face and literally beaten with boards and a leather whip (in public). I had also been belittled, screamed at, brainwashed, and completely stripped of any self-worth I had. They had forced me to do hard labor, stripped me of any sense of individuality, and they had let friends of mine suffer and hurt. They had put us in the same category as prisoners and screamed in my face that I was a slut and a harlot (and I was still a virgin!). I had a right to want to go home.

\

Better watch what you wish for.

I was shocked when I got a letter back from my mom saying she was going to come and see me and was bringing my brothers and sisters, too. It wasn't what I really wanted, but I was excited all the same.

I was really shocked and excited when Granny told me they were going to allow my family to stay out back in one of the old trailers (which weren't even used by then). She even let me and a few of the girls go out and clean and ready one of the trailers for them to stay in. The pregnant girls didn't stay out there anymore because they had gotten their own place by then.

Before I knew it, my mom, brothers David and Billy, and sisters Shelley and Darla were there. They had driven all the way from Tucson to Texas and had all grown so much in two years. They were now seven, nine, eleven and thirteen, and I was almost sixteen. I got hugs from all of them; they hadn't forgotten me, and I'd never stopped thinking of them once.

My mom was as young and beautiful as I remembered her to be. Her grandmother, my great grandmother, had been almost full-blooded American Indian, so she had gotten the dark hair and dark features from her. She was a striking woman.

My aunt Martha was Brother Roloff's personal secretary, so she had some pull around there. I saw her every Sunday at church, and quite often in general. Once, she even came and took me to town for a few hours, after I became a trustee. She even took me to her office at the corporate headquarters; that was when I saw all the women opening envelopes and making three piles: money, checks, and letters! She took me to her apartment, bought me things and took me out to eat once. She was my inside link to the outside, someone to look for on Sunday and say hello to. She often took pictures of me and the girls and gave me copies of them. That was how I got all the pictures I have of me at the home. I believe my aunt Martha talked them into letting my family stay out in the trailer. It was so neat to see them all.

During the days, I did all the stuff I had to do, like Bible study, choir practice, work and broadcasts, but both the girls (Shelley and Darla) got to go with me to almost everything. My two little brothers (David and Billy) weren't allowed in the dorm building, except for when we had church, even though Granny and Poppa had a son who lived there. Like I said, we didn't see him very much, but when we did, we didn't like him. He was treated so differently than all of us, and he was mean, too. Like one day when we were all outside having our free time on the tarmac, he was out there washing the bus, and a bunch of us had found a kitten (there were cats up at the barn). He grabbed the kitten from us and threw it over the bus like a baseball, then tried to run around the bus and catch it. Well, of course there was no way he was going to, and the kitten died. We couldn't even go tell, because you couldn't say anything bad about him. We all hated the fact that he was allowed to watch when we had to lift our dresses up and get whipped.

Anyway, my two little brothers weren't allowed in the dorm most of the time. It was great to have my brothers and sisters there, though, and they loved it, too. All four of them played with the goats and all the other animals we had there, and we all had a blast exploring the barn and playing on top of all the hay.

Granny and Poppa always acted differently whenever a parent was around, so I was being treated better during their visit. My brothers and sisters weren't getting left there, so their memories of those few days aren't the same as mine. Billy and David loved plucking chickens, but to all us girls it was a nightmare, and I hated it! So of course my brother's account of that day differs greatly from mine. They just loved the big machine with black nubs that went around and around to beat the feathers off those dead chickens. It's funny how different people can have such different perceptions of the same event.

While they were there, my mom got to take me to town without anybody coming along with us. With five kids, there was no room in the car for anyone else, so Granny let me go by myself. We went to the beach, even though it was still winter, so we didn't actually get in the ocean. We still walked along the beach, where my brother David found a big blue crab that bit him on the finger. If there was ever an animal around, David would find it. I know I've said he looked so much like Huckleberry Finn, but maybe he was more like Arliss in "Old Yeller".

I was so grateful for the distraction while my family was there. My mom and I talked a lot about my family back in Oklahoma while we were riding in the car. I guess Grandpa and Kari Jo were doing well. I was able to ask about Grandma's funeral (who all went, and stuff like that). I couldn't get enough of what was going on in the outside world and what I had missed. I wanted out of there so badly. I wanted Mom to keep driving and take me home with her.

Their visit was over so quickly, and they were leaving soon. I started dropping hints as much as I could. I didn't want to tell her horror tales, because I was afraid she might confront Granny. I was already terrified I would be punished for something I wasn't aware of after she left. I didn't want her to tell Granny I said anything bad about the home, but I finally flat out asked her if I could go home. She told me she'd already talked to Granny and they didn't think I was ready yet. I was devastated. I asked her when I would be ready, and she said it was up to Granny. I couldn't believe it. If Granny had her way, I would be another Elaine. So they left, and my heart left with them. I was sure now I would never get out of there.

I went back to my regular routine of broadcast, choir practice, Bible study, work, board meetings and school; you know, good old brainwashing and all that implies.

The "Rebecca Home for Girls" continued to grow by leaps and bounds. In fact, even with the new dorm, we were overloaded with people, so they started construction on a whole new dormitory, even bigger than the original dorm. It would be two stories tall and have a giant kitchen in it, one that would feed up to five hundred people. They were going to build it right next to the original dorm, on the other side, in part of the watermelon patch. It was under construction for months.

A few months after my visit from my family, right before the new dorm was completed; I got called to the office. I went to the office expecting to be in trouble; instead, I was shocked when Granny said to me, "April, your mom and your church in Tucson are going to hold a fundraiser to furnish the new kitchen in the new dorm. How would you like to go home for a short visit?"

My mouth dropped open; I just stood there and shook my head up and down with this "in awe" look on my face.

Granny said, "Your church is going to have a week-long event to furnish the new kitchen. They want you to speak and give your testimony. You will be a representative of the home, AND YOU BETTER NOT LET ME DOWN! Remember, this is just a visit. You will be back. You will be allowed to take one suitcase with you. You leave one week from today, stay for Easter, and then you will come back. So you will be gone for almost two weeks, and I can guarantee you, April, that anything you do while you are there that is against our rules will be dealt with as soon as you return. Your mother has promised to inform me of any indiscretions, so don't think that you can do anything you shouldn't and get away with it. This is a big test for you, and don't even think of betraying me. Now go to your room and pray about this."

I left the office, unable to process what had just happened. A visit! Two weeks! I was in shock! Could it be true? I would believe it when it really happened.

For the next week, I was on cloud nine. I was giddy with joy and thought of getting out of there and going home, even if it was only temporary.

I had to pack everything I was going to take into one bag – I was coming back, remember?! You must know I was planning to do everything in my power to make sure that didn't happen. At least I was going to try very hard to make sure it didn't. This was my one chance at freedom.

As I prepared to leave, I had to say goodbye to almost 300 girls. Of course, this was just a visit, mind you, but in my heart I was hoping it was more than that. Even as much as I wanted out of there, it was sad to say my goodbyes. This place had been my home for two years, and these girls weren't getting their chance to leave. I could see the desire in their eyes, and everyone of them was wishing they were going with me. I so desperately wanted to save them all and take them with me.

The morning they took me to the airport was very nerve-racking. It felt so strange to be driving to the airport; I was shivering, I was so excited. As I looked back on the home driving away, I had the most mixed emotions running through me – that is, until Granny and Elaine started in on me, repeating over and over the retribution I would feel on my return if this didn't go perfectly. The entire trip to the airport, I was terrified she would change her mind and turn around. She sounded so mad that I was going, even though it hadn't even been my idea.

Once we were at the airport, I was prayed over, then yelled at, then prayed over some more, and yelled at some more. The last thing Granny said to me was, "You better not make me sorry I did this, April, because if you say anything bad about me or the home, I will hunt you down and make you sorry you were ever born. Remember, April, God is a god of vengeance, and even if I don't know what evil you are up to, He does. Remember that."

I knew the moment I stepped on that airplane and she stepped off, I was going to try very hard not to go back to that place, no matter what they thought. Sitting on the plane waiting for take off was excruciating. It seemed like an eternity, and I kept waiting for Granny or Elaine to run on the plane and pull me off. I just wanted to be off the ground and out of the state of Texas.

When we finally did take off, do you know what I was thinking? I was thinking that even if the plane crashed and I died, at least I wouldn't have died in the home! I was one month away from turning sixteen years old, and even at that young age, death was very prevalent in my mind.

Freedom?

It was such a neat feeling to finally be flying away from that place. I felt more freedom at that moment than at any other time in my life. Even though I was going to a place that wasn't really my home anymore and leaving a place that called itself home – but definitely wasn't – at least for the next few hours I wouldn't be at either place; I would be free. No Granny, no Poppa, no Mom…just me. It was exhilarating!

I wish someone had told me just what a neat person I was, something I didn't find out until many years later. What a shame.

My plane landed in San Antonio, TX, for a five-hour layover. I was in the outside world, all by myself for five hours. I had been given ten dollars to eat on. It was the first money I'd touched or seen in two years. Finally, I got off the airplane and went into the terminal. I was in awe of everything, and everything was eye candy to me. The San Antonio Airport is really neat; at least it was to me. It was like being in a mall; there were shops everywhere. I fell to temptation and bought a tube of mascara. I felt like they were going to ask me for my ID or something, and I was sure the lady who took the money for it was a spy for the home. I went into the bathroom and put some on. After that, for the rest of the time I was there, I thought everyone who saw me knew I had just done something that would send me straight to hell. I was sure they were all looking at me and thinking what a hussy I was. That was one of Granny's favorite words to call us girls.

When it was time to get back on the airplane, I was terrified God would crash the plane to punish me. In fact, I was terrified of everything. If I wasn't wondering if God was going to get me, I was terrified my mom would see it on me and slap me across the face when she saw me.

My plane finally landed, and the moment of truth was here. When I got off the plane, my mom was waiting. I was relieved that she didn't hit me, but she barely said anything to me. In fact, when we got in the car, it was very awkward, like we were strangers. I guess we always had been, but the two-year separation had made the distance between us even wider. She didn't have any of the kids with her, and that was our only common bond. I don't think she knew what to say to me. I was like a foreign object to her, someone she didn't really know before, and knew even less now.

I had grown up and out and was much more submissive and quiet than I had been before. I was terrified of everything and everyone.

\

Unfortunately, it didn't help feeling like I was a stranger to her, and her to me.

When we left the airport, she took me straight to the church. I had to see the stuff they had collected for the new kitchen, and there was a whole giant room full of it. She also wanted me to see the poster they had made, to advertise about the home. It had my picture on it, and pictures of some of the other girls and the home.

I had to meet the new pastor and a bunch of women who worked there. It was all so foreign to me. The little church we had gone to when I left had grown a lot. They even had a bigger building. I must have met twenty people while we were there. My mom showed me off like a Miss America winner. It was exhausting.

When we finally got home, I was surprised to see they still lived in the same trailer as they had when I left. That was unusual, because we never lived anywhere for very long, but she had a surprise for me: Mom told me she was buying a house. I was shocked. She said I would have a room of my own someday. I was thrilled; I had never had a room of my own. It worked out perfectly so I could help her move while I was there. We had never owned a house before, so I was so excited.

Mom finally took me to see the house. It was a beautiful brick home, one block from the high school and two blocks from the church. It was even in a decent area. Someone had converted the garage into a den, so my mom turned that into a bedroom for the boys. Then there was a room for the girls, one for me, and of course my mom took the master suite. It was wonderful.

We spent the first few days of my stay moving into this house. It was great; a real house, a real yard, and it was in a respectable neighborhood, too. It really made me not want to go back to the home.

My mom watched me like a hawk, but one night I asked her if I could walk up to the 7-Eleven by myself; it was only a block away.

She gave me an accusatory look and said, "Why?"

I said, "Just to get out for a while."

She finally said (after a lecture of imminent doom if I did anything wrong), "I suppose so, but be back within an hour!"

So, I walked out into the real world for the first time in a long time, alone. It was a great feeling, I had no one to answer to, just for that moment. I had always been in awe of the world, but the deprivation of its wonders made me even more aware of everything around me. It was a beautiful night in Tucson. In my opinion, all life in Tucson should happen after dark; that's the only time the weather is bearable.

When I got to the store, I saw a girl I had known before I left. She wasn't from my church. There was always the church and all that entails, and then there was everything else. Seeing her threw me into a mountain of feelings to experience. I was overwhelmed by everything: candy in the store just to buy and eat; people driving in cars going anywhere they wanted to go; being able to walk out of a door without someone grabbing you and pulling you back in. It was exhilarating!

I talked to her for a little while. She asked me where I had been and said people had wondered where I went. I told her a little bit about the home and my life there.

"You poor thing!" she said.

So that life wasn't normal to everyone? I had forgotten life before the home. Everything was different now; it would never be the same. I had lost the "ignorance is bliss" factor. I now knew freedom was subjective and completely out of our hands and could be taken away from us at any moment. She was the first person I had spoken to in two years who didn't have something good to say about the "home". It made me feel good to know the whole world didn't see things like my mother, Granny, Poppa and Brother Roloff did. It was neat hearing about people I knew before I left, and about school. She freaked out when I told her we had "Bible" as a class at school.

I tried to be so good. Like, when my mom let me go to the store that night, I was back in the door five minutes early. I did everything she told me to do. I went to every church service, and I did all of the unpacking. I watched the kids, I didn't ask for anything. I just tried to be what she wanted me to be. The first few days I was back, my time was consumed by the dedication of the new dorm and all the things I had to do at church.

Things were very confusing to me. It was fun in a way, because I got to be around other people my age, including boys. My mom felt safe when I was doing anything with or at the church. No other association would be allowed. I saw that from the start.

I also felt safe there, or at least safer than out in the world. It was so hard to find people who lived as I had been taught to believe. I was definitely a minority. Yet, the people at church were the most conflicting of all. I was dizzy from the conflicts between them and the "home". I couldn't understand why the people from the church believed in the same religion as the home, yet they had televisions, ate fried food, listened to worldly music, ate pork, and drank sodas. The women even wore man's clothing (pants or shorts) and makeup. They had their ears pierced and adorned themselves with jewelry. It was a constant conflict in my brain. Why could they, but we couldn't? These people supported the home. So was it wrong, or wasn't it? Did they know something I didn't, or was Brother Roloff right? It was so hard. Some of the people even smoked cigarettes. I couldn't understand any of it. Every person there did something I had been made to believe would send you straight to hell – or worse, get you an immediate beating. It was all so confusing.

I then realized you can force almost perfection, if you control it hard enough, but the reality is that people aren't perfect. If you want perfection, then you want robots, not people. I felt very cheated and full of conflict. The home expected too much. People can't live like they lived, because they weren't in a controlled environment. No one stood over them and said, "Everything you do is bad, except what I say is right, and we'll beat you or lock you up if you do it wrong!" They just expected too much.

Finally, the big night at church came. I had to get up and give my testimony, something I was very good at by then. As I talked about the home, I talked all those people into donating money to the home. I felt like a traitor, to myself and the other girls at the home. I felt like I should have been up there begging them to get them all out, to go and save them all, but instead I said how good they were and how much they'd helped me become a better person, and how bad I was before they helped me. I said everything my mom and Granny had wanted me to say, everything expected of me. I had become such a good girl.

After the big event, I still had almost a week to go before I had to go back, so I started working on my mother. I was so good; I did everything I was told with no argument. I started hinting, just a little bit at first, but as the days flew by, I started hinting harder. Finally, I just broke down and flat out begged her.

"Please, Mom, let me stay! Please. I'll be so good. I can help you with the kids; I can clean the house and do all the chores. Please let me stay."

I begged and begged, without telling her anything bad about the home. At first she said no, but the day before I was supposed to go back, after much begging and pleading, she looked at me and said, "OK, April, you can stay, at least for a while."

I couldn't believe my ears – she had said yes! Could it be true? Was I home to stay? No going back? I couldn't believe it.

That night, Mom called Granny and told her I wasn't coming back, and Granny flipped out. She essentially guaranteed my freedom by fighting with my mother about it.

She said, "No! She isn't ready! You have to send her back. We won't let her stay!"

That right there did it; my mom wouldn't let anyone tell her what she could or couldn't do. They had such a fight that Granny refused to send any of my stuff to me, but I didn't care. I couldn't believe it. I was so happy, I cried. I couldn't believe it was over. Just like that! It was too good to be true! I was ecstatic and skeptical. I was always on the alert for the downside of everything. The home had turned me into a very subdued, timid and wary person, but it hadn't broken me completely. I wonder just how long that would have taken.

If Granny knew I wasn't ready after two years to be out of that home and be the way they wanted me to be, just how long would it have taken? I don't think 20 years would have been long enough. You can teach, you can show an example, you can inform, but you can NOT force people to be the way you want them to be. Not if they don't want to be that way. You may be able to physically force them, but you cannot force their mind, not without constant torture. So for my sixteenth birthday, I got a room of my own, and my freedom.

The world

Right around the time I left the "home" was when Brother Roloff was having all that trouble with the state. He was arrested and jailed. The state wanted a hand in his organization, but he fought them and used the ordeal to build his empire even stronger. He had pictures of himself taken behind bars and made into posters and flyers. He became a martyr, being persecuted by the evil government, and his plan worked. He used his broadcasting network to tell the world of his persecution.

As I said, the state couldn't do anything to him, because he had never taken a dollar from them. He ended up winning and getting out of jail. Brother Roloff used it for all it was worth, preaching that the world was ending and everyone but his followers were against him and God. He was a brilliant man, but he was kind of like one of those militia groups in Montana. This man had built a whole world that was completely self-sufficient. It was independent of the rest of the world, and he alone dominated it. Brother Roloff could feed, clothe, educate and house over two thousand people at a time. Besides, he had a worldwide broadcasting network to recruit new patrons and followers. He had Jim Jones and David Koresh beat by leaps and bounds in the numbers of followers he had.

Brother Roloff and his Honey bee quartet suffered an untimely death in a plane crash three years after I left the "home." I'm sure he would have gone down in the history books, but the question is "For what?" We'll never know. I remember him actually mentioning that someday we'd all die together if the world truly tried to step in.

He was a very charismatic man, though, and I completely understand why people of faith followed him. I have a scrapbook and photo album from when I was at the home, and it's filled with many articles and pictures. I even have one or two of those pictures of him behind bars in jail. It's strange to look at it all now, because it's like looking at another person's life.

Roloff Enterprises is still in business today. After being shut down for abuse charges, it was reopened a few years ago and is now fighting in the courts over a death that occurred there.

I'm not even saying everything Brother Roloff believed in or preached about was wrong, but I do think it got too big too fast and he lost control over it. He may have had good intentions; I just think he went about it the wrong way. I believe the physical punishment was wrong, and it's wrong to brainwash people. They are individuals and shouldn't be treated en masse, like one unit. You can force it as long as you have control over them, but if it doesn't come from the individual, it won't last. It wasn't real.

I think the sayings "Too much of a good thing" and "The road to hell is paved with the best of intentions" are very profound metaphors as far as the home is concerned. I also think that like a lot of good intentions, money can turn it bad, and Brother Roloff's Enterprises were bringing in millions a year.

You can't just take away the decision-making part of someone, especially where religion is concerned; it won't work. Faith and belief have to be genuine; if you cram them down someone's throat, then they'll gag. The truth is, I wasn't a criminal in need of imprisonment or a bad person in need of punishment. I was just a very young girl, with a young girl for a mother, who both needed guidance and love; that's all. Most of the girls in the home were just like me. None of them deserved to be beaten; just loved.

The whole time I was in the home, I never stopped missing my family or my freedom. You don't know what freedom is until you have it yanked away from you. Another saying, "You don't know what you have until it's gone", should be Webster's legal definition of regret.

My mom took me to school the following day and enrolled me in classes. What an overwhelming experience that was, but what a mess! They didn't accept "Bible" as a viable subject. "Credits", what was that? I had virtually missed the first two years of high school. I had some credits from all my correspondence schooling they would accept, but not many. Somehow, they accepted me and put me in the tenth grade; there were only six weeks of school left for the year anyway.

As I started back to real school, I found I had some real dilemmas. I couldn't do anything the other kids could do. My mom wouldn't let me wear the clothes they wore, and this was 1972, and hip huggers and bell bottoms were all the rage. Skirts were even shorter than they are today (if you can believe that). So, the first "bad" thing I did was roll up my skirts when I got to school; not much, just a little. It would be my first rebellious attempt at fitting in with everyone else. I also waited to get to school to put my mascara on. I was turning into a regular harlot.

My mom's life had changed while I was gone, too. Her dress was more modern, her car was more modern, and her house was more modern. She'd continued to go to school while I was gone and was more active in the church, "if that was possible".

Remember the McNealy's, her friend who was married to my high school principal? Well, somehow she'd talked them into letting her open and run a room at the high school called the "Opportunity Room." It was where you went if you got into trouble at school. It was an opportunity to complete your school work while you were suspended from school. You could come to school, go to the Opportunity Room and do your school work, but you couldn't go anywhere on campus or participate in school activities. The problem was, almost everyone who went there really didn't care if they did their work or not; most of them were the troublemakers of the school.

I really didn't see my mom that much at school, but everybody knew of her, and I definitely couldn't get into any trouble there. Everyone wanted to stay as far away from her and the "Opportunity Room" as possible.

\

At church there was a boy, and he asked me to go to a basketball game with him. I told him I didn't think my mom would let me go, but he talked me into asking her. I was terrified to do it, and I was shocked when I did and she said yes; she only let me go, though, because he was from the church and there were going to be other kids from church there.

My mom took me out and bought me a pair of jeans. I was shocked and excited, and I couldn't believe it. I guess it was only fair, since she wore pants all the time. It was the first time I had a pair of pants on in more than two years. It's weird to look back and realize what little things meant to me. I guess it wasn't such a little thing after all. I mean, I had just come from a place that beat it into me that wearing man's clothing would send me straight to hell. In one way, I was thrilled to be wearing a pair of jeans; then again, I walked around thinking God was going to strike me dead for doing it. The guilt complexes I had learned to carry around were astounding. They did gradually lessen as time went on, or maybe it was that I just wanted to be like everyone else. Believe me, everyone noticed I was different from them. I stuck out like a sore thumb: I was different from the way I'd been before I left, and I was different from everyone else at the school in almost every way.

First of all, I had hung on to my virginity, and from the way everyone at school talked, I was the only one in the world left who did. I didn't know it then, but they were more talk than action. We were in the "love in, love anybody, love everybody" era. Remember free love, before there was AIDS?

Even the kids at church were worldly, at least according to the laws of Brother Roloff. They listened to rock and roll, wore makeup, shorts and pants, ate fried food, chocolate, pork, and drank sodas. They even used slang and watched TV.

The night I went to the basketball game was a real culture shock. I had so much fun, though, being with people my own age and doing things without someone breathing down my back. It was freedom, and they were all fascinated about my stories of the home. It was amazing to them, but it was amazing to me that they didn't live just like me; I mean, they were from my church.

After the game, David, the boy I had gone with, took me home. He seemed really interested in me, which gave me so many conflicting feelings. I desperately wanted to be wanted, but on the other hand, I'd been told the worst thing you could do was look at a boy…well, that was what started the worst thing, anyhow.

My mom had told me to be home by ten, which meant we had to leave the game early, but he didn't seem to mind. After we got to my house, we stayed outside talking until after ten. Right at ten o'clock, my mom stuck her head outside and told me it was time to come in. I didn't want to; I loved having someone interested in me, and it was such a good feeling. After my mom shut the door, he kissed me. Now I was in trouble; I couldn't stop thinking of all those words Granny had used on us: "harlot", "tramp", "slut", and mostly "sinner".

The next time I went to church, David asked me again to go out with him, just to Denny's for some French fries and a coke. I was going downhill fast – and here I go again: I was breaking more than one of Brother Roloff's five thousand commandments. Boys, fried foods, carbonated beverages all in one night, and I was wearing pants while I was doing it all. I was going to hell in a handbasket and sinking so far down, it would take a lifeboat to save me this time. I almost enjoyed myself, but it would take years to overcome the inhibitions and guilt complexes the home had beaten into me.

So again I went out with a boy, and again my mom told me to be home by ten, so I was, and again we were standing outside – doing more kissing than talking this time. All of a sudden, an alarm went off; no, not inside my head, a real alarm. My mom had set an alarm clock and put it outside the front door. When it went off, we both jumped apart, and it was a good thing because at that moment my mother again stuck her head out the door and said, "It's time to come in, April."

I was so embarrassed, but it got me inside. I never went out with him again after that; my mom's Hitler-like control over me was hard for anyone to take for too long.

Coming home, I felt just like a kid who's been taken to a fair or a carnival and set loose with a hundred dollars to do anything he feels like doing. I didn't know which way to go first. It was like I'd been secluded on a farm or something (ha ha) and had never seen bright lights or ridden fun rides or eaten cotton candy. I didn't know which ride to go on first, and just like any kid at a carnival, they exhaust themselves and make themselves sick, but a week later they'd gladly do it again.

I made friends at school, but I was definitely a follower. I had no self-esteem, which was another sin ("Pride cometh before a fall"). Everything that tasted good, looked good, felt good or was popular was a sin and would send me straight to hell. Brother Roloff had preached of a very vengeful God, and he practiced what he preached. Conflict, conflict, conflict; everything I did, I anguished over. I was one week into my sixteenth year of life, and I never dreamed of or thought about tomorrow. I was just grateful to make it through each day.

While I was growing up, I never had anyone tell me I was worth anything, had value or potential, or was smart or good. I only had negativity my whole life. No one told me I would have to take care of myself one day, or maybe more than just myself. Or even that I could have a career or had potential for one. Planning for a career would mean there was a future, and the people in my life never even said the word "future". That's what poverty really is: people who don't know there is a future. They don't see one for themselves, so they don't see one for their children. Some people are so busy surviving each day, one day they just open their eyes and it's too late. The future is there, but at that point it turns into despair.

Can't blame mom for everything

All the bad stuff wasn't always my mom's fault. The lack of self-worth she instilled in us; no one ever told her of her worth either. The difference between her and us is she didn't have the hatred by her parents she directed towards us. Yes, she was poor and had little knowledge of a future, but she did have a sense of family and place, and she had both of her parents, "good or bad", to draw from, and they loved her.

I never invited any of my friends or acquaintances over to my house for many reasons. As I said before, I couldn't let them meet my mom because she would run them off, or worse, she would hit me or yell at me in front of them. Besides, I was so embarrassed by how dirty everything looked all the time. With five kids, my mom and a dog, our house looked like what it was, "poor white trash in a middle class neighborhood."

When we first moved into the house, we didn't have any curtains at all. I don't even know how we bought that house. It sat on the corner of a very busy, dead end street. So, everyone who lived on the street had to drive or walk by our house to get to their house. I know every one of them cried every time they went by it. No grass, toys everywhere (most of them broken), kids out there all the time with tacky clothes on and no shoes. We were an eyesore to the neighborhood.

One evening my mom was gone, as she always was. Three of the ladies who lived on our street came over and knocked on the door. I was a little surprised, but I let them in. They graciously and discreetly told me they could see in our house all the time and we needed curtains on our windows. The ladies were going to go in together and buy us curtains as a gift, and they wanted to know if they could measure the windows. I thought it was very nice and expected my mom would be pleased. So, I let the ladies in, and they got to work measuring the windows. I didn't tell my mom because I thought it would be a nice surprise for her. A few days later, the neighbor ladies brought some nice rubber backed curtains over and I helped them hang them up. They looked expensive and very nice. I thanked them, and they were so nice about it. I was so pleased about the privacy. In fact, I wished we could have put curtains around the whole yard, as I'm sure they did, too. Unfortunately, when my mom came home, you would have thought they had burned down our house or something. She yelled at me about it, for a month.

"They just think they're better than us! You should have told them no, that I would have bought my own curtains if I'd wanted them!" my mom screamed.

I didn't understand it at all. She had taken help from all kinds of people from our church, the state, or anyone else who offered it. I was grateful to the ladies, but my mom was pissed at me from that point on, and we gradually went back to a fight-building relationship. I just couldn't do anything right in her eyes.

There was always fighting at our house. Either my brothers and sisters were fighting among themselves, or my mom was fighting with one "or all" of us, and she didn't care who heard her. My house wasn't a place I wanted to be associated with, so I led a double life.

At home I was very quiet, I tried to stay out of trouble, I tried to do everything expected of me and keep out of my mom's line of sight, or avoid her as much as possible. I went to every church activity she requested, but away from home I was marveling at the wonders of life. I was inquisitive, funny, smart, cute and happy. I also discovered I could ditch church without her knowing it and go to the taco place down the street with a couple of other girls from church. We never got caught, either; we were always back before church was over.

I knew she could see some changes in me, because I was wearing my dresses shorter, wearing more makeup, and looking more like the kids around me. I was giving her no reason to ride me all the time, but she did anyway. I just tried to stay away from her as much as possible.

School was my escape. The kids from school always hung out at this drug store-restaurant, an old Walgreens or something like that. It was across the street from the high school, the place to be at lunch.

There was a math teacher at Flowing Wells High School who was so brilliant, he was stupid. He was like an idiot savant. Ask him any question that involved math, and he wouldn't miss, but at all other times he was just dumb. Once, the boys in class turned his desk around as joke, and he didn't even notice it the entire day.

Another time, he had driven over to the little drug store-restaurant to eat lunch with some of the other teachers. After school, when he went to leave, he thought someone had stolen his car because he had forgotten he had driven it to lunch. He had walked back from lunch with the other teachers and didn't even remember he had driven his car over there until they told him they had found his car over at the shopping center.

Another weird teacher experience I had at Flowing Wells was with this English teacher named Mrs. Stewart; she professed to be a witch. She even used to tell us stories in class about leaving her skin by the fireplace when she went on a witch thing. She also told us the only way to kill a witch was to catch her while she was out of her skin and put salt in it. The school fired her after she lifted a chair and threw it at a boy from across the room with one hand! I swear it's true; I saw her do it. She was definitely a weird woman.

Too much freedom

When I got out of the girls home and went back to regular school, lunch was my favorite class. It was my everyday fix of the normal world. No church affiliation and no mom affiliation; just a bunch of kids my age sitting around eating French fries and drinking Cokes. They all wore bell bottom jeans and listened to and talked about the Beatles, Jethro Tull, and Led Zeppelin (this was the 70s). A lot of them had black lights and black light posters. Of course, they all talked about sex like they did it every day, when actually it was just a lot of wishful thinking. Some kids did the most potent acid ever made. It was the orange sunshine era; their bodies were used as testing grounds for everything that would alter their state of mind. Peyote buds were eaten, mescaline was taken, and a lot of alcohol was consumed.

\

These weren't bad kids, just average kids of the time. Today they run our country, and at least most of the biggest companies in it. Funny how, at the time, they didn't believe in the system they run today. It sure was different from lunch conversation at the Heavenly Hayloft, I can tell you that. I just wanted to fit in, so I started by smoking a cigarette or two. One of my friends gave me a pair of bell bottoms to wear and a dress I couldn't wear to church, stuff like that. I was listening to rock and roll and committing those big sins like eating fried foods and drinking carbonated beverages. I even let one of my friends pierce my ears, and I let another talk me into lying to my mother so I could spend the night at her house and go to a party with her.

In the deserts in Arizona, they have these big outdoor parties called "Boonies." As many as 200 to 600 people get together (out in the boonies), burn a big bonfire, have many kegs of beer, play loud music, and do acid. Today, with raves, parties, and all the drugs there are today, it's nothing too shocking to come across a large group of partying young people, but in 1973 it was a shock to me, and oh so overwhelming. The other kids were at least led into it somewhat slowly just by watching TV or seeing these people in a mall or at the store. I was totally new to all of it, and in constant amazement.

I had just turned 16, and I was "well endowed", as they say, but very petite. I only weighed one hundred pounds. A couple of my girlfriends let me borrow some of their clothes, and I looked good. I have to say, I never thought of myself as ugly; worthless maybe, but not ugly. The natural curly dark red hair I hated as a child didn't look bad hanging down to the middle of my back at sixteen. Girls permed, crimped, and dyed their hair to get it to look like my mine did right after I got out of the shower. I was a quick learner, and I definitely didn't mind the attention I readily received from all the boys. I wanted nothing more than to be wanted by somebody.

Men in my life had until now always been a part of my mom's life, not mine, and then only temporary. She kept most of her boyfriends away from us kids, but I needed attention, and I wanted it from a man. I needed somebody to tell me I had something they wanted, desired, loved, accepted, and even needed. Of course, that's not what I really needed. Not that kind of love, anyway, but I didn't know that then.

When we got to this Boonie, I was very well-received. Guys came around and were sitting by me, talking to me, and looking at me. One of them gave me a beer; I hated how it tasted but drank it anyway. After I did, I was feeling pretty buzzed; I had never had a drink in my life. I liked the feeling, so I drank another one and felt even better.

A good looking guy came up to me and took my hand, pulled me up and said, "Let's dance." I told him I didn't know how to dance, but he pulled me up anyway. He pressed his body up next to mine, and we started moving as one. At that moment, I was experiencing so many new feelings that it was overwhelming. While we were dancing, he kissed me and told me to open my mouth, he had something for me.

"What?" I asked him.

He had this little pill that was half the size of a BB. I had never taken a pill before that I could remember and had no idea what would happen if I did, so I took it. It was so small, I couldn't even feel it in my mouth when I swallowed. I was so ignorant, gullible and easily led.

Fifteen minutes later, I had a permanent smile on my face. I felt so weird; it felt like my insides were moving. Voices took on an echo, and my vision was really doing weird things. I didn't feel bad, though. It felt strange, but I felt free and light.

The guy who gave me the little pill came over to me and said, "She's tripping, guys!"

They started moving their hands in front of me and saying things like "Are you tripping, April? Are you seeing trails?"

I thought everything and everyone was so funny. I couldn't stop laughing, and yes, I was seeing trails! Nothing is stranger than being on acid.

A really good looking guy from school came over to the group of people I was with. He started talking to me as he looked at the guys standing around me.

"What did you guys give her?" The guys just looked the other way. Before I knew it, this very attractive young man took my hand, pulled me up and began leading me away from there. "Let's go for a walk," he said.

I was already gone. He probably could have gotten me to jump off a bridge right then. I wasn't in control of myself at all. He led me to his car, where he opened the trunk and pulled out a blanket. He carried the blanket in one arm while he led me with the other, far away from the fire and people. Anything he wanted of me, I just smiled and shook my head up and down. I was in la la land. He was a good boy scout and always prepared! This handsome young man's name was Robert, and he was very popular at school. I didn't hang around him, but all the cool people did.

He put the blanket on the ground, and down we sat. He had two beers, and he handed me one. I drank it. This one didn't taste like anything, good, bad, or indifferent. I was so high, my eyes weren't even blue anymore, because they were all pupil. Then he leaned over and kissed me. I do remember everything. It's not like I was out of it; I was just out of control of myself.

He laid me down on the blanket and started touching me. I know this sounds stupid, but at the time I thought I was weird because I was a virgin. I didn't want to be different; I wanted to be normal, and I had no respect for myself. I didn't know what respecting myself was. No one had ever taught me to respect myself; I had only been taught I was worthless. This guy was telling me I was special and desired, and I couldn't believe he wanted me. I had no understanding of relationships, so I thought this was one.

As we got deeper into kissing and touching, he slipped off my shirt, then his. As this progressed, he also took off my pants, and then his. My senses were completely acute because of the drug I was on, and I was hungry for the one-on-one attention.

When he got more intimate, I did protest a little. I doubt most men understand protest, unless you yell rape or hit them. I had been very sheltered from sex. In the home, we weren't even supposed to think about it (like they could prevent that). The closest I had come was making out with Billy Mosley at the lake the summer I was 14. At that moment, I honestly didn't know what to expect. He wasn't rough or anything, just persistent, and I could tell he had done this before.

So, one thing led to another, and he did climb on top of me. As he tried to enter me, I gave a short yelp and tried to move away. It hurt, and what he used to do it with was terrifying. Surely, this couldn't be what everyone always talked about as being so good.

When it was over, I was glad, and he looked pretty pleased, too. Of course, I looked way happier than I actually was because I still couldn't stop smiling. This big grin was pasted to my face, like the Cheshire cat. My jaws actually hurt for days after that, and that's not all that hurt for days. I never told him it was my first time.

He helped me get my clothes on, and we went back to the fire and the people. I was sore and bleeding, and this trip I was on was intense. I left the group and waited by the car I had come out in until those who I came with returned a few hours later.

This just couldn't be the thing everyone raved about doing all the time. It couldn't be the great time I had been led to believe it was. I couldn't talk about it to anyone, because I didn't want anyone to know it was the first. The next day, I thought I was going to die. I hurt from my head to my toes, and my stomach was doing flip flops, but I survived and went home.

On Monday at school, Robert came up to me and said, "Are you all right? You were bleeding the other night!"

I was so embarrassed. "I know I started my period." I then slipped away and avoided him from then on.

To this day, no one ever knew it was my first time, not even the guy I had lost my virginity to. I kept so much to myself, I thought I would burst. Granny was right! I was a slut and a hussy! Oh well, she had told me that for so long, I believed it before I could even be one.

A couple days later, my grandpa and Aunt Kari Jo were coming to visit us in Tucson. I hadn't seen them for more than 2 years. The last time was when my grandma was in the hospital and she had her brain surgery. I was just 14 at the time, but I had changed so much since then. Two years at the home will change anyone.

The day they were supposed to arrive, I went to school. There were only about 5 or 6 days of school left. A friend came up and talked me into ditching with her. I was turning into a regular monster. She talked me into hitchhiking over to this guy's house with her. I had never ditched school or hitchhiked before, and now I was a slut. I was going to hell in a hand basket.

Anyway, there were three guys over at this particular house. They were all about 20 years old, which I thought was quite a bit older than us at 16 years old. We could see they had about 4 bottles of Boone's Farm Strawberry Hill wine. They gladly had us help them drink their wine, and oh my God was that stuff nasty (at least up until the 11th or 12th drink, anyway). I had never had anything but that beer a week earlier. This wine was so sweet that after a couple of drinks it wasn't so bad, and after a couple of bottles it didn't matter.

I was so drunk, I couldn't even see, and I definitely couldn't sit up. I remember one of them carried me into a bedroom, where I started to throw up all over the place. I can still remember the stink of that wine. I don't remember all of it, thank God. The guys weren't mean, but they definitely took advantage of the situation we had gotten ourselves into. When they were through having their fun, they took us (drunk, barefoot, and with my shirt inside out) and dropped us off in front of my high school. Unfortunately, school was just letting out and there were people everywhere. My house sat right across the street from the high school. I was so drunk, I started stumbling home. I could barely hold myself up, and I had to cross a very busy street to get to my house.

I was out in the middle of the street, when all of a sudden my mother drove right by me. She pulled over and stopped right on the road. As she was staring at me, I could see this look of revelation sweep over her face. She started yelling my name, and I started ducking down behind cars and laughing.

I began playing a game of hide and go seek with her, and I jumped up and said, "You can't find me, na ne na ne na na."

She crossed the road faster than lightning, dodging cars as she ran.

She grabbed me by the shirt, but I was laughing so hard, I said, "Whoops, I guess you did find me."

I could almost see smoke coming out of my mom's nose, she was so mad. She screamed, "What's wrong with you?"

I laughed and said, "Nothing" as I stumbled off the curb.

She pulled me across the road to the car, where I saw my aunt Kari Jo in the passenger seat. In my drunken stupor, I yelled, "Hi, Kari," as I waved my arms in the air; I was feeling no pain.

As we approached the car, Kari asked my mom, "What's wrong with her?"

"I don't know," my mom said. "I think she's on drugs." She stood me next to the car and started shaking me by the shoulders. "I demand to know what kind of drugs you've been given!" she said.

I laughed and said, "I don't know, no drugs, just a little bit of wine." I showed her with my fingers just how little I had had, and I couldn't stop laughing.

My mom said to my aunt, "Oh my God, she must be on some kind of drug, what am I going to do? I can't let Daddy see her like this."

She put me in the back seat of the car all alone, while they both sat in the front. I kept leaning over the back of the seat, trying to hug my aunt Kari. She had a smile on her face.

"She stinks to high heavens, like booze," she said.

My mom wasn't smiling at all, and she looked like the devil. I swear I could see horns growing from her head, smoke coming out of her nose and fire coming out of her eyes; it was spooky. Unfortunately, it didn't sober me up; it just gave me something to think about for years afterwards.

When we got to the house, my mom got out of the car and came up to my door. She opened the door, reached in and slapped me so hard across the face, I fell backward. Now, I'm not saying I didn't deserve that one, but thank goodness at the time I was feeling no pain. Mom started screaming in my face that my grandfather was in the house and she didn't want him to see me like that. I tried to get out of the car, but she shoved me back in and shut the door. It didn't help that I was still laughing. She told Kari to keep me in the car; she was going in to call a nurse friend of hers to see what to do.

As soon as my mom was in the house, I got out of the car. Kari was on me in a second, but I got past her. I had almost made it to the house when suddenly I tripped and fell as I was trying to get away from Kari Jo's grasp. I just kept going, crawling on my hands and knees into the house.

I stuck my head in the door and saw my grandpa sitting on the couch. I stood up (or tried to) and said, "Hi, Grandpa!"

He said, "Well, hello, kid."

I crawled, stumbled, and half walked over to where he was sitting. I tried to get up, but I couldn't.

Grandpa said, "What's the matter with you, kid?"

I just giggled. "Nothing, I'm fine."

He just looked at me and laughed. "You're drunk, kid!"

I couldn't help laughing and agreeing with him wholeheartedly, with a big smile on my face.

I picked up his crutches and started playing with them. I had my arms through the hand rests and was crawling on my knees (something I had done so many times as a child). My mother came out of the kitchen, where she had been on the phone; she yanked the crutches away from me and handed them back to my grandfather. She told Kari Jo to help her get me back out to the car. My grandpa asked her where she was taking me. She told him she was taking me to a friend of hers who was a nurse.

Grandpa asked, "Why are you taking her over there?"

Mom said, "Because she's on some kind of drug, Daddy!"

He just chuckled. "She's just drunk. You can smell it on her. Put her to bed, and tomorrow she'll never want to do that again."

My mom wasn't happy with that. "NO, Daddy. She's on something, and I'm going to find out what." She grabbed my shoulder, and with Kari's help she led me out to the car and drove us over to Mom's friend Dorothy's place.

Dorothy was her friend from church, and she was also a nurse. When we got to her house, I remember the first thing I did was run to the bathroom and throw up. The next thing I remember was falling down into a big easy chair in the living room, while my mom, Kari and Dorothy retreated to the kitchen.

Even in my drunken stupor, I could hear my mom and Dorothy in the next room talking about me. My mom was yelling, "How could she do this to me? My dad is here. I can't take her over there like this!"

I heard Dorothy tell her I was drunk and that was all. My mom was furious. I heard Dorothy tell her to leave me there for the night and sleep it off. I would be fine the next day.

The next thing I remember, it was morning and I was in a strange house in a strange bed. Dorothy came into the room with my clothes in her hand; they had been washed and ironed. She laid them on the end of the bed, then sweetly asked me how I felt.

"You know you had your mom pretty worried yesterday!"

I couldn't even see or think about my mom right then.

Dorothy patted me on the arm and said, "You wake up and get dressed. Then come to the kitchen, and I'll make you something to eat." She smiled, then turned and left the room.

I tried to sit up, but I was still so sick. I couldn't even look in the mirror; I was so ashamed and embarrassed. All of a sudden I realized I had more to worry about; there would definitely be retribution from my mother. I went into the bathroom and threw up, again.

I took a shower, got dressed, and timidly walked into the kitchen with my head practically down to my feet.

Dorothy greeted me with a smile and said, "Do you feel like eating anything? You should eat a piece of toast or something." Then she handed me two aspirin and some juice. She shocked me by saying,

"Your mom and I discussed it, and we think maybe you should stay here for a few days to let things settle down. Would you like to do that?"

I couldn't believe what I was hearing, "Yes. Please! I don't want to see my mom; she's going to kill me!"

Dorothy smiled. "Good. Then you'll stay here for a few days!"

I was thrilled. She told me to get ready for school and she would take me. I told her I didn't have any shoes, and she gave me some of hers.

I tried to apologize to her for the previous day and all the trouble I had caused, but she kept telling me stuff like, "It's OK, April. I got drunk when I was young, too. Maybe you'll learn something useful from this."

I had never been talked to like that from anyone before. She wasn't telling me I would go to hell or yelling at me; she was smiling at me and telling me it would be OK. It felt so weird.

Dorothy told me she had talked my mom into this and it would make things less volatile when I did see her again. They thought it was better for me to stay there until my grandpa was gone. I didn't want to face my mother, now or EVER. I wanted to put that off as long as possible. Dorothy suggested she go and see my mom during the day and get me some of my things. I felt so much better.

When I got to school, I saw the friend I had been with the previous day. She came up to me and said, "Oh my God! I didn't know if I would ever see you again! I couldn't believe your mom caught you yesterday!"

I told my friend I was so embarrassed about yesterday and asked her how those guys could do that to us.

She started cussing, "Those @$%& jerks! I'm ditching again today and going back over there. They have my purse!"

I realized I had left my shoes over there, too. I had to tell her I never wanted to go over there again because of how they treated us, but she begged me to go with her. The plan was that I could wait up the street and she would go in and get our stuff, but she pleaded for me to go with her. I really wanted my shoes back, so I finally said OK.

We started walking up the street, when all of a sudden this really neat, pale green 64 Impala pulled up next to us. It had been modified with loud glass packs and air shocks. It had nice mag wheels and a little steering wheel. There was the best looking guy driving it, and apparently my friend knew him.

He stopped the car and started a conversation with her. She asked him if he would give us a ride over to these guys' house so she could get our stuff.

He said, "Sure, get in."

So, my friend got into the front seat, and I got into the back. She turned around and introduced him to me. His name was Albert, he was two years ahead of us in school and he had already graduated; he was also 2 years older than me.

I can't explain my decision-making process, or lack thereof. I was brain dead, apparently. I had no roots or ties to school, and I had come in so late in the year that the teachers were just passing me so I would make it to the 11th grade the following year. Most teachers let me slide because I was just there for the last 6 weeks of school. I had missed my entire 9th and 10th grade and had no idea how important school was. I had no perception of the future, just the now. I went with my friend; I was so easily led!

As we drove, this cute guy kept trying to talk to me. I was being very quiet. I didn't feel good, and I was traumatized by what had happened to me the day before. I was still embarrassed, felt terrible about the entire thing, and just wanted to hide. I definitely wasn't going into that house when we got there (I told myself), I was sure of that. I was worried about ditching school again, and I had so much remorse.

This cute guy, Albert, kept looking back at me over the seat and smiling. He was really good looking. He had dark hair and a brilliant smile; it was actually dazzling. He was very clean cut and quite a charmer. During the conversation, I found out he lived one street away from my mom's house.

Albert and I sat in the car while my friend went into these guys' house to retrieve our things. He turned around, took my hand, and asked me if I would go to a graduation party with him the following night. I couldn't believe this guy. This really good looking guy wanted to take me somewhere.

I blushed and said, "I don't think I can go." I told him I had gotten into some trouble and was staying at this other lady's house.

Albert said, "Do you want me to ask her if you can go?"

I freaked out and said, "No! You can't. I don't even really know her." He offered to take me home and ask her. I couldn't believe this, he was so gutsy! I again said, "No, thank you. I'm sure she wouldn't let me go."

The whole time we sat in the car, he wouldn't let go of my hand. He leaned over the seat and tried to kiss me. I was being bombarded with this sex thing, and I did find him very attractive, but it was still overwhelming. Even after what I experienced the day before, I was completely controlled by the moment, with no thought of tomorrow. I was so desperate to be accepted by someone, and I wanted this attention. I really didn't even care who it came from.

Albert took my friend back to her house, then asked me again if he could go get permission from whoever I was staying with, if I could go. I finally told him I would go in and ask her, but I didn't think I could. He told me not to ask if I could go out tomorrow night, but ask if I could go swimming with him during the day. I agreed, so he drove me back to Dorothy's and I went in. She had been waiting for me and asked if I had had any trouble getting the bus back to her house. I told her I had met a boy and he had driven me home. Before I lost all my nerve, I asked her if I could go swimming with him tomorrow.

To my complete and utter amazement, she said, "I don't see a problem with that at all!"

Dorothy asked me if I had a bathing suit, and of course I didn't, but to my surprise she offered to buy me one. I told her I couldn't allow her to do that.

She just smiled and said, "I really want to. I've always wanted a girl to buy clothes for." Dorothy had four boys, and only one of them was still living at home. She said, "Come on, it'll be fun. We can make an afternoon out of it!"

I reluctantly accepted her offer, and off shopping we went.

I was so shocked when Dorothy bought me a bikini! It was so much fun. I knew my mother would never let me wear it, but I didn't care. I wasn't with her right now, and I had never been treated like this before. Dorothy would ask my opinion about everything. She also bought me a really cute pantsuit, a pair of sandals, a pair of bikini underwear and a bra to match. I couldn't believe it, I knew right then this was the way it was supposed to be. This was what I wanted out of life, someone who talked to me, asked my opinion, seemed to care about what made me happy, and didn't yell or judge.

She stopped at the grocery store and let me pick out what we made for dinner. I was so timid and quiet, because I was terrified of retaliation for any wrongdoings. It seemed so strange not to be afraid of the adult who had control over me. She was so kind and understanding. I wanted more acceptance, understanding, and genuine affection in my life.

Albert called me that evening and asked me if I could go swimming with him the next day. When I said, "Yes," he seemed truly pleased. We talked for over an hour on the phone.

The next day was Saturday, so there was no school. In fact, all we had to do on Monday was clean out our lockers and get our final report cards. Summer was here!

Albert called me at 9 o'clock that morning. Again, I was so pleased he even remembered me. I told him to come on over and get me. He was there in half an hour. Albert came in and introduced himself to Dorothy; he was a charmer for sure.

He said, "Did April tell you I invited her to go swimming tonight? Would it be all right if I take her?"

I was so sure she would change her mind and say no, but then she said, "I think that would be fun! Sure, she can go!"

I almost fainted. She told him to have me home by 1:00; again, I was shocked. She asked me if I would be home after swimming. I told her yes, I would be home, and then she asked me what I would like for dinner. This was too good to be true.

So I left with Albert to go swimming. He took me over to a friend of his who just happened to live almost right behind my mom's house. His friend's back yard touched the alley my mom's house backed up to, only it was about 5 houses down from hers. He had a pool in his back yard, but it was almost a little too close for comfort. Eventually, after we started swimming, I forgot how close I was to that hell hole.

Landry was his friend's name; there were a couple of other people over, too. I was definitely the youngest one there. Landry was 21, Albert was almost 19, and I had only been sixteen for less than a month. I was the only one there who still went to school, and definitely the most naive. I had never even had a two-piece bathing suit on, let alone a bikini. I have to say, though, I was shocked and pleased with the way I looked. It was almost enough to make me feel ashamed, but eventually I got up the nerve to go out to the pool with it on. When I did, all three of the guys whistled at me.

Albert came up, gently took my hand and yelled back at them, "Hands off!"

He walked me over to the edge of the pool and asked me if I wanted to get in; I shook my head affirmatively. It surprised me when he reached up with those big, strong arms of his, grabbed me by the waist and lifted me down into the pool. He was taller than me by a foot, and very muscular. I was in awe of him.

He swam over to me and put his arms around me. He kissed me.

"You're beautiful," he said. "I'm going to have to fight the guys off you, I can see that!"

I was mesmerized. I didn't take compliments as compliments, I took them as acceptance. They were the only positive things I had ever heard about myself from just about anyone. I was putty in his hands.

We stayed locked in each other's arms the rest of the day. It was wonderful. He knew all the right things to say, and even better, all the right things to do! He touched me just enough to make me enjoy myself. He didn't act pushy or selfish. His attention was undivided. He was *not* new to this, but boy was I!

Albert recognized my vulnerability, weakness, innocence, and low self-esteem. I was so perfect for this overpowering guy. He was built like a weightlifter, and I couldn't see an imperfection anywhere. Right then, he could have put a collar on me and led me down any street. I was like a little puppy wagging its tail all day!

Now, try getting that picture out of your head. We swam and made out all day, and I was in heaven. Before he took me back to Dorothy's house, Albert made a slight detour two streets over to his house. He still lived at home, with his mother and father.

I was surprised to see his parents were Hispanic. He didn't look it, or have an accent, but boy his mom and dad did. They had very thick accents; in fact, they didn't say anything in English the entire time I was there. They didn't seem too pleased I was there either. Even without understanding anything they were saying, I could tell Albert was extremely spoiled. He walked around the kitchen getting us something to drink, with them following him (speaking Spanish very loudly the entire time), but he barely acknowledged them. Finally, he sat me down on the couch in the living room, handed me a soda, then told me he would be right back. He headed back to the kitchen. While I sat there waiting, I could hear his parents following him around the kitchen yelling at him in Spanish, but he was ignoring them. I just wanted to leave.

I sat in his living room, getting a real culture shock. If I had ignored my mother like that, she would have hit me with a skillet or something. I sat there looking around this extravagantly decorated room. Compared to the way I lived, they were rich. His dad had worked for the mines for many years and had made good money. They lived like well-to-do Hispanics. Not a bad distinction; just a distinction. Plastic on the furniture, red, gold and black everywhere, velvet wallpaper, souped up cars. It was pretty in its own way. His parents lived true to their traditions and had both been raised in Mexico. Albert, on the other hand, was born and raised right there in Tucson. When I met him, he had what I thought was just a really good tan, but he didn't look Mexican. Living in Tucson, I saw Mexicans every day; I honestly never thought much about the fact that we were different races. As far as I was concerned, there was no difference between us, except that they held a unique look. Just like when someone looked at me, they automatically thought I was Irish because of my red hair. That's what I meant about Albert not looking Mexican. Of course, it was more than that, Albert didn't act Mexican, because he wasn't; he was an all-American boy.

I didn't like his mom from the moment I met her. Let me correct that: she didn't like me, but his dad seemed nice. As I would learn in time, his dad was quiet, but boy his mom would always be very outspoken. We didn't stay long, thank God; I was very uncomfortable there. I had never been taken to a guy's house before, let alone to meet a guy's parents, and it felt so strange. I could tell by the way Albert talked to his mother that he was very spoiled. He didn't talk that way to me, so I didn't think twice about it.

Albert took me back to Dorothy's house and kissed me before he let me go in.

"I'll see you at six. OK?"

I said, "Yes" and went inside.

Dorothy was waiting for me with a smile. She seemed genuinely interested in if I had fun or not, and I liked her very much. She had dinner waiting, and it was fun sitting and talking to her. She helped me get ready to go out that night and paid me some sincere compliments. I had an entire new outfit on thanks to her, something I had never experienced before either. Dorothy made me feel good about myself. She did mention seeing my mom, but she didn't dwell on it. I liked her a lot.

Learning my lessons the hard way

Being in the girls' home for those two years when I was fourteen to sixteen had put me in the strange position of what I call "The Castaway Syndrome." It was like I had been stranded on some island for years and years, then had been rescued, and the world had changed while I had been away. Everything was new to me, and I was being inundated with all these strange new tastes, smells, feelings and experiences.

Finally, it was six o'clock and Albert was knocking on the door. He was so handsome. His clothes were new and very sharp. He glided into the room and charmed both me and Dorothy. You must remember, I hadn't even watched TV for two years, and not much before that, so I had been very sheltered. Albert was overwhelming, even to the *not so naïve*.

We said our goodbyes to Dorothy, and I was out on my first real date. I seemed to do everything backwards. As soon as we were out of sight, he stopped the car, pulled me close and kissed me.

He looked at me with those gorgeous eyes of his and said, "God, you're beautiful! I couldn't stop thinking about you all afternoon. I didn't think you could look any better, but you do!"

I liked this guy more and more. He was so handsome, and I couldn't believe he was taking me to meet his friends. He actually wanted people to see me with him. Nothing like this had ever happened to me before. I was wanted! I was wanted! I just kept thinking that to myself. Someone was paying attention to me, like I was special! Just like jumping off a cliff, I was falling hard and fast! God, I was so inexperienced, gullible and naïve.

When we got to this party, I was a little freaked out when I realized it was just another one of those outside Boonies. There was a big fire and kegs of beer, although this time people were all dressed up, and we were out in the desert in the back of a big, grand house. There must have been over three hundred people there; most of them were from my school. They were all rich, preppie kids I didn't even know. Come to find out, Albert had been very popular in school. He was the drum major at our high school a couple of years earlier, and he was one of them, "The preppies."

Albert held my hand and led me through the crowd. He was introducing me to so many people, my head was spinning. I recognized one of the real popular girls there from school. I was shocked when she came over to me all smiles and said, "Hi, April!" I didn't even think she knew my name, because she wouldn't even talk to me at school. She was saying stuff like "April, I love your outfit! I didn't know you knew Albert!" Stuff like that. I meekly said hi, but all the time I was wondering why her and her rich friends were being so nice to me. At one point, I even wondered if this was some kind of a setup; you know, a "Carrie" story, or something weird like that.

As the night progressed, I tried drinking a little bit. Everyone was drinking, and I started talking a little bit. We were sitting around in circles, and different people were asking me questions. They all knew my mother as the "Opportunity Room" teacher, and they all voiced their fears of her. Some of them had heard about her beating me in front of the football team, so that got a few questions. There were comments like how they were terrified of getting in trouble and having to go to her class.

I said, "Yeah, you should try living with her!"

That got a laugh from them all.

I was asked about where I had gone to school for the last two years. I told them a little about the home, and they all seemed fascinated by it. They truly seemed interested, and it was so neat having people interested in me.

Albert came over eventually and took my hand. He said, "Come here," then pulled me up close and kissed me in front of all of his friends. We started walking, drinking, and talking to different people in the crowd. I was really starting to enjoy myself. He kept his hand on me at all times, holding my hand, touching my shoulder, or putting his arm around my waist. It was just the kind of attention I so desperately wanted. Not that it was the kind of attention I needed, but I didn't know that.

As the night moved to the eleven o'clock hour, he took me by the hand and said, "Let's go for a drive."

I said, "Sure." I just wanted to be where he was.

We got in his car and drove to a place called, what else, Lookout Mountain. The few moments I actually looked at the view of the city, it was beautiful. He didn't let me sit and just look for very long, though.

He said, "Let's get out and sit on the car."

I said, "OK." He was leading, I was following.

In Tucson, Arizona, at night, the weather is wonderful. From May till September, the night time temperatures run as high as 80 degrees, and you can see more stars than anywhere in the world. The nights are beautiful there, but don't forget the 110 degree days.

Once we got out of his car, Albert pulled a blanket from the trunk and laid it across the hood. I'm thinking to myself, *These guys all seem to have an emergency blanket tucked away.* Albert sat me up on the hood of his car. Remember, this was a '64 Chevy Impala; the hood was the size of a living room. He grabbed my shoulders and kissed me.

Now, he definitely knew what he was doing. That was the one, true, good quality about Albert. He was completely self-confident in his sexuality and masculinity, as much as I was the exact opposite. Every time he touched me, my body shook and tingled; I was a mouse, and he was a lion. He was the first person who acted like he cared how I felt, and he made me feel good. His self-confidence overwhelmed me, and he was full of it.

While we sat on the big hood of that Impala, Albert let me know he wanted me. So far I had had sex twice, and this was the first time I had experienced foreplay. He didn't just lay me down and jump on top of me, although I could tell he wanted to. He was slow and so gentle, yet he was very powerful. He definitely was experienced, and I was finally getting the gist of this "fun part of sex" everyone talked about.

I found out a lot about myself that night. I found out sex could be fun and I wanted it to happen again. I was shocked I liked it. I didn't know it, but it wasn't the sex that was so good; it was being desired. I wanted to be desired like this all the time.

Wow, Granny was right: I was a slut. Well, if you tell it that it looks like a chicken, and you tell it that it clucks like a chicken, and you tell it that it has feathers like a chicken, it must be a chicken! Might as well do what I had already been accused of doing.

After Albert took me back to Dorothy's, I thought about him all night. I hoped he would want to see me again. The next day, he was back over at nine in the morning. He asked if I could go swimming with him again, and to my delight, Dorothy let me go. We spent the next few days eating each other up. We couldn't touch each other enough; we couldn't slip away to a secluded spot with each other enough. We were like rabbits in heat. The contact was constant. If we weren't together, we were thinking about the next time we would be. We were in pure lust, but being the children we really were, we thought it was love.

I needed love so badly. I didn't know at the time what love was, but I knew I needed it. I wanted the dream of someone stronger than me, taking me away from my life and helping me deal with my problems. I wanted someone to make me a whole and happy person. I didn't know it then, but I had met the only person who could truly do that for me. I saw her in the mirror every time I looked into it, but that lesson would be long in coming.

I was a lost, unloved, unwanted, disturbed sixteen-year-old girl, and I knew so little. That saying, "Youth is wasted on the young"? How true it is. I, like so many young, lost girls, thought I saw it in Albert. I mean, he wanted me, he even acted proud of me, and I thought it was true love.

I had been at Dorothy's for well over a week now, and I had not seen or spoken to my mother since the "drunken" incident. My grandpa and Kari Jo had already left to go back to Oklahoma; I didn't even get to see them before they left. Little did I know then, I would never see my grandpa again. I wish I had known. I would have made an attempt to see him somehow. I loved him so much, and if I had known, I wouldn't have let the last time he saw me be when I was drunk.

One morning, Dorothy came into my room at 6 o'clock in the morning. I thought that was weird, because school had been out for a week and she always let me sleep in.

Boy, did my eyes pop open when she said, "April, you need to get up, your mom wants you to go home this morning."

I was so bummed out; God, I didn't want to go back there. I knew it would happen eventually, but I had dreamed it wouldn't. Once I had that taste of freedom, I liked it. I didn't want to go back to those problems, and her hating me.

I was still half-asleep, so I told her to give me a few minutes. I got up and packed my suitcase. I sure had a lot more to pack going than I had when I came. I just threw on my jeans and sandals, because I fully intended on going back to bed when I got home. I had been out with Albert the night before and hadn't gotten to bed until 1 o'clock in the morning.

I reluctantly loaded my suitcase in Dorothy's car. I told her I dreaded this, and she said she understood. We drove in silence. The closer we got to my mom's house, the more my stomach hurt. I didn't want to go back there, all the yelling and coldness. I had had a taste of a caring, sweet lady and a house where I never heard anyone yell. I had known it was inevitable I had to go back eventually, but that knowledge didn't make this any easier to take.

When we pulled up in front of the house, I saw a suitcase sitting on the porch. I didn't think anything of it, though, because at my house there was always junk everywhere.

When I opened the car door to get out, Dorothy said, "No, April, don't get out, wait here for your mom."

I said, "Wait here for my mom? Why?"

At that moment, my mom came out of the front door; she was dressed up and had another bag in her hand. She pulled the front door closed behind her and picked up the suitcase off the porch. I looked at Dorothy and asked her where she was taking me.

She said, "Your mom thought it would be better if you went back to the 'Home'."

I looked at her with tears welling up in my eyes. "NO! You aren't going to do that to me, are you? I won't go back. I can't! Please, Dorothy. Please!"

My mom was almost to the car. I looked at Dorothy again and begged her to help me.

She said, "I can't tell her what to do. She's your mother. I've tried to talk to her about this."

As my mom approached the car, I didn't even think; I just jumped out of the car and started running down the street, screaming, "NO!" over and over.

\

Like I said, our street was a culdy sack, but there were two little openings between some of the houses that led to the alley. I ran so hard and so fast, I literally left my sandals in the middle of the road. I heard Dorothy and my mother yelling behind me, but I was gone.

All of a sudden, I heard my little brother David running behind me. He was yelling, "April, come back. Please come back!"

Even though he was much faster than my mom was in high heels, he couldn't catch me. I was running for my freedom.

I ran with no direction, but I found myself in the alley at Landry's house. This was Albert's friend with the pool where we had gone swimming every day. I know I jumped his eight foot fence, but I can't remember how I did it. I ran to the back door and started pounding like a serial killer was after me. Landry's mom, whom I had only met twice, opened the door. I was hysterical as I pushed my way in; I just kept saying I had to see Landry. So, she took me to his room and woke him up. After his rude awakening, he could see I was hysterical as I begged him to help me. I told him my mom was sending me back to the home again and I had to get away. I was begging him to help me.

He asked, "Where's Albert?" I told him he was working the graveyard shift at the mine and wasn't home yet. After rubbing his head for a minute, he said, "April, I'm 21, you're sixteen. I could get in a lot of trouble if I helped you."

I was still crying and begging him to help me. Landry got up and went into his little brother's room. He came back and told me his 17-year-old brother could use his car and take me over to a friend of theirs. I could wait there until Albert got there. So, I got into the car with his little brother and he took me over to someone's trailer. I didn't know it, but my little brother David had been hiding and watched me leave.

When Landry's brother got home, the police and my mom were there. He told them he dropped me off at a bus stop. Even though they pressured him quite a bit, he refused to tell them more than that. So there I was, hiding out at this guy's trailer. His name was Dale; he was a strange little guy. His trailer was only 32 feet long, and it was full of weird stuff, like Nazi memorabilia and motorcycle parts. I spent the day trying to get a hold of Albert. When I finally did, he immediately came over to Dale's trailer. I told him my mom was going to send me back to Texas.

He said, "I won't let her!", then asked this guy Dale if I could stay there with him for a few days. Dale said sure.

So there I was, in this thirty-foot trailer with this little weird guy who rode around on a chopper and wore an old pointed Nazi helmet. He was short for a guy, only about 5'4", but very muscular. He was always nice to me, but he was the kind of guy who didn't really fit in anywhere. Sadly, he was the kind of guy people took advantage of. So he let me stay, which meant Albert stayed, too. Dale even lost his little bedroom, poor guy.

This was the kind of place where people hung out, because there was no supervision, we could do what we wanted. We smoked pot, and drank, didn't have to answer to anyone. Albert and I stayed in bed whenever he wasn't at work and had sex all day. He talked me into dying my hair black, because the police were after me and I was a runaway. The police had already been to Albert's parents' house looking for me. Most of the time, Albert would park down the street and then walk to the trailer. If we went anywhere, we always had to watch out behind us for the police, but most of the time we just hid in the trailer like scared animals.

By now, I was smoking cigarettes regularly. Albert kept me supplied with my cigarettes and food. We still drank, smoked pot and anything else that was going around. Albert kept me supplied with that, too. In fact, thanks to Albert, I was doing some real partying, having a good old time.

I can't even explain what was going through my mind; I was out of my mind, apparently. I just tried to forget about my life with my mom or the home. I was so pliable back then. If only the right person had come along right then and molded me differently, who knows? Of course, if that would have happened, I wouldn't be who I am today. Each and everything that happens affects other things that happen, so it goes.

We stayed together at Dale's trailer for almost three weeks before the police finally went to the mine where Albert worked. They told him he'd better find me, or they would arrest him.

So when Albert got off that day, he came to the trailer and said, "You have to go. You have to turn yourself in, or I'm going to get into trouble."

He drove me a block away from the police station and dropped me off. I had no choice but to go in, so that was what I did. I was scared to death, but when I got up the nerve, I told them I was a runaway and they were looking for me. They locked me up, and then they called my mother.

My mom arrived at the police station that afternoon. She was shocked when she saw me with black hair.

She said, "April. What have you done to yourself?"

I was expecting her to hit me, but she didn't. I kept waiting for it to come, but it didn't; I was shocked. She allowed me to talk all the way home. It was the first time she'd actually had a conversation with me that didn't involve her fist or a skillet. I told her I couldn't go back to the home, no matter what.

To my utter amazement, she said, "I won't make you go if you feel that strongly about it. I just thought, and still do, that that's the best place for you. If you'll live by my rules and try to change, then I'll allow you to stay here."

I gladly agreed to abide and change, as long as I didn't have to go back there.

I also told her I loved Albert and I had to be able to see him. She started yelling at me, telling me I didn't know what love was and I was too young to be in love. Of course she was right, but at the time I did think I knew what love was, and this was it. I had never learned love from her, so I thought I was learning something she knew nothing about.

I thought once about making a bumper sticker that said, "Ask a teenager while they still know everything," because it is so true. I thought I did know everything, but life would get out its Billy club soon enough and teach me my lessons the hard way. So try not to judge me here.

My mom told me she would allow me to see him, but on her terms. When she allowed, and where she allowed. Also, she had to meet him, to which I said of course. That was all I wanted anyway.

I couldn't believe she was giving in at all. This just wasn't like her. Someone had been talking to her; maybe it had been Dorothy. I was a happy camper that night. I was home, in my own bed, with no worries about the police coming to get me, or worries of being sent back to the Home. I was back with my little brothers and sisters. Of course, all I had as a guarantee was my mom's word, but I did sleep well that night.

For a week or so, things got better. It was summer, and school was out, so I watched the kids a lot. My mom always found somewhere to go to get away from us, but she did make a gesture or two towards my happiness. I loved animals and talked about them constantly, and one time she bought me a baby skunk. It was a little male, and I named him Costalot. Back then, thirty dollars to us at that time was a lot! I loved him; I love all animals, and I always have. I used to take him for walks on a leash. It also gave me an excuse to get out of the house. I could walk down the other street and see if Albert was at home or at Landry's.

Albert and I still got together on his days off, or after he was off work, but we weren't together 24/7 like we had been before. When we did get to be alone together, we would tell my mom we were going to a movie, but then we would go over to Dale's trailer and have sex, go to parties and drink, or both (honesty here)! He talked me into sneaking out of my bedroom window to see him. It got to be where I was sneaking out two or three times a week just to be with him. I only got caught once, and that was by my little brother David. When I crawled back in the window one night, he was sitting on my bed, waiting for me. It scared me to death. He was so ornery, he blackmailed me into doing his chores, or he would tell. David never told, but he would always hold it over my head if I ever did something to make him mad.

He would say, "I'm going to tell Mom on you!" So, he got me to do a lot of his stuff for him.

One day, my mom got a phone call saying my grandpa was very sick, so she went to Oklahoma. She wouldn't let me stay home alone with the kids, even though I did it every day. So, she got different people from the church to take us in. I don't remember why, but I ended up with my brother Billy. We went to stay with this woman from the church named Marilyn. Her and her husband had two small children of their own. It was okay for a couple of days, but she refused to allow me to see Albert, and it wasn't even that. One night, her husband Dale got mad at my little brother Billy for something, and he started beating on him. Marilyn and I had a terrible fight over it. I was very protective of my brothers and sisters, because I was more like their mother than their sister. Besides, the incident never should have happened. It was over something trivial anyway. The man was just mean, and he beat Billy to the point of losing control of himself.

I called my mother and told her what had happened. She started screaming at me, saying I was just starting trouble with Marilyn, then asked to speak to her. I heard Marilyn telling her I was being unreasonable. I thought to myself, *I'm being unreasonable? I guess so. I guess it's unreasonable of me to care that a man not even related to us is beating up my little brother. Whatever!*

She got back on the phone with me and proceeded to tell me that if I caused any more trouble for Marilyn, she had my mom's permission to put me on a plane back to the Home.

There it was again, right over my head, just hanging there, like a guillotine ready to fall. I tried to tell my mom what had happened, but she didn't want to hear any of it. She told me they were the adults and not to question their authority again, then proceeded to tell me now she

wouldn't be home for at least another week or more. I felt betrayed.
Why didn't what I have to say mean anything? The rest of the day was
horrible, and they wouldn't speak to me at all. I dreaded having to stay
there for another week or two. I just couldn't. I wouldn't! So, that night
after we got to church and they were mingling, I took off and walked
over to Albert's house. He drove me out to Marilyn's house, and I got my
stuff. Off we went, back to Dale's trailer.

Now we were back to hiding from everyone. I felt justified in my
decision. Stupid is as stupid does, as "Forrest Gump" once said. I woke
up the next day and realized I may have just doomed myself, and there
was no going back. My only hope now was that my mom would be
logical about all this when she got back. Yeah, right! As I said, "Stupid is
as stupid does!"

I don't know on what day my mom got back, or even how long
she was gone. All I know is two weeks went by, two weeks of me and
Albert getting closer and closer. We were talking all the time about
running off and getting married. Of course, this was in 1973, so I would
have to have a fake ID to do that. Back then, they actually used to look
for runaways, and they found them! The world was smaller then, and
things were different; yes, they were.

Early one morning, Albert and I were out at the trailer, in bed
together as usual, when all of a sudden there was a big BANG BANG
BANG on the door. This deep voice yelled, "Sheriff's Office!" BANG
BANG! I freaked out! I was stark naked, and there was nowhere to go.
Albert opened the closet door, and there was a small roll of carpeting. I
literally jumped into the middle of it, stark naked. I fit right down in the

middle of the roll; it was about four feet tall or so. Albert pulled his shorts on and answered the door.

I was shaking so badly and hunkered down in the middle of this roll of carpeting. There were five sheriffs at the door. Two of them came into the trailer, and the rest took Albert outside. I could hear them moving stuff around and opening cupboards. I was terrified. Finally, he opened the closet I was in. I froze! I didn't even breathe. I was stark naked and kept saying to myself, "Please don't find me. Please. Please!"

I couldn't believe it when he shut the closet door without finding me. By then I was shaking the whole trailer, I was shaking so badly. I heard them leave the bedroom, then they went out of the trailer. One of the sheriffs was telling Albert that if he knew where I was, he'd better turn me in, or he would go to jail. They gave him until noon, then they were gone.

Albert came back in and helped me get out of the carpet. I thought I was going to have a heart attack, I was so scared – and then came the words I didn't want to hear.

He said, "Did you hear them? I can't go to jail, April. You're going to have to go!" True love reigns!

So exactly at noon, he dropped me off in front of juvenile hall. I went inside and thought it would again be as it had been the last time. I would wait, my mom would come, and I would go home! No such luck.

As soon as I went inside and told them who I was, everything was different. Instead of calling my mom, they put me through booking. They hadn't done that the last time I came in here.

A man came into the booking room and said, "Hi, April. I'm your probation officer. My name is Mr. Reed."

I begged, "Can I please call my mom and have her come get me?"

He smiled and said, "Nope! We have orders from your mom to keep you here, so here you'll stay! Once you go through booking, I'll come and see you again."

He got up and left. I was so bummed, but it would get worse.

I sat there and cried. They came and got me and took me through a horrible experience. If the cops had found me naked in the closet, it couldn't have been worse than this. I got the whole thing, from a FULL body search to a de-licing in the shower. It was horrible. I was then given some orange coveralls to put on, and no underwear.

Now, I do know today they may even find stuff hidden in body cavities, but I still think a lot of it is a power trip. They definitely at that moment have full control over the situation, and they enjoy proving it to you. Of course, today we have ten-year-olds killing five-year-olds on purpose, so I guess you have to be ready for anything. Still, it wasn't a pleasant experience.

After that fun ordeal, they gave me a bologna sandwich and put me in solitary confinement. They left me there for 48 hours. At least they weren't pulling up my dress and whipping me with a piece of leather or wood in front of everyone. Solitary confinement is cruel and unusual punishment, in my opinion anyway. I just sat there, by myself, with only a metal toilet, a metal cup, a cement cot, one thin mattress, one blanket, one pillow and time to think. The only time I saw anyone was when they put the food through the door.

Now, I'm in no way saying I didn't deserve some sort of punishment. I had made some pretty bad choices up until then. It was still a horrible experience to be locked up all by myself, with no one to talk to and nothing to keep you occupied. At least that's what I thought, until they took me out of solitary and put me in with the rest of the prison population; nope, then I was ready to beg to go back to solitary. There were between one and two hundred girls there, and most of them were real troublemakers. This was definitely not the Home! Most of them were really mean, bad people. We all wore the same thing, we all ate together, we all showered together and we all had to brush our teeth together…wait, maybe this *was* the Home! Anyway, it was no fun; I know that.

On my third day there, my probation officer came to see me. He told me I had to promise not to see Albert anymore, or they weren't going to let me out.

I said "No! I can't promise something like that. It would be a lie!"

He said, "Oh, yes you will! Or you'll stay in here!"

After that, he told me all the other requirements my mom had in order for me to go home. I cried, and he left saying he would be back in a few days to see if I had changed my mind.

Well, he was right; after two more weeks in that place, I was ready to tell them anything they wanted to hear to get out of there. I promised not to see Albert anymore. I promised this, and I promised that. I didn't know what choice I had. They put me in that predicament of saying whatever they wanted me to say in order to gain my freedom, just like the Home. I don't know how long she would have left me there; forever, maybe. In the three weeks I was in there, my mom didn't come once.

At this point, I didn't trust any adult. I was sick of being locked up. I wasn't a bad person, really. Why was it she always found someone who had authority to correct her problem? All I really needed was for her to believe I was a person, with feelings and a brain. She needed to understand the things I was doing and feeling could have been completely corrected with some love, understanding, and acceptance. I know she had so many problems of her own. Unfortunately, we, her children, were her biggest problems, instead of being her biggest blessings. I wish that could have been different for all of our sakes.

After three weeks, my mom finally showed up. There were no tears or hugs this time. She just looked at me with a smirk on her face and said, "Are you ready to live the way I tell you?"

I said, "Yes."

She said, "OK. Let's go," then drove me home.

Unfortunately, nothing had changed on her end. There was a huge pile of dishes waiting for me, and loads of laundry. Within two or three hours, she was gone to church and I was left to watch the kids.

As soon as she was out the door, Albert came over and I let him in. I hadn't seen him in three weeks. You didn't really think I wasn't going to see him, did you?

My brothers and sisters were running around him, saying, "I'm going to tell Mom on you."

I asked them if they wanted me to go back to jail. They said no, so I told them if they told, I would go back jail, so they promised not to tell. They were more afraid of me getting a beating than going back to jail anyway.

Albert and I put the kids to bed and went out on the porch. We talked for over an hour, then he told me he wanted to marry me.

I said, "You know my mom would never allow it."

Suddenly, Albert had this great idea. "I know, but she'd have to if you were pregnant! Let's get you pregnant!"

I said, "OK!"

That's about as much as I thought about it. At the time, I trusted him completely; I thought it sounded like a solution to my dilemma. You know the saying, "What you don't know won't hurt you"? What a crock! Knowing what can hurt you is the only way to avoid being hurt. Now, being smart enough to realize what can hurt you, and avoiding that, is the real key. I never said I was a genius.

The next day, Albert came over and knocked on my door, and my mom answered it. He quickly handed her a vase full of roses and asked if he could come in and talk to her. She told him she'd wanted to talk to him anyway, so she let him in.

We all sat down, and Albert put on the charm. He was very good at that. My mom started off by telling him I was too young to be seeing him and we didn't need to be together.

Albert said, "Myrna, I know you're worried about April, but we love each other and we want to see each other. We need to be together. You can stop us from seeing each other for a while, but not forever. I'm asking your permission to see April, instead of going behind your back."

She gave him a smile and said, "You have guts, Albert. I have to say that. I'm sick of fighting with both of you. I'll allow her to go out with you two nights a week, and if you want more than that, you can come to church with her on Sundays. I want her back in this house when

I say, and no later. Don't come asking for more than that, because you won't get it. Now, if you're willing to go by my rules, then great; if not, get out of here and don't come back."

He said, "No. That's fine. That's all I'm asking for."

I truly don't believe anyone had ever told Albert no to anything he wanted. By making me unattainable, she was feeding his need to conquer, and he was determined to get what he wanted. Albert had done it his whole life. I was the forbidden fruit, and he was going to get some, come hell or high water. In fact, it was the chase he was after; it always had been, and always would be.

Albert did come to church with me once, and true to her word, my mom did let me go out twice that week. It was hard, though, because she wanted to know where, how long, with whom, and what we were doing. If we said we were going to a movie, she wanted to know what movie and what it was about. Since we didn't watch any movies when we went out, that was tough.

I was finding out more and more about my mom. I had been gone from her really most of my life; even when she was there, she wasn't home. If I wasn't living with my grandparents, then I was in the home, but I was old enough by then to notice more about her than I ever had before.

Now, I wasn't perfect either. I'm the first to have and admit to 20/20 hindsight. I realize what I was doing was as wrong as what she was doing, but she was the mom. I was just doing what I had to do to survive, and maybe she was, too. I found out she'd met someone while she'd been in Oklahoma. She'd met a doctor, and he'd been taking care of my grandpa back in Oklahoma. They were having a long distance romance.

That was why she was allowing me to see go out and see Albert. She was preoccupied with Pat, the doctor, and at the time she was happy.

This only went on for a week or so until one day my mom got another phone call: my grandfather was dying. I told you the last time I saw him was when I was drunk. I had lived in a teenage fantasy world ever since my grandma's death; you know, that teenage fantasy where death isn't real. Where teenagers think they're all indestructible. I had yet to deal with my grandma's death at all. I treated the situation like all the other times I'd been separated from them for long periods of time, I was in denial that she was actually dead. I didn't really pretend, but I refused to think about the reality of her death. I still hadn't spoken of it with anyone, including my mom. Of course, my mom and I didn't talk about anything.

My mom had no money, and her car was junk. So, somehow Albert talked her into letting him drive her, me and my brother David to Oklahoma from Tucson, Arizona. It took us two days to get there, so we all got to know each other better. The time together also allowed my and Albert's relationship to show itself to my mom. It was a strange experience. My little brother loved him. David was just 14 and had never had a father figure to pay attention to him before, just as I hadn't. He sucked it up like a sponge. I mean, Albert was viral, a guy's guy, built well and strong. He was athletic, lifted weights, rode a motorcycle, had a nice car, was very good looking, and he paid attention to David. So David definitely liked him, and I, of course, liked him. My mom, on the other hand, was in a war of wills with him, but once we were one or two hundred miles out, there was no going back. We all arrived in one piece.

My sweet grandpa died the same day we got there. The next time I saw him, he was in a coffin and a suit. Probably the only time silk had touched his skin. He had never worn a suit that I knew of, and now he was gone. Both of the people who loved me unconditionally were gone. Truly, it was like losing my parents, because to me they were my real parents. I still don't understand the finality of death, but I guess none of us do.

I wish I hadn't gone to his funeral. I don't believe in them, especially one with an open casket. It's just not for me. When I die, I want no casket; just a bunch of people sitting in front of a big screen. I want a video of me laughing and waving, and I want the song "Memories" by Barbara Streisand playing.

After the funeral, we stayed in Oklahoma for a few days and saw a bunch of our relatives. The whole ordeal was a real culture shock to Albert. He'd never seen people who lived like this. Here we were in this little impoverished town in Oklahoma. He was in shock that there were outhouses everywhere, and he had been to Mexico!

I meet my father

The whole ordeal was very hard on me, so much finality to deal with. Never again would I have my grandma or my grandpa to run to. Never would they be waiting to see me. I hadn't been back to Oklahoma for more than two years since the summer I was 14, before I went to the Home. The only place I'd ever felt safe, and the only place I'd ever "wanted" to be, was gone.

I did get to see Kari Jo for a while, but it was bittersweet. It was just a sad time for everyone there. Death always is. Now, Kari had no parents either, and she was the same age as I was.

While we were there, someone told me my biological father lived in a town only 10 miles from where we were. Remember, David and I have the same father. I wanted to meet him, of course I did. I had some fantasy he would want me, and maybe even save me. I'd wanted to meet him my whole life. I'd fantasized about him, what he looked like, what he smelled like, all the things we're naturally curious about. I wanted him to love me, and David, of course, wanted to know him, too.

Somehow I got his home telephone number, but I was shaking so badly. I called his house, and his wife Juanita answered. I can't even begin to explain all the emotions I was feeling right then. I said hello, told her who I was, then asked her if she knew of me. To my surprise, she said yes! My dad had actually talked about me.

Juanita didn't sound shocked or anything and wasn't mean or rude to me. She just said, "He's at work. He works for his brother, 'Buddy', at his shop. I'll give you the address, and you can go see him there." I asked if she was sure it would be OK. "Yes, don't you worry; I'll give him a call to let him know you're coming."

Albert drove me and David over to the shop. I was so nervous by the time we got there, I almost didn't get out of the car. It was an auto parts store with a service center attached. I went inside to ask if there was a Jim Martin there.

The guy at the service desk said, "He sure is. I think he's outside working on a car," as he pointed his greasy finger in the direction of the front window.

I went outside and saw two feet sticking out from under a car. I cautiously approached the man and said, "Excuse me, are you Jim Martin?"

He pushed himself out from under that car, on one of those rolling bed things, then stood up and said, "I guess you're April!" He looked me up and down and said, "Well, I guess there's no denying you're mine! Is there?" and he laughed.

I took that to mean I looked like him. He did have red curly hair like David and I had. I did look like him, and David really looked like him. He had on dirty coveralls, and his hands were black from working on that car. He was wiping them on a red rag.

He said, "I would shake your hand, but I'm pretty dirty."

It definitely wasn't the meeting of my dreams, but it didn't matter, he'd smiled at me. I couldn't take my eyes off him. He was really nice, and I could tell right away he had a good sense of humor. He asked about David, and I let him know he was in the car. My dad walked to the car where David was waiting.

Dad opened the door, grabbed David's hand and said, "I guess I'm your old man, son."

David was in love with him from that moment. He'd waited his whole 14-year-old life for this moment. Both of us had wished our whole lives for a dad just like any other child who didn't have one. We were no different from any other children anywhere.

I honestly believe most of the problems in this country today are due to the lack of fathers in our society. The inner city shootings and rampant crimes are committed by young boys who don't have a father in their lives; so, they turn to gangs. They have no role models or guidance in their lives, and no sense of family. The lack of family is the lack of structure. If you don't have family to help raise you and give you roots, a sense of where you came from, and a place to always come back to, then you become lost. We need structure, at least while we're children, so when we're adults we can function and don't have to depend on the government to repair the damage caused by the lack of family...oops, off the soapbox.

Anyway, we went to his house that evening after he was off work. It was a weird experience; we met his wife again and his four girls. I now had 4 more sisters, Carol, Terri, Chris, and Jamie Dawn. The girls were fifteen, fourteen, thirteen, and nine.

I didn't know it then, but David and I showing up was life-changing for everyone there. It wasn't my fault; I didn't even know they existed until I met them, but the three oldest girls weren't my dad's, and they didn't know it. They'd grown up with him as their dad, and he'd been their dad since they were very little. You see, to me it was no big deal because all my brothers and sisters had different dads. David and I were the only ones who had the same parents at both ends. So, it was normal to me, but it wasn't normal to them; to them it was a major big deal. I mean, so what if he wasn't their biological father? He raised them; I felt more distanced from him than they did. So I deduced from talking to all of them that they'd been together since my dad had gotten out of prison, about 13 years earlier.

Terri, the second to the oldest, put two and two together right away because of our ages; she figured he couldn't be in two places at once.

David and I were only in Oklahoma about 5 days or so, but we went to their house every day. During the entire time of our stay, nothing was mentioned about the 'Dad isn't mine' thing. I truly enjoyed myself. It was great being around him, and great getting to know the girls. I fell in love with Chris and Jamie. Terri and I got along OK, but I could tell I wasn't her favorite surprise. Carol and I didn't really interact. I guess the dad thing came up after we left. I wouldn't see them again until a year later.

My guess was he never had any intention of looking for me or David, but when you meet your dad for the first time at sixteen, you don't really think of things like that. You tell yourself that once he's met you and he seemed to like you, now he'd be in your life. I convinced myself there was a good reason he never tried to find us or be a part of our lives. The sad truth is that there are so many people out there who just don't care about the offspring they leave in their wake, but I wasn't old enough or cynical enough to think like that then.

Even though we were there for a very short period of time, I got to know the girls. They looked like my dad because they all had red hair. It wasn't curly like his, but still it was red. Maybe that was why I thought of them as being his.

I truly fell in love with my dad; this stranger I'd met only days earlier had endeared himself to me. He was so funny, and the type of guy almost everyone who meets him loves immediately. You couldn't help it, because he was so charismatic. I liked his wife Juanita, too; she was nice to us. She was very tiny, even smaller than my mom, who was tiny, too. My dad must have had a weakness for little women. Dad, Juanita and their family lived in the same little town I'd been born in. It was quaint, peaceful and pretty, with all the greenery and lushness, rivers and ponds I remembered. Unfortunately, if it wasn't for the tornadoes and poverty, I would still live there today.

That trip was so full of emotion for me. I'd lost my grandpa and found my dad, all in the same three days. I wasn't able to meet them at the time, but I learned I also had grandparents, aunts and uncles I hadn't met.

\

What a strange experience for me to see myself so prevalent in the face and actions of a person I'd known only three days. I couldn't seem to get enough of him. I noticed my dad treated those girls like they were his, and he seemed to love them very much. I envied them having his love, and I wanted to be loved by him. I wondered how this loving, jovial man could have deserted me so easily. As I got to know him, I couldn't help liking him; in fact, I knew I could forgive him for almost anything. Even though they were very poor, they seemed happy and they had a dad. Now he was my dad, and we were a complete family.

Eventually, we went back to Tucson and resumed the battle of wills between me and my mom. Every time I fought with her, she would jump on the opportunity to restrict me from seeing Albert. It wasn't long before I started sneaking out almost every night to see him. We kept talking about getting married and being out on our own, even going out looking at trailers. We knew once we were married, getting credit would be easy with Albert's job at the mine. We even went driving around and looked at lots to buy, but my mom was going to be tough. Remember, I'm not proud of a lot of the choices I made. I'm only stating which choices I did make.

Big mistake

One night, Albert and I were at a park with a bunch of his friends, doing acid and drinking. I had only had my first drink three months earlier and had only tried doing acid a couple of times. Albert had given it to me, so I just did it. I knew I shouldn't have right away, because I just couldn't deal with it. I started freaking out, laughing and crying at the same time.

All of a sudden, Albert walked up to me and slapped me really hard across my face. "Stop it," he said.

I laughed even harder, but then he hit me harder. This progressed to the point where it got out of hand and he really started slugging me. Amazingly, I just kept laughing, I just couldn't help it. Albert started laughing as he was hitting me. I know a lot of it was the acid, but there was a moment when I saw something in him that was very scary.

Finally, one of the guys with us saw what was going on and pulled him off me. He said, "Albert, hey man, you're going to kill her."

Albert stopped hitting me and pulled away, but I continued to laugh and cry hysterically. One of the girls with us sat with me and calmed me down; time eventually did the rest.

That was the only time (up to that point) Albert had ever hit me. I was sore and bruised the next day, for sure. I told my mom I'd fallen in the park, and she didn't ask anymore, but I had a black eye, busted lip and a very sore face.

The next day, Albert was so sweet and apologetic. He told me how sorry he was, and that was enough for me.

After we got back from Oklahoma, my mom seemed to accept Albert being around more. He would come over and take David and Billy for rides on his motorcycle, but we had to continue to sneak out to be together.

One day the same week school was starting, we were at Dale's trailer going at it, and I said, "Ouch! That hurts. Be careful."

He said, "What hurts? What did I do?"

I said, "I don't know why, it just hurts. I've been sore lately." We both looked at each other and at the same time had the same realization.

He said, "Do you think you're pregnant?"

I said, "I don't know. Do you get sore when you're pregnant?"

He asked if I'd been sick. I said no, but my breasts had been hurting lately.

He smiled. "I think you're pregnant!"

I'd never kept track of my periods, because at the Home I'd gone 9 months without having one. I'd never been regular there, and I'd only been home 5 months, so I didn't know if I was regular or not. I hadn't given it another thought. My mom had never talked about anything with me, especially anything personal. In fact, she got mad and yelled when I got my period and had to have tampons.

Here I was trying to get pregnant, and I didn't even know the first thing about being pregnant. Naïve, Naïve, Naïve! I knew that when my mom got pregnant, her stomach got big. Eventually the baby came along, and then there were diapers. That was about the extent of my pregnancy knowledge. I wasn't completely ignorant, but almost. There was no such thing as sex ed or parenting classes back then.

Albert said, "I'm going to find out who my mom's doctor is and take you to see him."

I said, "NO. You can't tell your mom!"

He said, "Why? I want them to know. I'm going to marry you."

I hadn't even thought ahead enough to realize we'd have to tell our parents, or what the consequences would be. I was naïve and ignorant. OK, I admit it.

Albert dragged me to his parents' house kicking and crying. We went in, and he proudly said, "April is pregnant, and we're going to get married. Mom, I want you to set up an appointment for her with your doctor."

That woman said every cuss word known to man, all in Spanish, while she looked straight at my face. Finally, she took a breath and continued to look directly at me and said (in English this time), "Well, I guess you got what you wanted!"

trailer we'd wanted and helped us get a lot to put it on. His mother continued to say cuss words to me in Spanish. She hated me, but I kept telling myself that once we were married, all that would change. I wouldn't see her, and we'd have a place of our own.

His parents picked out the lot and made most of the decisions for us, but I wasn't going to argue; it was a brand new mobile home. Also, because we were getting married, the place that sold us the trailer gave us all the decorations that were in it. The plants and candles, pewter mugs and stuff like that. Even the rugs on the kitchen floor came with it. The lot was so nice; it was fenced, landscaped, and even on a corner. I was in seventh heaven. I had never lived in anything so nice before. It had leather furniture and a little fake fireplace in the den. It was so fancy compared to what I had lived with.

In the meantime, we planned the wedding, if you could call it that. My mom planned everything, with no consultation with me. She bought me my dress, which was red, and she made me wear it. I was pregnant, you see; not so pregnant I would show (I was only 8 weeks), but she was bound and determined to make me pay for my sins. Mom also dressed appropriately: she wore black!

The church my mom went to let us get married there, even though first the minister had to bring me in his office and tell me how bad I had been and if I would please change my mind. It was fruitless, because all I saw was Albert, a baby and a home of my own. It was a much better option than my mom or the home. I wasn't going to change my mind.

So, we set the date for a month later. It would be a quickie! I lived at home with my mom during this time. She wasn't about to give up one moment of control over me.

About 10 days before the wedding, I talked two of Albert's sisters into going to a church watermelon social with me. The church was only a block from our houses. They weren't Baptist, but they went with me anyway. At the church, they had this big wagon full of watermelons. There must have been hundreds of them. We all decided to snatch a couple of them and take them back over to Albert's mom's house. Well, we got caught by one of the church deacons. He hauled me into the church office and called my mom, along with the minister. Once everyone had arrived, they proceeded to tell me that if they wanted to, they could press charges against me. I mean yes, it was wrong to take two watermelons out of two hundred, but come on. Call the police? God! Later, I wished they'd let the cops deal with me, because when I got home, my mom beat me and told me I was grounded for a month.

I looked at her and said, "I'm going to be married in ten days!"

She said, "Fine, then you're grounded for 10 days, and then I'm through with you!"

She didn't waver either; I wasn't allowed to leave the house (that she knew of) until the day I got married.

Reality

The wedding, what a mess! We got married at my mom's church, and I wore the red dress. While I was getting dressed, my mom told me I was a slut and I should dress like it. She definitely made a fashion statement with her black number!

I felt sick to my stomach. I think I was having motion sickness, because my life was moving so fast, or maybe it was morning sickness! Whatever! Although I felt terrible, Albert looked great in his white tux; he was a very stunning young man.

What an eclectic group of people were there. Albert's good friend Joe stood up for him. I had a woman who was a friend of my mother's who stood up for me. I didn't even know her name. I had no say in anything. The only people who were there from my side were my brothers and sisters, my mom and a few friends of hers from church. All the rest of the people who were there were friends or family of Albert's, and there were probably 60 people there. Talk about being outnumbered; 50 Hispanic Catholics in a Southern Baptist church. It was almost hilarious!

My mom never stopped giving me the evil eye, and all of Albert's people disliked me. I could tell, because they were whispering among themselves in Spanish. I felt like the last man standing at the Alamo. Enemies on every side, and this was my wedding! Doomed from the beginning, the wedding was awful. No. I'm serious. You'd think I could take a hint and call this fiasco off – but NO, I just kept on going.

I was standing there taking my vows (that I didn't even understand what they really meant), when Joe, the best man, started swaying back and forth. At first I thought he was fooling around, but I was completely distracted by his movement. All of a sudden, he fainted and fell hard flat on his face. People came running up; they picked him up and carried him outside. I just stood there the whole time, looking straight ahead, wishing I could crawl in a hole and die. There were people sitting behind me whispering and talking between themselves, but no one came up to me to tell me what to do, so I just stood there. Talk about an America's Funniest Home Video winner! It was a disaster, and this was just the beginning. Eventually, they brought Joe back in and the fiasco continued.

It definitely wasn't a dream wedding. Well, maybe it was a dream wedding, on a night when you ate Mexican food right before going to bed. It was a nightmare.

We did have a reception of sorts. Someone (I believe Albert's mom) got us a cake, then I had to go among the lions and meet them all. Then my mom signed the marriage license.

When she did, she looked at me and in front of everyone said, "Well, I hope you're happy, April. Don't come crying to me when it falls apart, and it will."

Those tender moments between mother and daughter can really tug on the old heart strings. I just wanted this nightmare wedding over, so I could have my happy, perfect new life. I'd show her. My life would be so different from hers.

Finally, the whole event was over. Here I was, a married woman with a baby on the way at sweet sixteen, and as naïve as I could be. At that moment, I had it all. I had a diamond ring, a handsome husband, a baby on the way, a new home of my own, and I would never have to answer to my mother again. What more could I want, right? It was more than I'd ever hoped for, but most of all I had my freedom. That's all I really wanted, wasn't it?

The trailer still needed to be hooked up to power and water, so we went to Joe's that night, after the wedding (as did all of Albert's friends). It turned into quite the party; Albert was having a good old time, and he was drinking pretty heavy. It had been a long day for both of us.

At 2:00 in the morning, I saw it wasn't going to end anytime soon, so I went to Albert and said, "I'm really tired. Do you think we could ask everyone to leave and call it a night?"

I didn't even get the word "night" out when he hauled off and slugged me in the mouth. I wasn't drinking, so I was completely sober. I was in shock, bleeding from my busted mouth, tears running down my face. What had I done? I completely didn't understand this. He told me to cut the crap and let him party. I went off to a corner and cried myself to sleep. My brain was on overload. I often wondered later if I'd hauled off and hit him back that night, would things have been different? But I didn't. I'd been trained by my mom and the Home to take what I got and be submissive, and I did it so well. I was a prime target for an abusive relationship. This was the second time he'd hit me.

The next day, he was so apologetic (again), but I was very wary of him from then on. How could I trust him now? I told myself he wouldn't do it again, but I wondered after that memorable wedding night just what fire I'd jumped into, out of my frying pan.

We finally got into our trailer. The first thing I learned was that married life wasn't going to be what I'd expected. It wasn't going to be me lying around the house having sex all day and having Albert telling me how beautiful I was and doting over me; instead, he acted like a stranger to me. I didn't know this person I was now bound to.

From day one, there was no honeymoon period; instead of things getting better, they got worse. My breasts were sore, my stomach hurt, sex hurt and every morning Albert insisted I cook him breakfast. "Chorizo and eggs." I hated the smell of it. It made me throw up, but he insisted. I only complained once, but once was enough; I was a quick learner.

The one time I did complain, he busted my mouth open again and gave me a black eye. Then he said, "You'll do what I say and like it!" Wow…déjà vu; he sounded just like my mother.

I swear, the minute we signed that marriage license, he was a different person. It was like night and day. By the time we'd been married a week, I had a black eye, a busted lip, was missing a wad of my hair, and had bruises around both wrists from him grabbing me. I could do nothing right in his eyes either.

Sex had become, not sadistic, but definitely one-sided. He wanted to be pleasured when he wanted to be pleasured, with no regard to me. If I complained about not feeling good or even acted disinterested, it infuriated him. It quickly became almost a punishment to me.

I had no one to tell and no one to talk to. I couldn't talk to my mother. She'd just told me not to come crying to her. I only knew two or three girls from school, and none of them that well. I'd only been out of the home for 6 months, and I'd been with Albert for 5 of those 6. We didn't hang with anyone but his friends, and now that we were married, I hung out alone, at the trailer. Oh, Albert went out, all the time. I just didn't go with him.

One day, Albert came home from work early and I didn't have his dinner ready. When he came in, I was on the phone with one of the girls I knew. Her name was Sandy Holley (her dad had something to do with Holley carburetors). Albert must have had a really bad day, because he walked up to me, yanked the phone out of my hand and then yanked the cord out of the wall. He started beating me with the phone while he was screaming at me to get up off my lazy ass and fix him something to eat. I did as I was told, with him following behind me, hitting me. Albert finally took the phone outside and threw it in the trunk of his car. He didn't bring it back in the house for over two months, and it wouldn't be the last time he would take it. Albert even refused to let me have a key to the trailer, because he didn't want me to go anywhere without him, or with him for that matter.

Now, for those who are saying, "I would have left him"...really? In the exact same circumstance, where do I go? Who do I call? Back then, they didn't even have women's shelters. The only place I was allowed to go was with him to his mother's, and that was only when he decided he wanted to take me. Even though my mom lived one street over, I never went over there; I missed my brothers and sisters.

It's hard to say why I did the things I did. Maybe I told myself life at home was just as bad or my mom wouldn't take me back. Besides, every time he was mean to me, he was so nice after that, making promises I wanted to believe. I knew the old Albert was in there somewhere. I had known him, or at least I thought! Every once in a while, he would be the old Albert I knew. I (like so many women in my same situation) had hoped the bad would end and it would be as it was before.

On one of these good days, he came home all smiles and in good spirits. He had a little tiny puppy in his arms, which he gave me, then said, "This is for you!"

It was the cutest thing I'd ever seen. It was part-miniature dachshund and part-Chihuahua. I could hold her in the palm of one hand. I named her Bohonkus and fell in love with her from the moment I saw her.

She filled my days while Albert was at work. She was only about 9 weeks old, and she couldn't even get up on the couch or up a stair, she was so little. I carried her everywhere I went. As she got older, I would take her outside and walk her...until one day when Albert came home and found me three trailers down from ours. He beat me and locked the dog in the bathroom all night. He told me he never wanted to catch me away from the trailer again. God, this was worse than my mom. I was fearful, but I left the trailer anyway, and only when I thought he wouldn't catch me. We were a mile from the nearest 7-Eleven; where did he think I was going?

God, that dog made me happy. I should have told him I didn't want it from the first day he brought her home, but I did want it. I was so lonely, and she loved me, unconditionally. I think he knew I would love her and got her for that one reason. Then again, maybe he was truly being thoughtful and kind at that moment.

I don't know why Albert changed so much once we were married, but he did, and the change was severe. I, of course, have all kinds of 20/20 hindsight theories. It may have been the sudden thrust of responsibility, or maybe it was the physical changes in me being pregnant. It may have been that the conquest was over, or it may have been that he was a psychopath looking for a victim. In the end, I deduced that Albert was just a classic macho, self-centered, controlling, spoiled, wife abuser with a lot of mother issues. He didn't respect any women, for reasons I can only guess. It wasn't that Albert's mother didn't deserve respect; quite the contrary, she demanded it. She was the matriarch of a very large family, and she definitely dominated his father. That's what I truly think the root of his problem was. He'd watched his mother treat his father like shit for as long as he could remember. That was why he hated women.

I also believe he was looking for someone exactly like me, who was weak, meek, and lonely. I was pliable, no one wanted me, and we were a perfect match for disaster! That was then, and I didn't grow a brain until years later, but at that moment in time I truly believed he was growing a brain (a brain tumor!).

One night after we'd been gone to his mother's, we came in to find the dog had chewed up a Kleenex on the living room floor. We'd been fighting all the way home, so he was already in a pissy mood. Albert grabbed the puppy and threw her against the wall. I heard her yelp in pain; she only weighed four pounds. I screamed and ran towards her to save her, but he grabbed me and knocked me down. He picked her up with one hand and held me off with the other.

He said, "If you can't teach your dog not to trash the place, then you don't deserve a dog!"

He took her outside, threw her in the car and took off. I would never see her again. Albert told me he killed her, but I found out later he gave her to one of his mean aunts who hated me. I never forgot Bohonkus. I wonder about her still today.

When he got home, he actually smiled while he was telling me he'd killed her. He was a very sick person. By now, I'd been married for about 4 months, but I was six months pregnant and huge. I had weighed 105 lbs when we got married, but now I weighed about 135 lbs.

He still wouldn't let me go anywhere or do anything. So, I just sat around and got fat. He bitched about that, too, and he didn't want anyone to look at me but him. I was a possession, his alone to own, hurt, kick, lock up, yell at, threaten, control, use, punish, and keep hidden.

The only place he would let me go was to his mother's, and that wasn't every time he went over there. Goody, goody, something to look forward to. It was always fun going over there! NOT! Those people hated me.

\

His mother would still sit in front of me and talk about me in Spanish. I knew she was talking about me, because I would hear my name and then she would laugh! His family was a very tight knit group. They thought of me, and treated me, as an outsider.

They believed I'd tricked Albert into marrying me. Even Albert treated me like that now, and he was the one who came up with the "I'll take you away from all this" idea!

One day we were going over there for one of those fun visits, when he suddenly pulled off the road. He got out of the car and came over to my side. I was afraid he was going to hit me, but it was worse than that.

He said, "Move over, I want you to learn how to drive."

I looked at the highway, with traffic whizzing by, and said, "Na huh. I don't think here is a good place for me to learn to drive."

That just infuriated him, and he started demanding I move over. I'd already learned that I didn't say no to Albert, so I moved over.

First of all, this was his 1964 Chevy Impala he'd spent most of his life and a lot of his money making perfect. It had overhead cams, glass packs (which only made it noisy), air shocks and a little 8-inch steering wheel. It was also a standard shift, which I'd never even driven before. We were on a major highway, and I was scared to death, but I tried. He told me what to do, and I tried to do it. I killed it twice, and I absolutely could not get the clutch pedal down at all. As soon as got it on the highway, I ran it up against the curb. It only took about three minutes for him to have amassed enough reason to beat me for at least a year. Albert reached over and yanked the wheel out of my hand. He steered the car partly off the road, backhanded me across the mouth and yelled at me to GET OUT, so I did. As soon as I closed my door, he moved into the driver's seat and took off, leaving me there standing on the highway.

I watched him as he spun the tires all the way down the road, then I just stood there and cried. I started walking, not knowing where I was going to go. After I'd walked about a mile, Albert came screeching up beside me.

He opened the door and said, "Get your ass in here."

Before I could even get all the way in, he took off. As soon as I was in the car, he reached over and slugged me. I covered my head and cowered in the corner, but he could still reach me. Every few seconds, he would reach over and slug me again.

In-between punches, he was getting the speedometer up to at least one hundred miles an hour. I started begging him to slow down, but that just made him go faster. The more I begged, the faster he went. I was an emotional wreck, but we did survive and make it to his mother's. Once we were there, he immediately changed back into Dr Jekyll. That was the first time I really started thinking he had a brain tumor. Surely, he couldn't just be this mean and crazy.

Albert came over to my side of the car and opened the door. I cowered and covered my head. He leaned in and sweetly said, "Come inside and wash your face, April" (which was bloody and swollen). I am so sorry. I didn't want to hit you. You just make me so mad sometimes." He held my hand and touched my face with tenderness. "I shouldn't have made you try to do that on the highway. I'll take you out to a dirt road and teach you to drive. OK?" Dr. Jekyll said...

Every time he had one of his "fists of fury" bouts, he would be nice to me for a day or two. He would be the Albert I'd previously known, the one I thought I'd fallen in love with. It was just enough to give me some hope and make me believe things would be better. I was in so much trouble. I was pregnant, sixteen years old, and had no one to go to or call. Even though my mom lived just around the corner from his mom, he never took me over there. I hardly ever saw my brothers and sisters. At first, I didn't mind. I didn't have any friends anyway, but it got old real fast. Even if I had had a friend, he wouldn't have let me see them, and here I was with a big stomach; I had nothing in common with any other sixteen-year-olds anyway.

Albert started staying out all night, every night, and when he did come home, he was always drunk. It was getting worse every day, and the hitting was always worse when he'd been drinking.

Instead of getting married giving us our freedom, it had given him responsibilities he apparently didn't want. He let me know in no uncertain terms I was the cause of all of his problems. I found myself dreading him coming home, no matter when it was. I was getting beaten on a regular basis now.

One day, a girl I'd been in the home with came to Tucson and called my mother. My mom gave her my phone number. Now, Albert never allowed me any contact with anyone, but for some reason when she called, he seemed pleased. He insisted they come over.

She was with her fiancé (I'll call them Jan and Joe). Albert liked her immediately. Why not? She had long blonde hair, and she was gorgeous. Now, I'm no dog, but I was six months pregnant and definitely not at my best. So, it was no wonder Albert liked her, but I didn't care. I was starved for a friend, or any companionship. I knew he went out on me all the time, but I didn't care. In fact, I used to wish he'd find someone else and leave me alone.

Most nights, he didn't come home until three in the morning. At first I'd wait up and worry he'd been in an accident, but if I was up when he got home, he would beat me. I started wishing he wouldn't come home at all. At least when he was gone, I was safe.

I started pretending I was asleep when he came in, but that didn't always save me. Most of the time when he came home drunk, that meant he would drag me out of bed and beat me anyway, then force me to fix him something to eat. He was officially crazy by the time Jan and Joe came into our lives.

Jan and Joe started coming over every day. Then one day, Albert talked them into moving in with us. We had an extra bedroom and they were looking for a place, so they moved in. It was just until they found a place of their own. They'd been staying with Joe's parents up to this point.

This was a good thing and a bad thing. It was good because I was desperate to have other people around to talk to, and he didn't hit me as much when other people were around. In fact, for two or three weeks, the only time I got beat was when they were gone and we were alone, or when we were in our bed room alone, so that was good. On the other hand, Joe worked a lot and Jan didn't, so she was home with us all the time.

It gave Albert and Jan the opportunity to party together. I wouldn't party because I was pregnant. At least I was smart enough to stop doing anything once I knew I was pregnant, but that didn't stop

\

Albert from doing it. He was 20 years old and partied all the time. He always had acid in our freezer, to take or sell.

So Jan and Albert dropped acid together, drank and smoked pot. They were having a good old time together. One night, ritualistic partying was going strong in our den, at the opposite end of the trailer from the bedrooms. I was asleep in our room, and Joe was asleep in their room because he had to work the next day. I'd gone to bed hours earlier because I didn't feel good. I just left Jan and Albert to their trails and colors.

About three in the morning, I awoke to screaming and yelling. I got out of bed and went down the hall towards the den, where all the commotion was coming from.

The first thing I saw was Albert sitting on the floor stark naked, and Joe was in his underwear standing over a naked Jan, holding tightly to a handful of her hair. It didn't take much imagination to figure out what was going on.

Joe was screaming obscenities at both her and Albert. He was trying to drag Jan up and out of the room. He told her to get up, get dressed and pack, because they were leaving. They did just that, in the middle of the night, but not without Joe trying to apologize to me, like he should have to apologize to me.

I just turned around and went back to my room. I could hear them throwing their stuff in their car, and then they were gone. After they left, Albert came in the bedroom; he started in with the "I'm sorry" stuff. I said it didn't matter, and it didn't. I was already trying to figure a way out of this nightmare. I was just glad he didn't take it out on me. I'm sure he could have rationalized some reason to blame me for his indiscretions.

We never spoke of the incident again (because I didn't bring it up), and I never spoke to Jan again. I don't know whatever happened to her. That's not quite true; they sent me flowers when I was in the hospital.

Once, my aunt Kari Jo came to Tucson to visit me, and Albert did let her come to the trailer to see me, but not very much. He kept me stuck way out of town in that trailer. I was always glad to see anyone.

My days were long and lonesome, and I was miserable. I was getting bigger every day. I could use my stomach as a table; I could set a plate on it. I was uncomfortable and ignorant of the changes taking place in my body. I had no one to talk to about being pregnant. I honestly had no idea what to expect or what to prepare for.

I did go to the doctor once a month, but I couldn't talk to him. He was very handsome, and I felt uncomfortable even seeing him. I needed someone my age to talk to, but that wasn't going to happen. Back in 1973, there weren't the epidemic numbers of teenage pregnancies there would be in the years to come. I'm sure I wasn't the only 16-year-old pregnant girl out there, but I felt like it. I didn't know any of them anyway. I'd never been able to talk to my mom, so that was out. My grandma was gone, and if she had been alive, I'm sure I would have been with her instead of Albert anyway. I didn't know my dad, and I was all grown up now anyway. Wasn't I?

I spent my days watching soap operas and cleaning the trailer…well, at least as much as I knew about cleaning. No matter what I did, it was never good enough for Albert. After he left in the morning, I would have my safe time. I felt such relief when I didn't have to worry about doing something wrong or being punished for something I didn't even do. Once the afternoon rolled around, I would start watching for him and worry about him coming home from work. I would have to make sure dinner was ready on time, but more often than not Albert wouldn't get home when he was supposed to. Of course, then dinner would get cold, which gave him a good excuse to beat me again. It seemed like I could never escape his wrath. Albert's mood would change so suddenly, and for no reason. I couldn't believe a person could be so mean just because they were mean. I've since learned there are mean people everywhere.

One night, about a month after the Jan incident, I was just into my seventh month of being pregnant. Albert had some of his friends over, so there were probably six other people with us. Everyone was sitting around partying (drinking). Except me, but I was laughing and truly enjoying everyone's company. It was one of those rare times he was letting me be with other people. Everyone was laughing and in a good mood.

I must have said something wrong, because all of a sudden Albert hauled off and slugged me in the mouth. Everyone in the room shut up and looked at us. It took me so by surprise, because I didn't usually get hit in front of people, so I felt safe. I started crying, then got up and ran down the hall to the bathroom. I was so embarrassed. I was standing in front of the mirror, wondering how I would ever be able to go back out there in front of any of those people again. I looked up at the mirror and saw Albert standing in the doorway behind me. I turned around and tried to get out of the bathroom door past him. He moved in front of me. I tried to go through on the other side of him, but he moved over in front of me. I then tried to push past him, but that just infuriated him. He picked me up like a toy and threw me down in the bathtub. I knew I was in real trouble when he turned around and shut the bathroom door behind him. He came at me like a mother bear protecting her young. He got on top of me in the tub and let loose with his fists.

Now, Albert worked out and was a well-built man. His hands were huge, and he knew how to use them. He used his feet to kick me while he was yanking my hair out of my head. How he maneuvered in that tiny area, I'll never know. I tried to cover my face and stomach as I stayed rolled up in a ball at the end of the bathtub. Any part of me that wasn't protected was fair game.

After Albert was spent from all that exertion (poor baby), he left the bathroom. I stayed there in the tub, cowering and crying. A minute or two later, he came back into the bathroom screaming and yelling.

"You bitch! You made me look like a fool out there! My friends are gone all because of you!" Then he came over and started hitting me again.

This went on until after midnight. He would leave the bathroom and leave me there in the bathtub, then he would pop back in just to slug me in the back again.

After hours of this, he came in and said, "Get up and get to bed! I have to work tomorrow!"

I didn't want to leave the safety of the bathtub, but I did what I was told. Once we were in bed, he left me alone! Poor thing, he must have been exhausted after expending all that energy.

About three or four in the morning, I woke up because my side of the bed was all wet. I got up and went to the bathroom. All the way there, I couldn't quit peeing. I sat on the toilet for a while, but every time I would stand up, there I'd go again. I wondered if the baby was sitting on my kidneys or something. I never speculated any other options. I was only 7 and 1/2 months pregnant. I wasn't in any kind of pain (at least not from this). My back, sides, and my scalp all hurt, but I was in no stomach pain. I had known nothing about pregnancy, but I was learning fast. I didn't know much about anything, but what I did know was that Albert was going to kill me when he woke up and the bed was wet. I got a towel and folded it into a square, then sat on it out on the couch. I sat there crying and wondering just how I was going to go in there and say, "Albert. I can't stop peeing!"

It didn't stop, because as soon as I stood up, there I would go again. I waited until after six am, then I had to go wake him up for work.

I stood over him for a while, debating any other alternative. I was petrified, but I reached down and gently shook his shoulder, preparing to be hit in the face.

I said, "Albert, something's wrong. I can't stop peeing."

Surprisingly, he got up and acted concerned. He didn't yell or hit me, which was a pleasant surprise. His mood swings were so weird. There was no mention of the night before.

He jumped out of bed and went to call the doctor, who then told him to bring me in to his office. Our car was up on blocks for some reason; Albert was adding some new gadget to it. He'd been riding into work with a friend of his, so he called his mother. She came out and got us, she was so concerned that she brought a stack of towels for me to sit on; she didn't want me to ruin her nice car seats. I don't blame her, although I had my own towels.

A mother at sixteen

Children having children

When we got to the doctor's office, I waddled in. I was so embarrassed; I was always embarrassed in front of my doctor. Like I said, he was a very good looking man. I had always felt self-conscious in front of him. Of course, I felt self-conscious in front of anybody.

My doctor put me on the table and started to do a pelvic, but as soon as he did, water gushed everywhere.

He looked at me and said, "Young lady. You're going to have a baby today!" I told him it was impossible, because I was only 7 and 1/2 months pregnant. He said, "Well, your water broke, so it's coming today! Sorry, no stopping it now."

I wonder if that's where the saying "getting the living shit kicked out of you" came from.

He sent me across the street to the hospital, and they quickly admitted me. The doctor sent orders to induce labor, so they did. At first I lay there thinking this couldn't be happening. I wasn't ready; I still had almost six weeks to go. It didn't take long for me to stop thinking that and start thinking this was going to hurt.

They started my labor at about 8:00 am that morning, and by 3 in the afternoon I'd ripped a bed sheet in half and cussed out everyone, including my mother. God, I was in some major pain. Nothing even Albert had done to me had hurt this bad.

By 5 pm, my pains were, like, 3 minutes long and 30 seconds apart. It was ridiculous. I thought I was dying, or it sure felt like it. I was starting to look and act like Linda Blair in "The Exorcist".

I could hear the nurses whispering among themselves about how I was supposed to be dilated to some degree or another, but I wasn't dilating. Finally, the doctor came over to the hospital at about 6 or so and gave me a check-up.

He said, "We're going to have to get an X-ray to see what the problem is." The next thing I remember is him standing over me saying, "April, we're going to have to do a cesarean section. You aren't dilating, and the baby hasn't even dropped yet."

I remember saying to him, "Do whatever you have to, to get this baby out of me."

I remember the operating room and looking at a big clock on the wall; it said 8:50. I remember them putting something in my IV and telling me to count backwards from 100, and I got to 99. The next thing I remember is waking up the next morning and Albert was there.

I said, "What day is it? Did I have the baby?"

He said, "Yes, a son. He's fine, just little; he only weighed 5 pounds." I asked if I could see him, he said, "No. He's in an incubator."

\

The next thing I wanted was some pain medication. I remember every time I had to cough, I had to hold a pillow over my stomach to do it.

Later that morning, they brought the baby into my room and let me hold him. God, he was so tiny, and hairy. I swear. He was bright yellow because he was jaundiced, and one of his little ears wasn't quite perfect, but the doctor said other than that, he was very healthy for being so little. No respiratory or heart problems, and that was very good. He told me he couldn't go home yet because of his weight, but this was back when they actually let women stay in the hospital for a week if they had a C-section. Not today, boy! Today, it's like a conveyer belt. Get 'em in, get 'em out.

I really enjoyed my time in the hospital, six days of people waiting on me. I got to hold the baby two or three times a day; he was so cute and so little. He would fall asleep in my arms, and I would just stare at him and touch him. I couldn't believe how delicate he was, and I was terrified of squeezing him too tightly or dropping him. I learned quite a bit, too, about taking care of him, and I got to see my brothers, sisters and my mom. It was a really good week.

The best part was that Albert was very nice to me the whole time I was in there. He brought me flowers and came to visit me, he was so proud of his son. We decided to name him Michael. It was a good time, but over too soon. Eventually, we had to go back home, and that meant back to real life, but it was good while it lasted. I believed things had changed now; this was what we needed. Now that the baby was here, things would be good for us.

The day we went home was awful; I did get to bring Michael home with me. He'd reached and maintained his weight, but when we got home, Albert's mother was there. She'd cleaned up my entire house and gone through my things. She proceeded to tell me I was a pig and I took terrible care of her son, and she wouldn't allow me to be like that with her grandson. God, I wasn't that bad; she was just obsessed. Albert's mom used to make me help her move her fridge and stove once a week to clean behind them, which I did on my hands and knees.

After his mom left, I had this overwhelming sense of reality. Here I was, a little mommy at sweet sixteen. I was really glad Albert was there to help me the first couple of days, because it was really overwhelming.

Michael was so premature; he had some digestive problems at first. We had to take him to the doctor quite a few times until they got him on soy milk. During this time, Albert was almost pleasant to be around. He showed real concern for me and the baby, but it didn't last long. After a couple of days, he was back to his sweet old self. His big hands seemed so funny handling that tiny baby. One time, he was changing a diaper and Michael peed in Albert's mouth. Way to go, Michael; it was actually pretty funny.

A week or so after I'd come home from the hospital, Albert started going out again and partying, not coming home till the wee hours of the morning, but I didn't mind. It gave me all kinds of time with the baby, and I was still happy and safe when he was gone.

For a while things were tolerable, even when he was home. There was always that glimpse of hope, but it was just a glimpse, though. By the time Michael was three or four months old, Albert was back to giving me regular beatings. It seemed like he had to do it every once in a while, even though I was careful not to give him any reason to be mad at me. During this time, I hardly ever saw my mother, brothers or sisters, besides the fact that Albert just didn't let me see them. My mom was involved in a love affair with the doctor in Oklahoma, and she was going back and forth quite a bit.

One day we went over to Albert's mother's (which was just one street over from my mom's house). We were sitting in the kitchen with Albert's sisters at the breakfast nook, while the baby was asleep in one of the bedrooms. Albert's parents were away somewhere. Albert and his sister Julie went from joking to fighting. All of a sudden, Albert jumped up and grabbed Maria by the hair. He picked her up like a doll from across the table and lifted her above his head, bent her over backwards and broke this pearl thing she had on around her neck. Pearls went everywhere, and I thought they were her teeth! I thought he'd knocked out her teeth! When you've been a victim of violence, you're very sensitive to any violence that springs up around you. My mind saw, and expected, the worst.

She was screaming, and it was very physical. I tried to get on him and make him put her down. I was screaming for him to let her go, so was his other little sister. He (without dropping Maria) picked me up and threw me down on the floor. I thought he was going to kill her, then me. I'd been on the receiving end of his rage many times. Anytime he freaked out, I wanted to run for cover; even if I wasn't the object of his rage at the moment, I soon would be.

I grabbed the phone and started to dial the police. Albert grabbed it away from me and hit me with it. So, I did what instinct demanded: I ran. I ran outside, then over to my mother's house. I banged on the door and the window, but she wasn't there, so I ran to her next door neighbor's house. I banged on that door until someone came. I was hysterical and scared, and I freaked out this woman who answered the door. I told her to call the police, Albert was killing his sister.

This same women who was now dialing the police had sent me screaming from her house one day a year earlier, right after we moved into that house. The neighbor had come over and asked if he could pay me to sit with his wife after school every day, so I did. I went over there and watched TV with her. I was never told why I needed to be there; he just wanted me there. She was a nice lady, pretty quiet, and she didn't get up off the couch very much. I didn't know anybody or have anything to do, and it was something to get me out of my house, so I didn't mind doing it.

Well, after a week or so of sitting with her after school, I was sitting by her on the couch one day and we were watching TV, when all of a sudden she fell on the floor by the coffee table and started thrashing back and forth against the couch and coffee table, hitting herself in the head. I didn't know it, but she was in a grand mal seizure. It freaked me out so bad, I tried to pull the coffee table away from her so she would stop hitting her head on it, but it was too heavy. I ran out into the street and started screaming and knocking on doors. Within a minute, I had everyone on the street over there; the adults dealt with it and got her an ambulance.

Well, needless to say, I was scared of her after that, even though they sent her home from the hospital one day later. Her husband had come over and interrogated me about what happened to her. I told him I didn't know. I said she'd just freaked out and started hurting herself. My

\

mom and the husband told me she'd been going through withdrawals from prescribed meds and it was a freak thing and wouldn't happen again. He asked me to come back and sit with her again. I was scared to. It was a very scary thing to deal with that. I was sitting on the piano seat, trying to get out of this. The women and her husband were sitting on the couch, and my mom was in a chair to my side. We were talking, and I was telling them I might try it again, when all of a sudden she did it again. Thank God her husband and my mom were there, because I ran outside and hadn't been back until I ended up knocking on her door, asking her to call the police on Albert.

She let me in, and I waited there for the police. The police came and put me in the patrol car, then drove me back to Albert's mom's house. As we pulled up, Albert and Julie were walking out of the house with their arms around each other, all smiles. They actually told the police they'd just been joking around and I'd freaked out over nothing. They said everything was fine and they were joking and laughing together. They even came up to me and said stuff like, "We were just kidding you, April," "Albert would never hurt me," "We're sorry you took it like that," blah, blah, blah. So, the cops believed them and left, leaving me there with them. That bitch Julie; I'd tried to save her, and she was standing there telling me I was crazy. They were good; they were so convincing, they almost had me believing all was fine and maybe I'd overreacted. Ha!

I knew I was in big trouble as the cops were driving away. Maria gave me the evil eye and said, "You bitch, you called the cops on MY BROTHER!"

Albert grabbed me by the arm and dragged me into the house. As soon as we were inside, he started pounding on me.

He said, "God dam it! Don't you ever call the cops on me again, (POW) ever!"

Point made! Point taken! The whole time, Maria was yelling at me over him (God, how they stuck together, even when they were killing each other). I was an outsider, and I'd just committed the ultimate sin: I'd gone against one of them, with the rest of them watching me do it.

His whole family was as guilty as he was for his abuse, because they knew he did it, and they covered up for him. To them, he could do no wrong! They could fight with him, but God forbid anyone else does.

He finally stopped hitting me and went into the bedroom, where the baby was. A moment later, he came out of the bedroom holding Michael, who was now crying.

I immediately jumped up off the floor, ran over to Albert, and said, "What are you doing?"

He looked at me with hate in his eyes and said, "What I do is none of your mother f**king business!" He then pushed me away and went out the front door with the baby.

I ran after him, trying to grab Michael, but Albert knocked me to the ground and told me to stay there if I knew what was good for me. I just got right back up and chased after him, and I kept asking where he was taking the baby.

He smiled at me and said, "You'll never know, and in fact, you'll never see him again!"

I frantically clung to Albert's arm, but he kept shaking me off. I kept crying and begging him not to take him, but he just started laughing as he put the baby in the car. I was like a mother bear protecting her young as I jumped on Albert's back. He threw me on the ground and put his foot on my chest.

"You'll pay for today, April!"

As he tried to move towards the car, I was up and on his back again. This time, Albert picked me up over his head and literally threw me at least, what seemed like, 8 feet away from him onto the ground. The wind had been knocked out of me, and I was trying to catch my breath.

I heard Albert saying to me, "You better say goodbye to the baby, because you'll never see him again."

He jumped into the car and started backing out of the driveway. The baby was crying, and I was hanging onto the car for dear life. Albert pushed me off onto the ground with no effort. His sisters were just standing there watching all this, and then he tried to peel out. I mustered my last bit of strength, then got up and clung to the car again. With one more punch, I fell down onto the ground for the last time. I didn't try to get up again. All I could do was watch as he drove away with my baby in the car. I just sat in the driveway crying.

Not three minutes later, my mom pulled up. She was in her Volkswagen van and had my little brother David with her. One of her neighbors had told her about the police when she got home. My mom came up behind me, grabbed me by the arm and pulled me up off the ground.

"Get in the van, April." I was still sobbing as I tried to tell her Albert had the baby and we needed to go after him. "No!" she said. "You're getting a divorce from that maniac right now! Get in the van".

So, I did. My mom drove me straight to a lawyer's office, but all the way there I couldn't stop thinking of what Albert was doing to Michael. I knew his wrath, and I was terrified of him. The last time he'd taken off with something I loved, I'd never seen it again. Why should I believe he wouldn't hurt Michael?

All my mom did on the way to the lawyer's office was scream that I was going to talk to this lawyer, divorce Albert, and move back home with her. I heard her talking, but I wasn't really listening.

Once we got to the attorney's office, my mom did all the talking. She told the man more than she knew, as usual. He called Child Protective Services and put an APB out on Albert. Honestly, I don't remember much. I was in a daze.

The next thing I knew, my mom had me back in her van. She was saying to me, "April, we need to go out to the trailer and get your stuff. We also have to get the baby's stuff; we're going to need it."

I said, "Mom, I don't have the baby!"

She said, "Yes. But you will, and when you do, we're going to need his stuff."

In my mind, I wasn't so sure about that. I couldn't keep from thinking about the puppy. Albert had taken it away, and it never came back! Besides, I knew right then that even if I did get Michael back, Albert would always use him to hurt me, just like he had the puppy. Let me have something to love, then make sure I couldn't love it. I knew he'd never allow me to have anything to love, without threatening its safety just to hurt me. It was a very sad realization.

When we got out to the trailer, I told my mom, "I don't have a key!"

She said, "What do you mean you don't have a key?"

I told her Albert wouldn't let me have one. She proceeded to tell me how she'd warned me this would happen. "Didn't I tell you?" She told me how, if I'd listened to her, none of this would be happening, on and on and on.

Mom proceeded to break one of the little windows in the front room, then we helped my little brother through so he could unlock the door. Once we were in, we just started loading everything we could into the van. We grabbed everything from the high chair to my clothes. We even got the baby's bed in there, and the van full.

I was walking from the bedroom to the front door with an armload of stuff when my mom came running towards me yelling, "RUN! Albert's here!"

I dropped what I had in my arms and took off out the back door of the trailer, but I didn't get three steps out the door before he was on me. Albert picked me up by my hair and started slugging me in the mouth. He was like a wild animal. My mom jumped on his back and my little brother wrapped himself around his leg.

My mom only weighed about 105 lbs, while my little brother weighed about 75 lbs, so they weren't much more of a hindrance than a heavy coat would be. At least they tried to protect me, but Albert didn't miss a beat. My mom sunk her teeth into Albert's shoulder, causing him to drop me. He tried pulling her off him, but she was still attached to his shoulder by her teeth. So, he tried slamming her into the side of the trailer a few times. When my mom finally went flying, she had a chunk of his shoulder in her mouth.

\

Now it was me and my brother David who were on Albert, trying to get him off my mom. I was screaming, and David was screaming. By this time, there were people gathered all around us. I guess it's the same way today, but not ONE of those people stepped in to help us. I ran up to a man who was standing in the crowd and pleaded with him to help us, but he just stood there like he was watching something on TV. At one point, there must have been at least 20 people standing around us, and not one of them even tried to intervene.

Albert hit my mom against the trailer, breaking her breast bone. Once she fell to the ground, he was back on me. Still, no one helped us! This is how I know when you see someone on TV who's committed a heroic act and is being celebrated for bravery; he probably deserves it, because not everyone will.

Albert dragged me by my hair around the trailer to his car (we were now driving a 1968 Camaro instead of the '64 Impala). Albert tried to shove me in the car through the window, but for some reason there was a guy sitting in it. Albert opened the car door and told this guy to get out, but whoever it was tried to tell Albert he was very upset at the moment and maybe he should cool down. Albert just reached in without saying anything and yanked this guy out of the car, still never letting go of my hair. The whole time, my mom and brother were trying to pull me away from him, but he was too strong and in a fit of rage!

Eventually, Albert was able to push me into the car and slam the door. Immediately, I tried to climb out the other side, but before I could, he'd run around the car and pushed me back in. Albert jumped in and held me back with his arm as he started the car and backed out. Even though it would be a fruitless act, my mom and David tried to hold onto the car, and for a little while they did. The doors weren't even closed all the way, but they shut on their own once he punched the gas. We were doing at least 100 miles an hour, and it seemed like we'd achieved that in about 10 seconds.

I just knew I'd be dead in a few minutes, either from a car wreck or he'd kill me some other way! The possibilities were endless. The only possibility I couldn't envision was me surviving this. The entire time he was driving, he was also swinging his fist and hitting me. A few times, he even got his foot up and kicked me while driving 100 miles an hour. Albert kept telling me I was going to die. I had no problem believing him, but he kept repeating it, like I wasn't listening to him.

I did get bold enough to ask him where the baby was, so between slugging me and pulling my hair, he told me he'd taken him to Mexico, where he'd given him to some guys to hold. Albert proceeded to tell me that if he didn't come back to get him by a certain time, they would kill him, and I'd never find his body. Why should I doubt him? We lived just miles from the border, and he had relatives there.

Albert was driving like a maniac the entire time, doing what seemed to me like 100 miles an hour around sharp curves on winding foothill roads. One of them is called "Roller Coaster Road", and it was named correctly. I was so terrified of dying right then. Seventeen years old, and I'd faced death because of this man at least as many times as I was years old. This time was completely different, though, because now other people were involved. My mom, the neighborhood, and even Albert's friend he'd yanked from the car had witnessed it. Albert kept screaming these obvious facts at me.

All of a sudden, Albert pulled off the road onto the shoulder and screeched to a stop. He looked at me and said, "There is one thing you can do to get Michael back alive."

Of course, I told him I would do anything. Albert had never made an idle threat to me; if he said he would do it, he did it. He was telling me over and over I was going to die today, and he constantly carried out his threats. We were less than an hour from Mexico, so why wouldn't I believe him? I wanted my baby back, I wanted to live, and I would have said or done anything to get him to stop hitting me.

Albert said, "OK. Remember, you have to do everything I say, or I *will* get you, April. If it takes the rest of my life, I *will* get you. You know I mean it. Don't fuck with me. You know you can't hide from me. Do you hear me?"

I said, "Yes. I hear you."

Albert drove up to a 7-Eleven, pulled in front of the telephone, and said "Get out!"

So, I did. If it hadn't been for the baby, I would have tried to run from him at the store, but I didn't have anywhere to run to anyway. He told me to call the police and tell them my mother had broken into our house and we wanted to press charges. Also tell them to come out to the trailer, because she was there right now. He made me tell them I wanted her arrested for it. I said everything he told me, too. The woman on the phone said someone else had already called and there were officers on scene. I didn't tell Albert this.

Albert hung up the phone and placed me back in the car, then said, "OK, we're going back to the trailer, and you're going to convince them this is all your mom's doing. If you let the police take them to jail, I will kill you, April, and you'll never see Michael again. Do you hear me? I mean it. I *will* get you, even if it takes me years. You know I'll do it!"

I knew in my heart he meant it.

As we drove back to the trailer, he would reach over every now and then to slug me in the side for good measure, all the while reminding me how this was all my fault.

When we pulled onto our street, there were at least five cop cars there. Albert looked at me and said, "So help me, God. If I go to jail, you will die. I mean it, April. They can't protect you forever. Remember that!"

At that point, the police all came to the car and drug him out. They handcuffed him, but I swear to you it took every one of those officers to get him down. Albert was so brazen, even after they had him handcuffed, he was screaming at me in front of the police, saying, "April. I mean it. You know I do. I mean it."

Some of the police and my mom came up to me and asked me if I was all right. I couldn't stop shaking and crying, of course, but I managed to tell them yes. My mom was barking orders to me and the police, telling me this was it, I was getting a divorce and pressing charges, and she was pressing charges.

This was in 1973, and the laws dealing with spousal abuse were almost non-existent. I had a police officer tell me one time, right in front of Albert, "You're 16, he's over 18, you're married to him, and you're his property!" I swear to you, he said that to me. So in 1973, they told me I had to press charges against him or he wouldn't go to jail, even though I was standing there with my eye swollen shut and my lip bleeding. Even though 50 people had witnessed him beat me. They would do nothing if I didn't press charges. Yes, the law is different today, but this wasn't today; the police put the responsibility on me. I was scared, seventeen, and I wanted my baby back. All I could think of was Albert having Michael killed, or he would eventually kill me. I told the police I wasn't going to press any charges.

My mom just stood there in shock. After what Albert did to her, she couldn't believe it.

She started screaming at me, "If you do this, April, I will never help you again, ever!"

The police were trying to tell me that if I didn't press charges now, he would do it again, but I said, "No. I can't. He'll kill me or my baby! He has my baby, and I want him back. If I put him in jail, he'll definitely kill me." The police tried to assure me it wouldn't happen, but I couldn't take that chance.

By this time, Albert had changed back into his old charming, sweet self Albert. He started pleading with me, "I love you, April. I am so sorry. It'll never happen again. I love you, I promise. I love Michael, we're a family, and your mom is just trying to break us up!" He started blaming everyone else for his actions, all of this while he was still handcuffed.

Finally, one of the officers asked Albert where Michael was. He told them he was at his mother's house and he was fine. He looked at me with those big brown eyes, pleading with me. I could actually see moisture in his eyes.

He started saying, "You know I'd never hurt him, April. I love him, and I love you. You know I do."

\

The whole time he was giving this Oscar-winning performance, I was looking into his eyes. I was so scared for my future and devastated at the knowledge I'd have to run from Albert, as I had my mother.

I was in no shape mentally to be making this decision, but the police were forcing it on me. As long as the decision was on my shoulders, I couldn't do it. If it had been taken out of my hands, I would have been so happy, but they were dooming me by forcing me to make that decision. I'm so glad the laws are different today.

The whole time this was happening, my mom was standing there telling me if I did this, then I deserved what I got, not to come crying to her anymore, because she would never help me again. I told her if I put him in jail, he definitely would kill me, and what if he hurt Michael?

She said, "He's lying, April. He'll be in jail, the only place that'll make you safe."

While she was telling me this, Albert was begging me and telling me how much he loved me, how we were a family, but the cops were telling me that in their opinion, I should file charges.

I looked at the police and asked them, "If he goes to jail, how long will he be there?"

They told me he'd be there until someone bailed him out. I knew right then he'd be out that same day – and that was the day I would die.

I had to tell them NO. I would not press charges. I told my mom I was sorry and asked her to forgive me. Then I told the police to let Albert go, so they did.

My mom yelled at me the whole time we unloaded the van. The police stayed until she was gone. Finally, even the police left, and I was once again alone with Albert. We went inside. He raised his hand to me

\

but stopped short of hitting me. He shut up and put a piece of wood up in the window we'd broken to get in. He kept telling me tomorrow I was going to call the police and tell them to charge my mom, and she was going to pay for the window.

He was so stupid. It was my house, too. I was with her. The police weren't going to do anything to her, but I was so tired. I agreed with anything he said. I just wanted him to go get the baby.

Finally, Albert said he was going to get Michael, and he left. The entire time he was gone, my mind went wild. I was still terrified he had taken him to Mexico or was going to use Michael to hurt me by keeping him from me somehow. Albert was back in forty-five minutes, and of course he'd been lying about the killers in Mexico. Michael had been over at his mother's, like he said.

Albert didn't speak to me the rest of the night. We were both exhausted, and that was fine with me. I had Michael back, and now I started biding my time. I'd decided I wasn't going to stay and put up with him killing me. He would go to work the next day. I just tried to stay out of his way and not make him any madder.

I truly believed if I stayed in Tucson, Albert would find me and eventually kill me. I knew I had to get away from him if I was going to live. I honestly believed I could run from my problems.

The next day, right after he left for work, I called my mom and apologized. I told her I had to get the baby back before I did anything. She was so mad, and hurt, both physically and emotionally. She had had to go the emergency room the night before. Albert had broken her breast bone and pulled a big wad of her hair out. She had bruises all over her. My mom was just realizing what I had been living with. She told me I had to get away from that maniac. I totally agreed with her and asked her if she could help me at all. She told me to call her back in half an hour. After I hung up with my mom, I called my aunt and uncle in Oklahoma, who was my mom's sister Reta. I told them I was in trouble and asked them if I could come and stay with them for a little while. They were so nice and told me of course I could come stay with them. I couldn't believe it.

I called my mom back, and she told me she could borrow the money to get me a plane ticket. I told her Aunt Reta and Uncle John had said yes, I could come out there. My mom drove out and got me and the baby. I packed one suitcase for me, and one for Michael. I was terrified Albert hadn't gone to work and was watching me from somewhere, but truthfully, I don't think he really believed I would leave him.

My mom took us to the airport in Tucson and put us on a plane. The whole time I was waiting for take-off, I was terrified he'd somehow followed us. At any moment, I expected Albert would charge onto the plane and drag me off, but he didn't. Finally, the plane took off. Again, I found myself with this strange sensation while I was in the air. I had such a sense of freedom, a sense of peace. As we got closer to landing in Oklahoma City, I got a wild idea Albert had somehow gotten there ahead of me and would be waiting for us. I know that sounds silly now, but when you live in constant fear, no horror movie is too far-fetched, including reality.

What I wanted was a constant feeling of that peace and lack of fear; I didn't want it to end. The only two times in three years I'd felt like this, and I had to be off the ground to know that feeling. I guess I couldn't live in-between problems, but the idea of it was wonderful.

When I landed in Oklahoma City, Albert wasn't there, of course, but my aunt Kari Jo and my cousin Kari Lavern were. Kari Jo is my age, and my cousin Kari Lavern was three years younger than us. So, the oldest of this group was a whopping 17. My uncle had let them drive the one hundred and fifty miles to Oklahoma City to get me and the baby. It was the closest airport to them.

We were all excited and happy to see one another, and I was so glad to be somewhere Albert wasn't. Just to know that at least for tonight he wasn't going to come up behind me and say, "Boo!" Then POW!

The four of us piled into my aunt Kari's 1968 Oldsmobile, which was a monster of a car. We proceeded to drive out of Oklahoma City and back to Wilburton, which is a little town in southeastern Oklahoma where my aunt and uncle lived.

We had just gotten to the outskirts of Oklahoma City when Kari's car broke down. We made it to a gas station parking lot, but it was closed and we weren't in the best part of town. Kari Lavern ended up calling her father, my uncle John, in Wilburton. Uncle John got a friend of his to go with him, and they drove up to get us. It was horrible waiting in that car for hours, though. Michael was fussy, and we were all a little bit scared. There was never a dull moment where I'm concerned; nothing just happens like it's supposed to.

Of course, I bore the guilt that this was entirely my fault, a real symptom of spousal abuse. Albert had knocked all the self-esteem out of me the Home hadn't stolen. He'd turned me into someone who goes around constantly apologizing to everyone, even if it wasn't my fault. Between him, the Home, and my mother, I was terrified of being punished.

\

When Uncle John and his friend finally arrived, we were so glad to see them. Luckily, it only took them five minutes to fix the car; it was only a loose wire. Being the good-hearted person my uncle was, he didn't even act mad or put out. It was so good to finally get to their house, among familiar surroundings and feelings of family and acceptance. I was back in Oklahoma, and Albert wasn't.

The first few days of being at my aunt and uncle's house were great. I was free of being terrified every minute, scared of doing something wrong, or being punished for something I didn't even do. Everyone helped with the baby, and they all acted like they wanted me there. That's love, right? Acceptance? Of course, I never stopped warning them that Albert would find me. I was so young and so naïve; I figured he hadn't been to my uncle's before, so he wouldn't think of it. I was just hoping he would forget about me altogether. Yeah, right!

Every time the phone rang or someone knocked on the door, I would run and hide. This was what I did all the time. I would always say, "I'm sorry," even if I was across the room from whatever had happened. I jumped every time someone came up from behind me. This really bothered my uncle, when he would innocently reach for something and I covered my head or cowered.

Most of the time, I did normal teenage stuff with my cousin and aunt. We drove through the Sonic drive-in and ate onion rings. We fixed each other's hair and took movies of the baby. It was fun with all of us in the kitchen cooking together. So far, my life had run in the wrong sequence. I skipped childhood, so I was having one now. What am I saying? I was still a child myself at seventeen.

\

My aunt and uncle lived in a rural town, much like where I'd grown up; lots of trees and water, hunting and fishing. In fact, it was less than 200 miles from my hometown. Most of the homes had a garden somewhere in the yard. It was definitely not like living in a big city like Tucson. I loved the simplicity of it, with no pressures, just life. I could have stayed right there forever.

I talked to my mom on the phone, and she told me Albert had been there, of course. He'd given her the "I'm sorry and I love her" thing. She'd threatened to call the police if he didn't get off her property. Albert told her he would find me, with or without her help, and he was right.

On about the fourth or fifth day of my "flight for life", I was sitting with my aunt and uncle, playing with the baby and watching TV. It was about 8 in the evening when someone knocked on the door. Before I could react, my little cousin Melissa (my aunt and uncle's other daughter) jumped up and opened the door. There stood Albert.

I froze. My uncle went to the door and said, "What do you want?"

Albert looked past my uncle at me and said, "I want to talk to April."

My uncle looked at me and said, "Do you want to talk to him?"

I shook my head no, so my uncle told him I didn't want to talk to him.

Albert looked at me with pleading eyes and actually started crying. "I love you more than anything, April! I can't live without you. You and Michael are my whole life. Please come outside and talk to me. I wouldn't hurt you, I love you!"

He was a charmer, and a good liar! Believe it or not, I felt sorry for him. When a woman is in an abusive relationship, they dream of

making it right. They believe they can fix it. I didn't say it was smart;
I'm just stating a fact.

I wanted and needed to be loved. In my heart, I thought I loved
Albert. I had this man's child, and I wanted nothing more than for life to
be the way I pictured it. I wanted so desperately for everything Albert
said to be true.

I told my uncle I would go out and talk to him. As I stepped
outside, I noticed there was someone else in the car. I asked Albert who it
was. He just said it was a friend of his who had driven to Oklahoma with
him.

When he finally got me all to himself, he told me everything I
wanted to hear: how much he loved me and Michael; how we were his
family; how sorry he was for losing his temper; how he would never do it
again. Albert said he'd been so stupid, we were all that mattered to him,
and he couldn't live without us. It was everything I wanted to be true. He
even told me he would go to a marriage counselor with me.

My uncle John came walking out onto the porch with his shotgun
in his hand. He asked, "Is everything all right out there?"

I told him it was. He then warned Albert that if he touched me, he
would shoot him.

Albert said, "I won't hurt her. I love her, and I need her and my
son to come home. I'll never hit her again."

My uncle had a few choice words for Albert, but then he left us
alone again and went back inside. Before he did, though, he reminded me
I didn't have to do anything I didn't want to. I thanked him and told him I
wanted to talk to Albert.

\

I stayed outside with Albert and let him continue to talk me into going back with him, which he did. After an hour or so, I went back inside and told everyone I was going back to Tucson. My aunt told me not to, but it was done. Apparently, I hadn't had enough yet. So, I got the baby and my few things and got in the car with Albert and his friend. I had high hopes and was pleased when he told his friend to get in the back seat so he could ride next to his wife. We all took off and headed back to Tucson.

We drove about ten miles or so, and the baby had fallen asleep in his car carrier. It was already dark, and the movement of the car had soothed him. It was around eleven at night by now, and Albert hadn't said anything since we pulled out of my aunt's driveway. His friend in the back seat hadn't said anything the entire time. Still, without saying anything, Albert pulled over to the side of the road. We were out in the middle of nowhere; there wasn't even a farm anywhere near us. He opened his door, looked at me and told me to get out; he said he wanted to talk to me in private. As soon as I was out of the car, he ran around the car and came at me like a wild dog.

He grabbed me by the hair, and his first loving words were, "You fucking bitch! How dare you even think you can take my son from me? Do you honestly think I would allow you to take my son from me? DO YOU? You're crazy if you think that (!*&*^*&*#@ %#%@!)..." and in-between each word, his fist was connecting to some part of my body. "If you ever try that again, I'll kill you."

That last statement gave me some hope. Did that mean I wasn't going to die tonight? I had, of course, realized my horrible mistake of again believing he wouldn't hurt me and that he loved me. I went into my now most common pose of cowering down and trying to protect my head with my hands. He was going wild, with his fists flying and feet kicking, and my hair was the handle that kept me within reach.

His friend got out of the car and said, "Hey, Albert, man, don't kill her."

Albert said, "Stay the fuck out of it." *Smack.* No, he didn't hit him; he was still hitting me.

The guy got back in the car, and Albert finally let go of my hair and let me drop to the ground. I was covering my face and trying to stop crying. He kicked me again and told me to get in the car.

He could have won an Academy Award that night, Doctor Jekyll and Mister Hyde. He was so brazen, he told this guy to get out of the car. We were on a dirt road in the middle of Nowhere, Oklahoma, at midnight. I thought he was going to leave his friend there, but no such luck; he put the baby in his carrier and sat him up in the front seat. Albert told me to get in the back seat, then told the guy to take a walk. He then forced me to have sex with him in the back seat of the car. When he was done, he was halfway nice again, then started giving me the "I'm sorry" routine.

He said, "You forced me to act like that. Why do you force me to hit you?" The same old crap, just another day in hell.

Now that I look back on it, the reasons he did it are sicker than the fact that he did it at all. He did it to reestablish his ownership of me and demean me, because he knew I didn't want him to. To him, those were reasons enough.

\

Needless to say, the rest of the trip home was hell. Once, he just reached over and slapped me while I was sleeping. He was such a sick man. That would be the first time I left him.

When we got back home, my mom wouldn't talk to me. Albert kept an even closer eye on me than before, if that's possible. Things deteriorated at home, if you can imagine them getting any worse.

My mom moved back to Oklahoma with the kids when Michael was about nine months old. I never really got to see her anyways; Albert made sure of that. My mom and I still weren't very close, but I felt even more isolated than ever. She was pursuing a relationship with the doctor she'd met when Grandpa was sick back in our little hometown. In fact, she was going to marry him.

Now my mom was gone, and I was pretty much alone in Tucson. In reality, I was alone even when she was there. I'd been uprooted so many times in my life. Like I said, I never had the chance to make lifelong friends or establish roots anywhere, except in Oklahoma, and those roots were weak and getting weaker. My grandparents were both dead now, and I'd been buried in this marriage for sixteen or seventeen months. Here I'd been a mom for nine months, and I was all of seventeen. Looking back, I'd been in fear for my life, every day, for over a year and a half. Let's not forget the two years at the home. There, I woke up thinking about surviving that day and went to bed every night surprised and grateful I was still alive.

Sometimes just going to bed was a real nightmare. Albert would do things like come home drunk and wake me up just to fight with me. Or I would just wake up to him hitting me, without bothering to wake me up first. One time, he got out his pool cue and started poking me in the back with it.

He told me, "If you go to sleep, I'll kill you." Then he'd poke me in the back with it and say, "Are you awake, April? Don't go to sleep, April, or I'll kill you." He would eventually fall asleep and leave me alone in my terror.

Even worse than a beating, Albert would come home drunk and want to have sex with me. That had become the worst punishment of all. I'd rather he beat me than receive pleasure from my misery. Sex had lost all its pleasure; it was torture, and he knew it. That made it worse.

I had become so submissive that I gave up reasoning with him. It was just useless, and it would antagonize him. Those of you who are at the point of judging my ignorance, or will as you read this, just don't understand. I hope you never have to. The choices I did make were the wrong choices, but I didn't have the knowledge to make the right ones. I did try to learn from my mistakes.

Things weren't always bad, although they definitely progressed on a downward slope. I had Michael, and he was such a sweet baby, a happy baby. He was physically beautiful, because of Albert's dark skin and my light skin; Michael had what they call olive skin. That baby had a head of hair most women would die for.

Albert's mother doted over Michael as much as she hated me. She wanted nothing more than to have me out of the way, and she acted like Michael was hers, not mine. He was the first born of their first born. You have to understand the Hispanic culture. They're very family oriented. Not that we couldn't learn something from them, but sometimes they were obsessed with it. Albert, as I said, was their first born. His parents were raised in Mexico, and they were very race-oriented. Albert was, of course, trying to break away from that. That was why he chose me instead of a Mexican girl. It infuriated his mother, and she felt betrayed by me. I had lured her son away from his race, and I wasn't even Catholic. I knew I wasn't up to her expectations, but she truly hated me.

One day, she had me down on my hands and knees cleaning her kitchen floor. As I was cleaning, I had done something not to her liking, and she threatened to hit me with a forty-eight ounce 7 Up bottle. Now, this was before we had plastic bottles.

Sometimes, for no apparent reason, she would go off in Spanish and scare the shit out of me, mostly because I didn't know what she wanted from me. I couldn't understand her and dreaded going over there, even though it was just about the only place I ever went.

Albert did take me grocery shopping, but of course he decided everything we bought. I was never allowed to touch money.

As he would say, "What do you need money for? If you need something, I'll get it for you." He had to have total control.

During the day, while he was at work, it was my time. He would never even consider letting me get a job; it was too much out of his control, so it would never happen. When he was gone to work, it was just me and the baby. Michael was my only company, and he kept me very busy and took my mind off other things. By now, he was using his walker and into everything. He was trying to walk on his own, and he was even saying, "Mama." Michael was now old enough to cry and scream whenever Albert started in on me. Amazingly enough, Albert was never abusive to the baby. I was very glad of that, because I wouldn't have let it go on so long if he had been. I'm not saying he didn't get mad at the baby; he would just take it out on me. If Michael cried excessively or was teething, Albert would hit me and say, "Go do something about that." At least he kept it focused on me for the time being. Michael wasn't even a year old yet. Who knows what Albert would be like later in life?

One day, Albert came home from work, drunk and late as usual, and I knew I was in for it when he came through the door. I honestly don't know how I survived some of the beatings he gave me. I'd learned to hide my head and take it in the body; it's amazing what our bodies can take. This night, he was particularly rough. I never even considered fighting back, because I remember trying to fight him off before, and it just made it worse.

I lay awake after he was finished and had passed out. I was wondering how to get out of this mess alive. I couldn't go to my mom, especially after the last incident when she got her breast bone broken. Then I'd gone back to him from my aunt's house. I'd barely spoken to my mom since she'd moved back to Oklahoma. She was going to school at the University of Oklahoma now, and she lived right next to the college in Norman, Oklahoma. Mom was finally working on a new life, again, and she'd told me she wouldn't help me again. I couldn't blame her.

The day after this particular beating, I called my dad in Oklahoma once Albert had gone to work. I'd only met him that one time, after my grandpa died, and I hadn't spoken to him since. He was surprisingly nice to me and told me I could come there if I wanted to.

I don't remember how I got the money, but somehow I got a bus ticket to my dad's house in Baxter Springs, Kansas. Michael and I left while Albert was at work again. It was a horrible trip, because the baby was almost a year old now and was into everything. He became real fidgety if he wasn't constantly moving. The trip took 36 hours, and I had no money to buy us anything to eat or drink. By the time I got to my dad's, I was out of diapers, formula and patience. I was ready for a hug from someone, and I was pleased to get one from everyone when I got there.

It had been a little over a year and a half since I'd met my dad and his family, but things were pretty much the same as when I'd first met him. They lived in the same little house, and I think he had the same job. They were still pretty poor, but they seemed happy.

On top of that, my little brother David was staying with them. It seems the relationship between my mom and the doctor was blooming, but it didn't work as well with a fourteen or fifteen-year-old boy around. So, David gladly went to my dad's. Dad and David had formed a real bond. Out of all the kids my dad claimed or raised, David would be the only boy.

I liked being there. They treated me as if I was welcome. I loved my little sisters, and it was so nice to be around people again. The girls and I had fun. They loved the baby. He took his first steps on his own while I was there. It was strange getting to know my dad. He's the most personable man you'll ever meet. He's funny and bright. He just had a real problem with his stability and growing up. He could charm anyone into anything. Some people would call him a con artist, and in a way he was. He's so charming, people who are used by him can't even hate him when it's over.

I got to meet a lot of my newfound relatives while I was there, like my dad's brothers and sisters, their children and even my paternal grandmother. I was able to see Kari Jo. My aunt Kari Jo was living on her own now that my grandpa and grandma were gone. Remember, my grandparents were her parents, poor Kari Jo. She'd been raised by dying old people whom she had to take care of most of her life, and now she was seventeen and both of her parents were gone. She was more like my sister than my aunt. I always loved seeing her. She had her own apartment in a little town about five miles from my dad's. She lived across the street from Paul Thomas' funeral parlor. It was such a unique experience for me to see someone my age living independently on their own. She had a job and was going to school; she also had a car and a boyfriend. It was like Kari Jo knew from the beginning she would have to take care of herself someday, and when that day came, she easily stepped into the role. She'd lost both of her parents at too young an age.

When I got to meet my father's mother, I was pleasantly surprised to see she was a real grandma type. She was a big woman; jolly, I guess you would call her. She didn't seem to be interested in me. Of course, she had at least eight kids, and I couldn't tell you how many grandchildren. Now that I think about it, I'd made her a great-grandmother by having Michael. I don't know if I was the only one or not. I don't even remember if it was mentioned. Anyway, I had fun there. I especially became friends with my little sister Chris, and she would follow me everywhere. I think she was twelve at the time. Carol, the oldest, was sixteen. She was already married and gone from home. Terry, the now sixteen-year-old, didn't seem to like having me around very much. Jamie Dawn, the littlest one, was nine. She was a doll and spoiled rotten. Then there was their mother, and with David, me, and the baby, it was a full house.

Since the little town they lived in was also where I'd been born, it was like home to me. We didn't talk about the future; they bought my baby food and diapers, fed me and gave me a place to stay. I know it was a hardship on them, but they didn't confront me on what I was going to do. They didn't really mention Albert.

A week or so after I got to my dad's, Albert pulled into my dad's driveway. I was at the park with my sister and the baby. My dad told him he didn't know where I was. He told Albert I had an uncle in Tennessee, and maybe he should try there. I should have known he would think of my dad eventually, because he'd met him the same time I had.

Two or three days went by, and I didn't hear any more from him. One day after lunch, I took the baby out to swing him in the tree swing in the front yard. All of a sudden, Albert pulled up in the yard right in front of me, and his mother was with him. My dad was at work, and the girls were in school; it was just me and Michael. My stepmom was in the house, but she was only four-feet-ten, and she weighed about ninety pounds. My mouth dropped open as his eyes met mine through the window of the car. I shut my mouth and tried to get out of the swing, but he was there before I could. He grabbed the baby from me and handed him to his mother. We stood there and argued, but he didn't hit me. Albert was yelling at me, telling me he'd driven all over the country looking for me. Apparently, he'd driven to my Uncle David's house in Tennessee and had as an afterthought stopped by my dad's house again there in Kansas on his way back home. He'd all but given up hope of finding me, and he almost didn't stop there. I was shocked he had his mother with him; they were in her Camaro.

Albert told me, in no uncertain terms, that they were going back to Tucson and they were taking the baby with them. If I wanted to go, I'd better get in the car, but no matter what, the baby was going. I couldn't just stay there and let them take my baby, so I got in the car. My stepmother came out and asked if I was all right. I asked her if she would bring me the diaper bag, which she did. Albert peeled out, and we were off, back to Tucson and my life of hell.

Albert didn't hit me right away, but he and his mother gave me a verbal beating all the way back. Poor Michael; even though he wasn't physically abused by Albert, he had to hear all the yelling aimed at me. This is just as traumatic to a child as a beating.

Once we stopped at a gas station, I ran around the building to the bathroom. Albert snuck up behind me and slugged me just once, while we were out of his mother's sight. He then walked away without a word; just a warning of things to come.

Run, run, run away

When I got back to the car, Albert's mother didn't ask me what happened to my face, because she knew. I think she enjoyed it. I know from her verbal thrashing, she thought I deserved whatever I got. So I was back, and Albert had more ammunition to hate me and punish me for.

Sometimes, everything would be fine and he would just lay into me because he'd remember one of the times I'd left him. Over the next few months, I left again two or three more times. Each time I left, he found me, and each time he found me, he hated me more and more. The beatings grew more intense and more frequent. Every time he had to find me, he immediately had to reclaim his property; so, sex became torture, and driving with him in a car became torture, because he loved to terrify me by driving like a maniac.

One of the times I left, I'd gone to my Aunt Kari Jo's little apartment in Picher, Oklahoma. Picher was the center of the "heart of poverty." This little town was so dead, it's now been declared a legal ghost town. To tell you how ghostly it was: the only thriving place of business was Paul Thomas' Mortuary, across the street from her apartment.

Albert showed up at her apartment, looking for me. Actually, he was never looking for me; he wanted Michael. By now, he would have been happy to have me out of his life, or out of the world, but he wasn't going to let me take Michael. Again, he'd left Tucson for places beyond, looking for me and his son. I was over at my cousin's house visiting when he showed up at Kari's. He cried to Kari Jo and made her believe he loved me so much, and he eventually talked her into telling him where I was. A little while later, Albert was chasing me down the street in front of my cousin's house, threatening to kill me.

I was running out of places to run to. I had run to my poor aunt and uncle more than once. I'd even run to my cousin Ellen's once, and he still found me, even though he'd never even heard of her before. He was resourceful and persistent. As far as I knew, my mom was still in Norman Oklahoma, going to school, and she was still planning on marry the doctor...

Speaking of doctors, I didn't tell you what happened to my good looking doctor, the one who delivered Michael! I was scheduled to go to the doctor's office for my six-week check up the next day. Albert and I were watching the news on television that evening, and all of a sudden this story came on about a prominent doctor who had been shot and killed by his estranged wife. She then shot herself; I believe their twelve-year-old daughter was there. They then said his name, and Albert and I looked at each other with our mouths open. It was my doctor, Louis Bronstein, Jr. The next day, I called and found out it was true. I never did go back for my six-week check up.

Another time I left Albert, I ended up going to my mom's wedding to the doctor, in Norman, Oklahoma. I know at that time it was over Michael's first birthday. Albert really hated me for that one. When he got me back again, he almost killed me. We'd celebrated his first birthday with my dad and his family, but Albert's beating schedule didn't seem to coincide with birthdays or weddings.

I didn't stay with my mom, of course; I stayed with my aunt in Picher, about one hundred miles away. I drove down with her and went to the wedding. When I saw my mom right before her wedding ceremony, she sat me and my aunt Kari Jo down and told us how happy she was. She was going on and on about how much of herself she'd given to us kids, and now it was her turn.

Mom actually said to us, "I've devoted my life to these kids, and now it's my turn. I won't let anything get in the way of my happiness."

Well, I couldn't believe my ears. She'd devoted her life to us? I hadn't even lived at home for a third of my life. My youngest sister, Darla, was only eight years old, but she'd devoted her life to us? Whatever!

I got to meet her almost-husband and his parents for the first time. His name was Pat, and he was the exact same age as my mom; they were either thirty-three or thirty-four. He'd never been married before, and he was marrying a woman with five kids, all by different men, and now she had a grandchild. Pat was not only a doctor, he was also a lawyer. He'd spent his whole life going to school, one of which was Vanderbilt University in Nashville, Tennessee. He was the only child of very prominent parents. Pat came from old southern money, while she came from absolutely no money. They were so different.

They were like night and day, but she seemed happy, so I wished her the best. Their wedding was beautiful, and the reception was held in a hotel. I'm not sure I'd ever been in a hotel before. Her wedding cake had doves on it, and little pearls. I was very impressed, but I didn't get to enjoy much of the festivities. Once they were married, I had to continue my mad dash from Albert. Of course, he would find me; he always found me.

One time when Albert had brought me back home from one of my attempted escapes, he either lost his job or got demoted at the mine. I paid for that one. Things really got bad when he didn't have anywhere to go all day. The meaner he got, the more I tried to run away. The more times I'd run, the more times he'd have to lose time at work or spend money looking for me. Eventually, we lost the trailer and had to file for bankruptcy.

It's hard to believe things could get worse, but they did. Our finances were deteriorating quickly. Albert moved us into his mother's house, and oh God, it was awful. Even Albert couldn't take that for long. When he was at work, she made my life hell. They watched me closer than he did.

Finally, Albert had a big fight with her and we moved in with some friends of his. Their names were Donny and Babe, and they had an apartment on the third or fourth floor of this building. It had a balcony off one of the bedrooms.

By now, Michael was sixteen months old. He was walking and trying to talk, and he kept me sane. He was so adorable, but Albert and I fought constantly. I make it sound like I yelled at him, but no way! What I mean is Albert fought with himself, and he used me to do it. I was miserable; things were getting worse, if that was possible.

Albert was under a lot of pressure. He'd gotten himself another job, but he still blamed me for losing the other one. He'd been without work for a month or two.

We were living with people, and that meant he had to keep things bottled in more. Oh, he didn't stop beating me; he just had to hold it in until we were alone. There were a couple of times he beat me in front of people, but not very often. This was nineteen seventy-four. In the eyes of the law, I was his property. He could do what he wanted to me, up to murder, and he pushed the limits more than once.

One time, we went to the wedding of one of his relatives. He beat me when we got home, because he swore up and down some guy looked at me. Hell, I wouldn't have known if he did. I never looked up anymore.

Albert told me over and over I'd never leave him, especially not with Michael. I knew he meant it, because every time I had tried to get away from him, I would pay the price. There were no abuse shelters back then, not that I knew of. I'd called the police on him more than five or six times, and I always got a beating for it. Right or wrong, I'd been led to believe I didn't have any legal rights. I was legally his property, pretty much to do with as he pleased.

Albert was almost twenty-one, and he had parents who would do anything for him, and had; they would back him against me in a minute. He had friends and family, a job, a car, and of course he had his temper. One day his temper got the best of him, and he started hitting me in front of Donny and Babe. They didn't know what to do, but they sympathized. Donny started talking to me about options. He told me I should leave him, but I told him I'd tried. He didn't have any solutions, but it was nice to have someone to talk to who cared.

Life is change..

One night, Donny called me from a party he, his wife Babe and
Albert were at. He was telling me, Albert was drunk and maybe I should
watch out. The rest of the conversation went something like this: I told
him I didn't know what to do; I talked about divorce and running away
again; he said he wished he could do something to help me, he was truly
sorry for me; I told him I wasn't going to be able to take it much longer
and I couldn't live in fear anymore; I even said I thought Albert would
kill me soon. I was dumping on a sweet guy, or anyone who would listen.

An hour later they all came home, drunk. Donny whispered to me
as he walked by that Albert had been listening on the other phone at the
party. He'd heard everything I'd said. I started going into heart failure; it
felt like it anyway. I saw Albert come out of the bathroom carrying a tall
Budweiser can in his hand. Before I could flinch, he grabbed my hand,
dragging me into
Donny and Babe's bedroom. Their room was the one with the balcony
off it. The baby was asleep in our room. He shut the door and smiled at

me with every one of his pearly whites showing. I didn't say anything; I was just trying to back up. As soon as he stopped smiling, he laid into me with the beer can. I knew from the start, this was going to be special. He wasn't just being his mean old self; he was pissed, at me. From the first blow, I was hurt. I tried to cover my head, but he was yanking my hair, using it like a handle and slugging me in the face. When I did get my face buried, he went to work on my back. He slugged me, hit me with the beer can in his hand, and when he got tired, he used his feet. He had on big clutter boots, or hiking boots.

I was in trouble! Albert was extremely drunk and had gone out of his mind with rage. He was beating me with complete purpose, and the purpose was to make sure I didn't get up again, ever!

After some time (I don't know how long), he left the room and went to the bathroom. Albert left me literally gasping for breath on the floor. I couldn't walk, so I crawled out of the bedroom and into the living room. Donny and Babe were both passed out on the living room couch. I crawled to Donny and grabbed his leg. I shook him and tried to ask him to help me. I was in real distress; I couldn't breathe. I finally got him to wake up a little.

As I did, Albert came out of the bathroom. When he saw me on the floor at Donny's knees, he freaked out and grabbed my leg, dragging me back to the bedroom.

Donny followed. "Stop! Let go of her! You're gonna kill her!"

Albert said, "Keep the fuck out of it, Donny."

He pulled me back into the bedroom behind him and slammed the door. Donny tried to open it, but Albert pushed him out and locked the door. All I could do was brace myself for what was about to happen.

Albert quickly turned his attention (and his fists) back on me. I really couldn't breathe, and I knew I was going to die. At one point, I almost wished for it.

Babe was still at the door yelling, "Albert! Let her go! Open the door now! If you don't, I'll break the door down!"

Albert reciprocated with threats of killing me and killing himself, but Donny and Babe continued to beat on the door and try to talk some sense into Albert.

By this time I was in extreme distress. I was gasping for air. Something was really wrong. I couldn't even stand up, and I couldn't breathe. Every breath I did get came with excruciating pain. Donny started throwing his body against the door, trying to break it down. Albert dragged me and the telephone out onto the balcony.

He was trying to shut and lock the sliding glass door behind us, but the phone cord stopped it from closing all the way. Albert had to let go of me while he was trying to close the door over the cord. When he let me go, all I could do was fall to the floor. We were up on the third floor of this apartment building; otherwise, I would have tried to get away – but I couldn't stand up, let alone run.

Eventually, Donny and Babe broke the bedroom door open. We could see them through the glass door. They ran through the bedroom to the sliding glass door and tried to yank it open. Albert was having a hard time holding onto me and holding the door shut at the same time.

I couldn't stand up, but he kept yanking me up anyway, and every time I tried to lie down, he would yank me back up.

He gave me the ugliest look and said, "Stay there, so help me, God."

He was holding the door shut, and the guys were trying to pull it open. I couldn't help it; I kept falling down. So, he took my left hand and slammed his foot against my hand, into the brick wall, trying to hold me up. I felt my hand break, but that was the least of my problems. I really couldn't breathe.

Babe finally pulled until the door jamb came off and he opened the door. When the door opened, Albert just dropped me and stepped back. He didn't try to fight either one of them; he just turned back into Doctor Jekyll again. He let Babe pick me up and carry me to the living room. Donny told Albert to give him his car keys, and he just did it, without an argument or anything. It was like he'd just reverted back to human form. It was weird to witness.

Albert followed us around like a puppy. Babe drove me to the hospital, and Donny stayed with Michael. Albert got in the back seat of the car and went with us. Albert never said a word the entire way to the hospital; he just sat quietly in the back seat. I tried to maintain while gasping for air.

Once we got to the hospital, Babe went inside the emergency room. Almost as quickly, a bunch of medical people came running out. As they put me on the gurney, the last thing I remember was this nurse asking if I'd taken drugs. Babe told her no.

The next thing I remember was waking up, with Albert standing over me.

He got down in my face and said, "Tell them you fell off the balcony, April. I swear to God, if you don't, I'll kill you. You know I will. No matter how long it takes."

\

I was hardly coherent. I couldn't deal with him all alone for long. I still couldn't breathe right. I was so relieved when a doctor came in, causing Albert to step back from me.

I was physically in bad shape; this time I got it in the face, as well as everywhere else. It was so obvious what had happened to me. I had handprints covering almost all of my body. I had three fingers broken, on my left hand; I remember that because they cut off my wedding rings and gave them to Albert. I had punctured my lung from a broken rib, and they thought my spleen was going to have to come out. Later on, when the doctor came in again, he was trying to ask me what had happened. Albert was standing right there, so that's what I told him. I said I'd fallen off the balcony.

Later, after Albert left, the doctor came into my room and sat down beside me. "You have to tell me the truth. You don't get handprints all over your body from falling off a balcony. I've seen people who fell off balconies, and they looked better than you do!" He knew I'd been beaten, and he suspected Albert.

I told him I couldn't do anything about what Albert had done to me. He was so nice, and he really seemed to care. He also told me he would help me and said, "You need to press charges against him. You're lucky to be alive. But don't worry about it right now; tomorrow is soon enough."

After he left, all I could do was lay there and cry. I was terrified to press charges against Albert. They didn't know him; he would kill me, no matter what they said.

The next day, the doctor kept Albert away from me by sending me to radiology and other places where Albert couldn't come.

My body was so bruised, a few days later there would be no part of my entire back that wasn't purple first, then green. I discovered my mouth didn't work right because my jaw was also broken. I hurt all over. They kept me in intensive care those first few nights.

On the third or fourth day, they put me in a private room and prepped me for surgery, again. They hadn't removed my spleen, but they prepped me for surgery every morning, just in case they had to. That meant no food either, a liquid diet only, but I couldn't open my mouth anyway, so I didn't care. I was so sore and tired, and most of the time I just slept.

On the 5th day or the day after, I really don't remember, Donny and Babe came to visit me. Donny sat down in the chair next to the bed I was in, and Babe sat on the empty bed next to me.

I was a mess; I was lying in this hospital bed with a catheter, two IVs in my arms and every other tube they could get in me. Donny and Babe were asking me how I was (like it wasn't obvious). I was crying and telling them the doctor wanted me to press charges against Albert. They were both freaking out at how bad my face looked. My eye was swollen shut, and my lip looked like the Elephant Man's, not to mention how bruised every inch of my body was.

I apologized for everything, like the broken doors, and they told me not to be silly. Donny apologized for not stepping in sooner. I was so grateful to them for doing what they had. It was that kind of conversation, pretty uncomfortable. They didn't really know what to say, and I didn't either.

I started crying and told them I didn't know what I was going to do. Donny took my hand and was holding it, trying to comfort me. I was explaining to them that the doctor was trying to talk me into filing charges against Albert. Babe said I really did have to stop him from doing this again. Donny was still voicing his opinion on the subject, when the door opened and Albert walked in.

Albert didn't even look to see that Babe was right there; all he saw was Donny sitting next to me, holding my hand. He'd brought me a dozen red roses in a vase. Albert glared at Donny, then at me. In another fit of rage, Albert threw the roses (vase and all) right at me. With a loud smash, the flowers and vase hit the wall over my head. Shattered glass, water and roses went everywhere.

Now, I was really up to something here. I was holding a guy's hand; I hope the tubes, IVs and urine bag didn't turn him off.

Before any of us could react, Albert literally flew across the room at Donny, landing on the bed I was in. I figured I was dead, so I was out of there. I yanked tubes and needles out of my body at lightning speed and took off running down the hall, screaming for my life.

I remember I had one of those hospital gowns on with no back in it, but I hauled my bare butt down the hall to an office and ran inside. There was a big desk in the room, which I was under in just a second. I was shaking and crying with fear, and I wasn't coming out for anyone.

Almost immediately, nurses and doctors surrounded me, trying to figure out what was happening. Just a second later, they knew why I was hiding under a desk, freaking out. Albert was standing there in the doorway. I started screaming at the top of my lungs, begging them to help me; please don't let him get me.

I don't know who or how they got him to leave, but they had to give me a shot to get me out from under the desk. Eventually, they sedated me and I slept. Later that day, I was awakened when my doctor came to my room. He had three police officers with him.

He said, "April, you have to press charges against Albert. If you don't, the next time he'll kill you."

The police talked to me for quite some time. They told me if I pressed charges for attempted murder, Albert would be arrested and go to jail. He wouldn't be able to get at me; they'd protect me. There would be a restraining order put against him that would keep him away. Remember, back then, if the victim didn't press charges, they didn't get pressed! That's exactly why the law is different now. The state presses charges even if the victim won't.

I told them about the baby, and they said, "They won't give your baby to a convicted criminal, believe me; this is the only thing you can do. Blah Blah Blah."

So, I finally said OK. They had me sign a bunch of papers, then they took a bunch of pictures of my face and bare back.

After the "vase of roses" incident, Albert had tried once to re-enter the hospital and was now banned from coming back in. After I'd signed the papers and the charges were pressed, the hospital put me in a storage room, I swear to God; they put me in a linen storage room. It was to protect me from Albert, although he was banned from entering the hospital; we all knew not much stopped Albert.

So there I stayed, in a linen closet, for almost a month. Maintenance eventually put a phone and TV in the room; like I had anyone to call.

The police came almost every day, and sometimes they put a guard outside the door. It was really embarrassing. I didn't have any

\

visitors anyway, no one who would come and see me. I did call over to Donny and Babe's a couple of times; other than that, the nursing staff were my visitors. The police made me go over and over every detail of what had happened to me. I was told that as soon as I was released from the hospital, I would have to go before a grand jury to get an indictment for attempted murder.

I tried to get a hold of my mom, but she was on her honeymoon with her doctor. No one seemed to know exactly where she was, because she and her new husband had decided to travel around for a few months after they were married.

Donny and Babe came to see me once or twice. They told me they were moving back to Pennsylvania soon, but I could come over and stay with them until they did. They were going back in less than a month. It was a good thing they offered, because I didn't have anywhere else to go.

They never did have to remove my spleen, but because I was prepped for surgery every morning, I lost over twenty-five pounds in the three or four weeks I was in the hospital.

The day came when they finally released me. All I had to wear were the cutoffs I had on when I first came to the hospital, and they wouldn't even stay up on me anymore. It had been a month since I'd worn anything other than a hospital gown. I just asked a nurse for a safety pin to hold up my shorts.

I had nothing else in the world that was mine at that moment; Albert had moved back to his mother's and had taken all my stuff with him. I hadn't seen Albert since the "roses against the wall" incident, but I was told he'd made numerous attempts to see me or call me. At least I'd been sheltered and safe for a month. Now I was being put back out there, on my own. I had no place to go and nothing to take there if I did. I was terrified Albert would be waiting outside the hospital when I came out, but he wasn't.

The hospital wouldn't discharge me if I didn't have a ride of some kind, so Donny and Babe got me money for cab fare, so I could get to their apartment. It was kind of scary, because I hadn't done anything by myself in more than two years.

I was still very sick and had only been back on solid food for a few days. I hadn't been out of bed in weeks until the end, when I was able to get up and go to the bathroom.

As I walked up the stairs to the apartment, I had a terrible case of déjà vu. I started looking over my shoulder again; Albert was never far from thought. It had been so nice for those last couple of weeks, not to have to deal with worrying for my life or terrified of moving wrong or opening my mouth and saying the wrong thing – or, God forbid, someone else looked at me or said hello.

I worried he would be at the apartment when I got there, waiting for me. Maybe he'd killed Donny and Babe and was waiting for me inside the apartment. It would be many years before those fears were gone, if ever.

When I got to Donny and Babe's place, it felt good to sit down; I was pretty weak. The apartment was full of boxes and activity because the guys were moving back to Scranton, Pennsylvania, where they were from. They were only going to be in town another nine days; after that, I wouldn't have any place to stay.

\

At the moment, I had so many other real problems. I didn't even have a change of underwear. I had to go before a grand jury in the morning, and I had nothing to wear except cutoffs. Thankfully, Donny got a friend of his to give me a couple of things to wear.

I was down to a hundred and six pounds again. That was nice; not the way I lost the weight, but it was nice. This girlfriend of Donny's was so sweet. She gave me at least three shirts, a pair of jeans, a dress, a bra and some underwear. I had the toothbrush, hairbrush, shampoo and lotion from the hospital. The shoes I wore were given to me by one of the nurses at the hospital. That was the entire list of my personal belongings, so I didn't take up much room.

The guys finally had all their stuff packed. They didn't have a bed for me, but they had blankets. I was able to stay there, and they fed me while they could.

The next morning, I went to the courthouse on a bus, again, thanks to the goodness of Donny and Babe. I went all by myself, and I was terrified. I thought a hundred times of getting off the bus and not going in, but I did.

So, I went before a grand jury; it was the strangest experience. This room was a big circle, and it had layers of chairs that graduated up in height. I was down in the center of this circle with a microphone, and all these people were seated above and around me. They asked me a lot of questions, like how many times did he hit you, how hard did he hit you, what did he hit you with. I had to go through the whole ordeal again with them. The officers who came to the hospital were there also; they brought the pictures they'd taken of me.

This took about an hour, and then it was over. The police told me to go home and they'd let me know when the jury had come to a decision, so I went back to the apartment. Less than two hours later, they called and told me they'd granted an indictment for attempted murder against Albert. They said Albert would be picked up and put in jail that day. The sheriff tried to tell me everything would be fine now, but I was terrified. I knew he was going to be so pissed at me, and I was right.

That night at eleven o'clock, Albert called the apartment. Someone else answered it and handed the phone to me.

Before I could even wonder who it was, I heard Albert saying, "April, you are a dead woman. Do you hear me, you bitch? You better get your ass down to that police station first thing in the morning and tell them to drop these fucking charges, or you're dead. You know I mean it. You will die, you bitch!"

I hung up the phone and went in and woke Babe up. I told him Albert had called and I was terrified.

He said, "He must have called from jail. They told you they picked him up, didn't they?"

Five minutes later, Albert was at the door. He was beating on it and screaming through it.

He was yelling, "April, so help me God, if you don't drop the charges against me, I'm going to kill you! You know I will. I don't care how long it takes me, you know I will. If they keep me there for ten years, I'll find you when I get out. I mean it, April; drop the charges, or else you're dead!"

In my mind, I truly believed he meant it.

I'd run in the bathroom as soon as I heard him and shut the door, and I was cowering in a corner. Of course, by this time Donny and Babe were both up and in the living room. One of them was yelling at Albert through the door, telling him they'd called the police and he better get out of there. Albert proceeded to scream back that Donny and Babe were dead, too, for helping me, or "fucking him over", as he put it.

Someone did call the police besides us, but he was gone by the time they got there. They told me that if he came back, call them and they'd drive by every once in a while and check on things. Boy, that made me feel safe! After they left, he started in on the phone, calling constantly; we finally took the phone off the hook.

The next morning, I called the prosecuting attorney. I said, "Look, he's coming over here and threatening me. You told me he would be in jail! You said he wouldn't hurt me."

The attorney said he was sorry, but Albert's parents had bailed him out immediately. The bail had been set high, so they didn't think he'd be able to post it. He told me Albert would be out of jail now until he went to trial, which would be a month or better.

I said, "I can't even see my baby, because he has him. If he isn't in jail, I won't be able to see him at all."

I asked him how I was going to get my baby back. He said, "Well, Albert's parents are apparently giving him full financial support."

At this time, the baby wasn't in need of anything and was being well cared for. If I would just wait for the trial, all my problems would be over. The attorney stated that without a conviction, Albert had as much legal right to him as I did. He also told me I had to get a job and a place to live for the baby and myself before the trial.

\

"I won't be alive for the trial. He'll kill me!" I told him. "The officer kept trying to tell me the law would protect me. Yeah, right!" I said. "I'm terrified! In a week, I won't have a place to stay anymore. What am I supposed to do?"

He asked if I had anyone who would help me, and I said no. I just hung up, in complete despair.

That night, Albert again came to the apartment. This time he didn't yell, he just kept saying through the door how he was going to kill me if I didn't drop the charges.

I called the police, and again he was gone when they got there. The police went to his mom's, and he was there. His mom swore up and down to the police that he hadn't left the house all night. He started in on the phone as soon as the police left his house. I didn't sleep all night.

The next day, I went to the police station. I told them I wanted to drop the charges. They begged me not to.

They said, "You can never file charges against him for this again. You'll be letting him get away with this. Don't do it, please!"

They even called the prosecutor and had him try to talk me out of it. They didn't understand. I wanted to live. The laws are different today; I wouldn't have a choice today. The state would prosecute him anyway, but they were forcing me to make the choice, and I chose life. I'd done what they said, and he was still after me. I just wanted him to leave me alone. So, I eventually dropped the charges.

I called Albert and told him I had. He never said thank you; all he said was, "If you hadn't, April, I would have killed you. You know I would." I asked him if he would let me see the baby. He said he would "if" I'd go talk to his attorney.

His attorney was a young guy who had helped us with a car accident we'd been in a year earlier. So the next day, I went to see him. He told me I didn't have a chance of getting Michael away from Albert, and he was right. I was only seventeen, homeless, jobless, and broke. Albert had his family, a good job, and a place to live. He also had his family's money to back him up.

The attorney told me I should sign the no-fault divorce papers, and I'd be letting Albert have Michael. Once I got a job and a place to live, I could come back in a few months and get Michael legally.

He said, "You won't have a problem getting him back if you do all these things, but without any means of support, you may as well forget it. If you sign these papers, you'll be divorced in twenty-eight days."

I was so tired, I had no answers, and I didn't even understand the questions. As much as I loved Michael, I knew at this time I couldn't even offer him a place to stay. I knew Albert's parents would see to his physical needs, clothes, food, and a place to live, and I knew he would be pampered and cared for. I even knew they loved him and wanted him as their own. I also knew Albert would never let me stay alive if I had Michael without him; not unless I had somewhere to go to get away from him. In my mind, I believed I would change my life and Michael wouldn't be there for long. I didn't see what choices I had.

Albert's lawyer convinced me to sign the paper. I'm sure it was a conflict of interest for him even to consult with me. There again is that twenty-twenty hindsight so clear today. It's so easy for me to sit here today and clearly see my mistakes and the ignorant choices I made, but that was then, and this is now.

I left his office and went back to the apartment. Donny and Babe were leaving in just a few days, so I had to find a place to stay. I called Albert and told him he'd won and I'd signed the papers. I ask him if I could see the baby. He said I could if I came to his mom's, but I could only see him there; I couldn't take him anywhere.

I had no transportation, so I hitchhiked over to his mother's house. I hadn't seen the baby since I went into the hospital over a month earlier. It was a strange sensation. Even though I knew I'd see Albert, I wasn't petrified; just a little nervous. I knew he'd gotten everything he wanted. I'd dropped the charges, and he had the baby. What else could he do to me?

When I went to the door, his mother answered it. She didn't say hello or go to hell; she just yelled over her shoulder, "Albert, she's here." She didn't invite me in; just looked at me and said, "You know, April, we'll take better care of him than you could."

I turned around. I didn't want to hear or see her self-satisfaction.

A moment later, Albert came to the door. His mother looked directly at Albert, ignoring me completely, and said, "The baby's asleep. I don't want you to wake him up yet."

Albert came outside and shut the door on her while she was still talking to him. We hadn't seen each other since the "roses on the wall" incident at the hospital a month earlier. He commented on all the weight I'd lost. I snidely remarked that I had him to thank for that.

He said, "Do you wanna fight?"

I said, "No." I told him I'd come all the way across town and wanted to see the baby.

He said, "When he wakes up, you can."

\

He made a nasty face and asked me if I was still staying at my boyfriend's house. I told him he was being ridiculous, and he made a fist and shook it in my face, gritted his teeth and forcefully said, "You are so lucky you dropped those charges, April, or right now you'd be dead. You're lucky I don't do it still…you never know, I still may."

I didn't even try to talk to him or rationalize with him. I asked him if there was any way he would let me have a few of my clothes. He said everything was stored in his parents' garage and it was too hard to get to.

He opened the door of the garage and said, "If there's anything you can get to without dragging stuff out, go ahead, but I don't want to drag anything out and have to repack it."

As he opened the garage door, I saw what used to be my life, stacked and boxed to the ceiling. I saw a stuffed dog I'd drug around with me before I'd met him; one of the only things I had from my childhood. I didn't ask for it. I didn't have any way to drag a bunch of stuff with me, and I didn't have a place to put it even if I did. I found a garbage bag towards the front of the garage with some dirty clothes in it, and I went through those. I couldn't even wear most of them, since I'd lost over twenty-five pounds. I found a few shirts and one pair of shorts and took those. I also found a purse and took that.

While we were alone in the garage together, he grabbed a handful of my hair and brought my face right up to his. He looked at me with so much hate in his eyes and said, "You are so fucking lucky you aren't dead. I'm almost sorry you didn't give me the chance to finish you off. If you hadn't dropped those charges April, I would have found you, and I would have killed you; no matter where you went or how long it took me. And you know I would have, don't you?"

I whimpered yes, and he clinched his fist and held it right up to my mouth. He wanted to hit me so bad right then, he could taste it. The fact that he didn't gave me a sense of finality. His brutal hold on me was diminishing.

Later, I asked him what had happened to my wedding rings. Someone had cut them off my finger in the hospital because my hand was broken and had swollen up around it. They'd given them to him at the hospital. He took me out to his car and showed them to me. They were hanging from his rearview mirror. He'd taken the stones out of the rings and had them made into earrings.

He said, "They're mine now. I bought them."

I didn't argue. They had no sentimental value to me; I was thinking of selling them so I could eat.

I said I wanted to see the baby and I had come so far to do so. He headed inside and told me to follow him. I reluctantly went into the kitchen with him, and he sat me at the breakfast nook. He left the room, and a few minutes later he came back with the baby in his arms.

Michael immediately stuck out his arms and said, "Mama." He had the biggest smile on his face.

I grabbed him and held him to me. At first, it was the best medicine anyone could have given me. I didn't realize how much I'd lived for this moment.

Albert's mother came in and sat right across from me. She wasn't even going to let me see him for a moment without her being right there. She saw my regret and second thoughts and started telling me how much they could do for him that I couldn't. I just wanted to take my baby and go home, but I didn't have a home to go to, and they weren't going to let me take him there even if I did.

His sisters, dad and brother were all in the kitchen with us by now. I felt so confined and outnumbered. I asked Albert if we could take him outside and sit in the yard.

His mother immediately said, "I don't think that's a good idea. He's had a cold, and I think he should stay inside."

They didn't trust me to be alone with him, even for a minute. What they didn't realize was I didn't have anywhere to take him and no way to get him there. Did they think I had someone outside waiting to help me? Yeah, right. I wish I did have someone to help me. If I had, I may have just taken him and run away again. It still hadn't hit me that I could never run from Albert.

Finally, I had to go; it was the hardest thing I've ever had to do. I had to put the baby in his mother's arms and walk away from him; he was screaming, "Mama, mama, mama" as I let him go. He started crying and reaching for me. I almost couldn't leave. I could hear him yelling for me as I walked down the street, even though they'd taken him back inside. I don't remember how I got back to the apartment; I know I cried all night long.

They're truly lucky I didn't see him before I signed that paper, or I never would have. My heart hurt so bad, it was worse than any physical pain I'd ever endured. It was even worse the next time I saw him.

The next day, I called a friend I'd known for a short time in-between the home and Albert. She'd lived by my mother, and I remember her dad was a building inspector for the city of Tucson. He also raised Weimaraner dogs. It was so sad; he raised them to sell them to

\

junk yards as guard dogs. Almost one hundred of them were raised in a giant pen together. This pen was circular and had wooden walls that had to be 8 feet tall. They weren't pets, and most of them were mean. They were so beautiful, though; they were silver and had red eyes.

Once, I remember being at her house and some of the dogs came meandering up to us; one of them had the leg of another dog in its mouth. They would get in terrible fights out in this pen. If one died in the fight, the rest of them would tear it apart, I guess that was part of their terrible existence. Being a compassionate animal lover, to this day I can't forget the lives of those poor dogs. Mary's property was very large and rural. It sat right up against the railroad tracks, and I remember a couple of the dogs got out one night and got hit by a train.

This girl's name was Mary; I told her of my predicament and asked her if there was any way I could stay with her for a little while. She said her dad couldn't know about it, but I could stay for a night or two. Her mother had died when she was very young, so she'd been raised by her dad and was very independent. Mary wasn't a makeup and dresses kind of girl; she wore jeans and had two horses. That was how I'd met her, because I love horses.

The night before Donny and Babe left to go back to Pennsylvania, they took me to the movies. We went to see "The Exorcist." When we were standing in line, people were giving out pamphlets, warning about the movie. That movie caused a lot of controversy when it came out, especially for me. After being at the home and having religion beat into me, that was probably not a good movie for me to see, but I was glad they took me with them. I'd only been to one or two movies prior to that, and all of them at the drive-in with my mom and the kids, or Albert.

\

The next day they left, and so did I. I only had one garbage bag full of stuff, so I took it and hitchhiked over to Mary's. Her dad was home when I got over there, so she had me put my stuff in an old car on the property next to her house. Actually, there was more than one abandoned car out there; the place was almost like a construction site, or maybe I should say "junk yard".

Her dad wasn't a very pleasant man; Mary never wanted to be at home when he was there. Luckily, he was gone a lot. She'd lived like that for most of her life; on her own, pretty much.

In Tucson, it's so hot during the day, you really shouldn't ride horses, because the heat can kill them if you ride them too hard. For that reason, a lot of people ride at night or in the evening. The first night I was there, we went riding on her horses. It was great! We rode until two or three in the morning. We rode over to some friends of hers who also had horses, and I met them. The horse she let me ride was twenty-six years old, but she could hold her own. I fell in love with her. I'd always dreamed of owning my own horse.

My mom used to tease me by saying, "April, if you ever find a horse walking along the side of the road that doesn't belong to anyone, you can have him." I actually used to watch for loose horses (when I was little).

The next few days, we rode every night and slept during the day while her dad was at work. On the weekend when he was off, I slept in the old car out in the yard so he wouldn't know I was there. One night when I was in her room with her, he came home drunk (I think he was drunk, anyway) and tried to get into her room. She had two locks on her door, and she jumped up and locked both of them. She told me to be quiet and he would eventually go away. He was banging on the door, saying she'd better let him in. I was cowering in the corner (I cowered at the slightest threat of violence. I would for years, thanks to Albert).

Poor Mary; I didn't realize at the time just what she was dealing with, or how long she'd had to deal with it. Thankfully, that's one thing I hadn't had to deal with in my short life. Apparently, Mary had put the locks on her door herself. So, we both avoided her dad as much as possible.

Each night we would get her friends who had horses together, and from five to ten of us would go riding together. We all cut through this trailer park because it was a shortcut to the riverbed through there, and the riverbeds were the best places to ride. They were all sand and easy to ride on, but the horses' hoofs made a lot of noise on the pavement in this trailer park, and this was, like, eleven or so at night.

One night, this guy came out of his trailer and started yelling at us. "Get those horses out of here! This is private property!" He was cussing and yelling, so we hurried through there.

After we'd ridden for four or five hours, we had to head home. We had to go back the same way we'd come, and the same man yelled at us again; he was really mad.

The following night, we again headed out on the horses, and they again headed for the trailer park. The path through the trailer park that led down to the riverbed was miles shorter than going around another way. I didn't want to go back through there, and I tried to tell them so, but everyone was saying, "Come on, April, there's no other way to get there." So, we all started back through the trailer park.

\

We made it through the park to this field behind it that led down to the riverbed. Again, the clip clop of the hooves was definitely loud. We'd just come to the edge of the field when two sets of car lights came on behind us. All of a sudden, this guy in a pickup truck and another one in a car came roaring out of the bushes after us. All of us started galloping as fast as we could, or as fast as our horses could. This idiot in the truck was driving as fast as he could, right on my butt; mine, because I was on a twenty-three-year-old horse, so I was in the rear of this herd of teenagers and horses. If it hadn't been for his headlights, I would have died for sure. There were holes and bushes, and cactus everywhere. I literally rode for my life; if my horse would have stumbled, the guy in the truck would have run over me for sure.

We all made it safely to the riverbed somehow. Needless to say, we never cut through the trailer park again. That was a terrifying experience, but I still rode every day and loved every minute of it.

Like I said, I'm not proud of most of the decisions I made when I was young; I'm just telling it like it is. I'm still trying to find out why I made most of them. I guess that's really what life is, figuring out what we did wrong, why, and what the long-term consequences are.

One of these times, a bunch of us went riding together and we were all doing acid; I told you I was a follower. We'd borrowed two horses so a bigger group of us could all ride together; there must have been ten of us there. We let a girl who didn't know how to ride very well ride the mare I usually rode, because she was so gentle. The horse I was on was a stallion, and this guy named Steve was also on a stallion. Unfortunately, the horses weren't familiar with each other, and from the start these two stallions didn't get along. The acid was starting to take effect as we were riding down the road together. All of a sudden, the horse I was on kicked at the horse Steve was on. It missed Steve's horse but got him right on the shin. It laid his leg wide open all the way to the bone. What I could see looked so nasty, and here we all were, tripping on acid; as I said, I'm not proud of that at all, I'm just being honest. We found something to tie around this horrific gash in Steve's leg and went on. We didn't know what else to do. None of us was in any shape to deal with hospitals or doctors. I don't know how he made it, but we rode the rest of the night with his leg going unattended.

After the sun came up and we were able to deal with reality, we took Steve to the hospital. His leg was broken and needed more than thirty stitches. Poor Steve; that had to be painful.

That wasn't the only time we were a group of stupid teenagers, and poor Steve always got the worst of it. We didn't always go everywhere on horseback. One time, we loaded eleven people and two dogs into a '56 Chevy and went to the foothills. We hiked in over rocks and up cliffs at Sabino Canyon. It took us over an hour to get to this particular place. There were cliffs people could dive into the water from; it was such a beautiful place. Tucson sits at the base of the Catalina Mountains, which has so many neat waterways that wind through the foothills. It's gorgeous! This was a popular place to go, apparently, and they all knew about it. When we got there, the guys had climbed up and started diving into the water below. These cliffs were pretty high up, so a lot of us stayed at the bottom and watched. We were lying out on towels, playing with the dogs and watching the guys dive off the rocks. It was a beautiful place, and we were all having fun. Steve (the same guy who had been kicked by the horse) did a cannonball; you know, you grab your feet and roll into a ball as you're entering the water. Unfortunately, when Steve hit the water, he hadn't rolled his legs up like he was supposed to and hit the water flat. After the water cleared, we could see Steve floating face down. He didn't move as he just kept floating there for a minute. At first, we thought he was kidding us. In fact, we were laughing and ribbing him to stop the shenanigans until we saw blood slowly surround him in the water. Some of the guys dove in and pulled him to the shore.

It was so gross: he had hit his knees to his mouth when he tucked, and his teeth had gone all the way through his lips. It was so scary. He was conscious and alert, but he knew he was hurt. Luckily, he didn't know how it looked; it really was hard to look at him.

So, we hauled all these people, dogs, coolers and Steve back the hour-long hike to the car. We had to go over rocks and ravines, and we even had to use ropes once in a while. It was horrible. Eventually, we got him to the hospital. Here we were eleven kids and two dogs, at the emergency room. They got Steve's teeth out of his lips. His biorhythms must have been down that year.

Another time, in that same '56 Chevy (we'd all been drinking), and again there was a record number of us in this car. We'd pulled over to the side of road so someone could throw up, and a police officer pulled up behind us, got out and came up to the door of the car. Lucky him; one of the guys in the front seat leaned out of the window and puked, right in front of the cop. I don't remember why not, but I'm pretty sure none of us was taken to jail or anything, at least I wasn't. Like I said, Stupid is as stupid does. I think the driver got some kind of ticket, and I think the driver was Steve. Poor Steve; all this stuff happened within a two or three-week period.

Anyway, Mary let me ride her horse over to see the baby one day. I rode over to Albert's parents' house all by myself. It was spooky because it was over five miles, and three miles of it was through residential neighborhoods, with traffic and people to deal with, but I did it.

Believe it or not, Albert didn't give me any grief when I got there. He even let me hold the baby and ride him around a field across the street from their house. The baby loved it. Albert's family even stood around outside and watched. They would never let me out of their sight with him again. They were right, too; if I could have, I would have taken him and never seen them again. Right or wrong, I can't help it. I would have.

It was hard to deal with seeing Albert or his family (it always felt like entering a lions' den), but seeing the baby was wonderful. He was walking without that baby wobble, and he was forming his own personality. I absolutely could not handle leaving Michael. He cried and yelled for his mommy, reaching out for me and begging me to take him back in my arms. It broke my heart, it broke his heart also, and it ate at me constantly.

Ten or twelve days after I moved into Mary's car, she told me of this older "cowboy-type man" who owned this cool house out in the desert. Mary said he may let me stay there if I would do some cleaning for him. So, I went with her out to the desert and met him. His name was Harold, and he was probably in his late fifties. The house he lived in had once been a beautiful home. It was made in a big, square horseshoe pattern. The house was built so all the rooms had a door that opened to a yard with a big swimming pool and garden at the center. It also had a little guest house, off to the side. It had been terribly let go and unkempt since his divorce six years earlier. What a shame; it could have been beautiful.

He told me he'd be glad to have me; he had a room for me and everything. When he showed me this room, I was shocked: it was all decorated in pink. It must have been his daughter's room at one time. It had a pedestal bed that sat in the center of the room, and of course a door out to the pool and garden. I was ecstatic. He wanted me to do his laundry and a little cleaning, and he seemed like a really nice man. He spent most of his time at the local country western taverns in the area and had a drinking problem.

His lifestyle also included allowing all these young people to hang out there. He had two twenty-three-year-old men renting the guest house out back. The two guys told me they would pay me, too, if I did some of their laundry and cleaning. This was too good to be true, plus I got to stay in this cool house. The pool was all green and looked like a pond, but I could go out and lay by it in privacy, and the house was so neat. It was out of town about five miles, so it was hard for me to go anywhere, but my options at the time were either staying at Mary's in the car or this.

I was happy; I had my own room, and a nice one at that. This man was once fair-to-do and upper class, but now he was a lost divorcee. He had once had a wife and three children. They were gone now, and so was his life. You could tell the house had been really nice once. As I said, the room I stayed in was pink in décor, pretty but dusty, and it just felt like it had been empty for a long time, but for me it was like a dream. This house had a couple of fireplaces and a lot of brick and rock work in it. Harold never bothered me; he was just a really nice man. I bet with my luck, you thought he would turn out to be a pervert, huh? There was always a party going on at his house. The way the house was built was party heaven, and because it was five miles out of town in the desert, no one ever complained about noise or traffic. The wall surrounding the house was about eight feet tall and a foot thick. At every party, people either walked on and sat up on that wall or pushed each other off it. They could get as wild as they wanted, and no one bothered them.

At some of the parties, people would get pushed into the pool, but no one got in it voluntarily; it hadn't been cleaned in years and looked and smelled like a pond.

Harold would usually go to the country bars in town each night, so he didn't really hang out at the house. A lot of the kids with no supervision would just trash the place. It was a sad situation that couldn't last very much longer. Harold's whole life, as well as his world and home, were hanging on by a thread. I never had any delusions of this lasting, but it was a temporary solution for me.   Since we were so far from town, I very rarely got to go to town and see the baby.

Mary would come and see me or take me to ride once or twice, whenever she could snag the truck from her dad. So, I stayed there for free and cleaned up after parties, and I did Harold's laundry. One time, Mary took me up to Mt. Lemon; her dad owned a cabin there. We stayed for a week and had one constant party. We ran out of gas and tried to walk through the woods down the mountain, but we got lost. It took us 8 hours to find our way out and back to the road. Another time, we ran out of gas and Mary coasted all the way down the mountain, 40 miles. She would let the truck get going at really high speeds so we could make it up the next hill. It was horrifying, but we made it all the way down. I don't know how I survived any of my ignorant antics.

The guest house guys who paid me to do their laundry were generous with their money, and their drugs. They showed me a new trick: running up. Yes, I mean using a needle. These two young men had money to spend, too; one of them owned a Corvette. What did they do for a living? Well, they (as I learned later) ripped off drug dealers. They would set up drug deals and then rip the people off instead of selling them drugs or paying them money. Apparently, they did this for a living. I really didn't know too much about their business, except one time they came home all out of breath and sweaty. They kept looking out the window and were apparently scared of someone. I'm lucky none of their ordeals ended in a gunfight out at the house. Of course, I wasn't there very long. I wonder if they ever grew old.

Those guys, like every young person I knew at the time, did every kind of drug there was, like acid, peyote, cocaine, speed, pot, liquor, but these guys did heroin, too. They were the only people I knew who had ever tried it. At first, I would go out to their little guest house and just watch them shoot up. They tried to talk me into trying it, but I didn't want to stick a needle in my arm. I did agree to snort it, and I liked it. After two or three times, I liked it enough to let them talk me into putting a needle into my arm. I hate to tell you this, but it was the most incredible experience I've ever had. I can understand completely how people can get hooked on heroin. I'm in no way saying this is a good thing; I'm just being honest and telling you my experience. The first few times I let them do it to me, then one time they helped me do it to myself. I'd only done it to myself that one time.

This house they lived in had big, high beamed ceilings; the whole place was very rustic. They would keep their spoon and syringe up above one of the beams in the ceiling. I watched them put it away once, and they got it down more than once. They would leave the cotton in the spoon and reuse it, because all the stuff in the cotton wouldn't always be used up. Now believe me, this isn't a pretty picture, but then not much of reality is. One day, knowing they were both gone, I went over to get their laundry, which was over at Harold's. Ignorance and curiosity got the better of me. I crawled up and got the spoon and needle down, added water to the cotton, and did it to myself using one of their dirty needles. I didn't even know what I was doing, really. This was in '73, and AIDS wasn't heard of. Unfortunately, AIDS isn't the only thing that can happen to you from being stupid with drugs and needles. Again, that saying from Forrest Gump comes to mind: "Stupid is as stupid does." Honestly, I was more ignorant than stupid, and I made some very bad choices. I cringe at some of the choices I did make, but that was then, and the cringing didn't come until later.

During my time at Harold's house, I tried to contact my mother more than once, but apparently she was still on her honeymoon, or whatever she was doing. Their honeymoon consisted of many trips, and I would later learn they'd taken my three youngest siblings on a two-month road trip of sorts. They'd stopped at one point in Rapid City, South Dakota, and while they were there they'd purchased a beautiful home. At that time, I didn't know where they were. I think I eventually found her through my aunt Reta, her sister. I believe I'd spoken to her on the phone when I was in the hospital, but I'm not sure of that. I did finally talk to her after I'd been at Harold's for over a month, and I told her of my predicament.

After all the "I told you so"s, I was shocked when my mom told me they were coming to Tucson in two weeks. She also told me she'd help me try to get Michael back and give us a place to live for a while. That was so unexpected, I couldn't believe it. I was ecstatic, and it gave me some hope.

For the next two weeks, I waited for her. I had something to look forward to. I went to town to try to see the baby at Albert's mother's house, but when I went there, they told me Albert was gone and I couldn't see the baby unless he was there.

I had to wait for five hours until Mary could come back and get me, and he didn't come back the entire time, so I walked around my old street.

One street over from Albert's house, on the street where my mom had lived, a guy I knew from my high school was out in his yard. He said hello to me, so I went over and talked to him. I was invited into his house, where gave me a beer. We started talking; he was a really popular guy when I was in school, and good looking. He saw an easy opportunity and took it. I was an easy opportunity.

Somehow, he talked me right into bed; I was so in need of someone to even pretend to like me that I was an easy mark for anyone. It was the first sexual experience I had had with someone else since the day I met Albert; it was a little ironic it was with a neighbor of his.

A week later, I got another ride into town and went back to see the baby. Again, I wasn't allowed to see him, so I went back over to that boy's house around the corner. For some reason, he wouldn't see me. His friend came to the door and told me he was sick. I was officially a slut now. I'd never been rejected by a boy before, and it was a weird sensation. It would be just another learning experience, and later I would understand more of his attitude problem.

One day, Harold came home with a puppy and asked me if I wanted the dog. I squealed with delight and said of course I wanted it. He said, "Then it's yours." I didn't think of the responsibility or how I would feed her; at the moment, I just knew I had something to love that would love me back. I named her "Brandy", because that song was very popular then. I enjoyed every moment of her company. She was about 3 months old, and the cutest thing. I don't know where he got her or why he gave her to me, but I fell in love with her immediately. She was a quick learner, and very smart. Brandy was housebroken within just a few days. We spent every moment together, and she even slept with me. Harold bought her a bag of dog food, and we both enjoyed playing with her.

Red-headed stepchild

My life from the divorce until now was in a sort of limbo;
actually, my entire existence had all been pretty much in limbo. I kept
telling myself that when my mom got there, things would be better.
She'd help me get Michael back, and we'd go live with her and my new
stepdad. I'd only met my stepdad once, at their wedding, six or seven
months earlier. He seemed OK, although I didn't talk to him for more
than a couple of minutes.

For the next two weeks, I didn't leave Harold's house at all; I just
waited for my mother. A few days before they were due to arrive, I
started feeling bad. I wanted to sleep all the time, I itched all over, and I
was again losing weight. Of course, my diet consisted of whatever I
could scrounge from Harold's fridge, which wasn't much; he hardly ever
ate there.

The day they were to arrive, I went to bed to wait for them; I
absolutely couldn't stay awake. Hours later, I was awakened by my
mother shaking me and the puppy licking my face.

The first thing she said to me was, "What's wrong with you? We've been banging on that door for thirty minutes, didn't you hear us?"

I was still groggy when I told her, "No."

I sat up and immediately started scratching my arms. My two little sisters came running up to me and gave me a hug. It was so good to see them; they'd both grown so much that I barely recognized them.

My new stepfather came over to us with a frown on his face and no hello to me. He abruptly said, "Where's your stuff?" I told him I didn't have much stuff, and he said, "Then get it together, now." He abruptly left the house and went back to wait for us at the car.

It wasn't the welcome I'd dreamed of. I didn't really know what to expect from him. He'd just turned into an instant father of five and a grandpa of one by marrying my mom. He'd never even been married before. I didn't know how he would treat me. I'm sure he wasn't thrilled to be dealing with my problems, but I never expected what I got.

It was horrible from the very beginning. As usual, there had been a party there at the house the night before, and there were beer bottles everywhere. I think there were a few people still passed out around the pool. My mother is so judgmental anyway, and it wasn't like she didn't have reason to wish things were different, but she ate this up. I hadn't seen my mom since her wedding, so I was hoping for a hug and some motherly comfort (I'd just been through more than most people would deal with their entire lives), but she started yelling at me from the time she woke me up. On top of that, I'd acquired my dog, so we had to deal with that right away. I don't know how I did it, but they allowed me to bring Brandy with me. She was all I had. Everything else I had fit into a paper bag. It didn't take long to get me and my stuff out of there.

\

I do realize everything she didn't like about my situation and life, but I was just trying to survive. If she'd come a month earlier, she would have found me sleeping in an abandoned car, and a month before that in a hospital linen closet. I thought I'd done pretty well for myself.

They took me with them to a cheap motel, and I do mean cheap. He drove to six motels before he found the cheapest one. We stayed there for a couple of days while they did the stuff they'd planned to do in Tucson. Remember, my mom had lived there off and on for a long time. She had friends to see and business to take care of while she was there; they hadn't come there just for me. In fact, I was only going with them "because" they were coming to Tucson. They wouldn't have come just for me.

One afternoon, they took me to an attorney and the courthouse so Pat could get copies of all my divorce papers, etc. The attorney told us it would take about a month and would cost about a thousand dollars to get Michael back from Albert. I was ecstatic; it sounded easier than I thought it would be.

I didn't know much about this man, my new stepfather, but I did know he was a doctor and a lawyer, and he had some money. My mother had said he was going to help me…or so I thought.

After we spent two whole days going to lawyers and the courthouse and doing all this legal stuff we'd done, Pat sat me down outside the county courthouse and said, "At this time, April, I don't think I want to help you with this matter. You don't have a job, so you have no way of repaying me, and I don't have a month to put into this."

So I sat there, stunned, wondering why he'd just gone to all the trouble of finding out what had to be done if he had no intention of helping me. I was devastated.

I said, "What am I supposed to do now?"

He told me he would allow me to come to South Dakota, live with them and get a job. Then I could do it for myself.

So, they wanted me to go off and leave Michael there. I suppose his offer was generous to someone he didn't even know, but it didn't make me feel good. I didn't understand why he'd made it seem like he was going to help me. I got the feeling he was enjoying this. I didn't know if that "constant smile" he wore all the time meant he was happy, or happy you were unhappy.

I went into a state of depression. I didn't feel good anyway, and I hadn't felt good since the last hospital visit I'd had. My diet had been either terrible or nonexistent, and I'd been drinking, doing drugs and living in people's cars since I got out of the hospital. I was down to under a hundred pounds and just feeling lousy.

I spent the next day in bed at the motel, and I mean all day. Mom and Pat went to see some people or something, and I couldn't get up. They left me with the kids at the motel while they were gone. Even with my sisters and the dog there, running around in a motel room, I slept all day. I was just so tired; I didn't even get up until they came in hours later and made me get out of bed.

The girls were sitting next to me on the bed, watching TV; all of a sudden, Pat grabbed the girl's arms, pulled them back off the bed, and told them to get away from me. My mother asked him what he was doing.

He said, "Look at her, Myrna, she's all yellow. I guarantee you she's contagious!"

Pat made me come into the bathroom, where there was better light. Once he inspected my eyes and skin, he loudly announced, "She has hepatitis!"

I was like, *OK, now can I go back to bed?* I really didn't know what it meant or what I was supposed to do about it.

Remember the needle and cotton I so bravely used without knowing what I was doing? When he asked me if I'd been using needles, I said "No." How could I admit to them I'd done that? So I lied and said no. I hadn't done it enough to have track marks on my arms or anything, and I have freckles.

Anyway, he took it for granted that I had the other type of hepatitis. Apparently, there are two types of hepatitis: one you can get by drinking after someone or eating something they made or touched, and the other kind you can get only by blood transfer or drinking yourself to death. I'm sure I had the second kind, but because I'd lied, he thought I had the other kind. So, he went to the pharmacy (he's a doctor, remember) and got some "immunoglobulin", then gave my mom and both of my sisters a shot to prevent them from contracting it.

From that moment, my color turned quickly; within a day or two, it was a beautiful lemon color, and it darkened day by day. I also had no energy, no appetite, couldn't stay awake, and I itched all the time.

As I stayed there, sick in the motel room, I started learning more and more about my new stepfather. I learned he didn't think much of taking on a woman with all these kids and their problems, and he had a real thing about money, especially parting with it. I found out he was the only son of a wealthy older couple, and his money was old money. They'd been rich southern plantation owners, way back before the Civil War, or at least his ancestors had. His father had owned one the biggest, and oldest, Ford dealerships in Oklahoma City for over fifty years.

He was so different from anybody in our entire family. His parents were well into their forties when they had him, and he was an only child. He'd never been married before, had gone to school almost all his life, had a medical degree and law degree, and he was also an ordained minister. Pat had more degrees than everyone in my entire family history put together. He'd graduated from Vanderbilt University with one of his degrees, and he'd been in a fraternity and all that goes along with that. I'd never really met anyone like him. I admired him and wanted him to like me, but that was not to be. He was very wary of my financial needs, and my lack of a future. He'd been raised in a lifestyle that was foreign to me, and mine was foreign to him, and it was also absolutely intolerable to him. In his world, everyone had gone to school and had future plans for financial success. Poverty was a mortal sin in his eyes. I was a failure in his eyes, even though I was only seventeen, and on top of everything else, I was now very much a burden to him.

The entire time he'd dated my mother, I'd been out of the picture. My younger brother David had been sent to my real father's over a year earlier, and he'd also been out of the picture since they met. Up until this point, he only had to deal with my youngest brother, Billy, and my two little sisters, Shelley and Darla. On this trip, Billy wasn't even with them; he was visiting his real daddy's family back in Kansas.

My mom's new husband had many issues. Pat didn't believe in divorce or second marriages, because of his religious beliefs; but somehow in his mind, he could rationalize, find acceptance and justification in this particular relationship. He even accepted the three youngest kids, Billy, Shelley, and Darla, because legally they didn't have fathers. Billy's father had been killed, and the two girls had never known their fathers, so he rationalized acceptance for them. The only reason he accepted my mother was that her last legal husband was dead. That made my mother a legal widow, not a divorcee; until death do you part.

Pat really had a problem with me and David, because our father was still alive. In fact, my new stepfather's religious beliefs had almost kept him from marrying my mom, because she'd been divorced before. Soon, he found a way to overcome that minor detail, because legally she'd been widowed, after she'd been divorced. Also, she'd become a Christian after her sinful past, so everything prior to that was forgiven.

I learned later that before they were married, Pat had gone to Tucson and spent a month talking to my mom's old friends and church mates. He went there to "verify" that the changes in her were valid and true.

I wasn't kidding around that he was a strange person, and he couldn't "forgive" me for having a father still alive somewhere. It didn't matter to him that I'd only met the man twice in my life. I really can't blame him for the way he felt about us, since he never had a child or had even been around many. I don't think he'd ever been a child either. His parents were old when they had him, and I don't think they were gentle people, at least his mother wasn't. He was an interruption in her life, and she treated him as such. Maybe I'm wrong, but I don't think he was a planned child. I know he had a lot of issues with his mother.

His mother was very dominant, and his father drank. I think his father was an unhappy man. I'm not sure of this; I only met him two or three times. His father was very nice to me, but his mother was a little cold. She was a prim and proper, old southern belle, and her son had married an ex-floozy who had five children and a grandchild. So, I almost felt sorry for the guy.

Anyway, he was a little strange, and he really had a thing about money. He would drive all over town to save two cents a gallon on gas, and he wouldn't take us out to eat, even though we were staying in a motel. He would let my mom get a package of bologna, bread and mustard, then he "allowed" her to make one sandwich apiece and we ate in the room. Nothing had changed for the better that I could see ever since I'd lived at home.

He made my mom make some tea at the motel, but he wouldn't buy sugar for the tea because it was too expensive. I didn't care much what we did or didn't eat; I was getting sicker by the hour and really didn't care much about anything but sleeping. I think we stayed in Tucson for about another week, and I slept as much as they'd let me. I just couldn't wake up, I stayed so tired.

One day, he came into the motel room and said, "We're leaving tomorrow, I have things to do." So at 4 am, we were on the road.

They'd bought that house in Rapid City, South Dakota, and Pat had gotten a job at Dow Chemical. I don't know what he did there, but he wasn't practicing medicine at this time, "except on us." He stated he needed to get back there and take care of business, but first we were going to stop in Denver, Colorado, so he could see his cousins there. I just wanted to get someplace where I could sleep a lot; I was really sick.

So, they loaded me and the girls, Mom, Pat, my puppy, everything I owned, and everything they'd brought for a month-long trip into my mom's 1968 Toyota and headed for Rapid City, South Dakota, via Denver, Colorado.

I hated leaving Michael there, but the last time I saw Albert, he told me not to get my hopes up about seeing much of the baby. His attitude was one of complete power. He told me I'd given up custody, and it was up to him when or if I saw Michael at all. Albert grabbed my hair again, put his fist in my face, and reminded me I was lucky to be alive.

He said, "I still haven't forgotten that you had me arrested, April, and I should kill you for that. I'll get you for that someday, April, don't think I won't..."

So, it wasn't going to be pleasant whenever I had to deal with him again. I'd been hoping someone else would help me deal with him. I was terrified of him, but it wasn't going to be Mom and Pat who helped me; they didn't want to deal with him either. Although I have to say, my mom wasn't happy Pat had decided not to help me fight for Michael. I think she felt the same way I did about it, but she herself was still just getting to know this man. Married or not, they hadn't even known each other more than a year or so.

Burning my fingers and still touching the stove.

The trip to Denver was horrible. We were riding in one of those little Toyotas, the ones that aren't much bigger than a Volkswagen Bug. The back seat had a hump in the middle of it, and there were five of us and a dog.

My sisters and I switched seats every once in a while, so none of us had to sit on the hump for the whole trip. I still just wanted to sleep, which wasn't easy to do in that little car. During the trip, I was learning more and more about my new "stepdad".

Pat wasn't very personable. He didn't like other people's children; in fact, he didn't like too much of anything. He wasn't happy about this addition to what he already thought of as "too many new people in his life." He wanted my mom, not her excess baggage, especially excess baggage with problems. I was hers before she was his, and I didn't have anywhere else to go. I didn't like the situation either; I also wished things were different.

He should have realized I would be a factor in her life before he married her. I guess she thought she was rid of us forever. We weren't even introduced to the guy, at least David and I weren't, and Pat was quick to remind me he didn't expect to be dealing with my problems when he married my mom.

Pat and my mother "discussed" or fought over what to do with me once we got to Denver the entire trip. He was adamant I was "not" going over to his relatives' house with hepatitis. She asked what she was supposed to do with me. At one point, he actually mentioned having me stay in the car while we were there, and they were going to be there for five days! My mom sarcastically asked, "Where is she supposed to go to the bathroom, Pat?" He decided he would have to find a cheap motel and put me there.

During the trip to Denver, I had a lot of time to think of the predicament I was in. I thought of the miles we were putting between me and Tucson. I was ambivalent about that, because I loved the freedom of not having Albert on my back, but of course I had a broken heart about the baby. I didn't want to be going back to live with my mother again, I physically felt terrible, and my stepdad didn't like me. I just wanted to get somewhere and lie down and cry.

The scenery coming into the mountains of Colorado was beautiful, but Pat wouldn't stop to enjoy any of it. He was on a mission to get to Denver without stopping at all. I swear, he only stopped twice from Tucson, Arizona, to Denver, Colorado, and that was because my mom forced him to get gas and let us go to the bathroom.

He refused to buy any fast food, so we again ate sandwiches prepared before our departure. I was noticing that Pat and my mom fought all the time; didn't they just get married a few months ago? Pat resented spending even a dollar if it wasn't absolutely a must (it was weird), so they fought over everything. Mom told him to stop and get gas; he told her he wanted to look for it somewhere cheaper. Mom yelled that the car was almost empty and we needed to go to the bathroom; Pat would tell her he could make it farther. During every battle, he would always have this smirk on his face. I'd been in many situations where people couldn't afford luxuries in their lives, but he resented luxury of any kind. In fact, he seemed to enjoy denying even the basics to us.

Once we arrived in Denver, he took us to the worst part of town possible. I swear, it was so run down and spooky, it's hard to describe. Pat found a motel on Santa Fe Drive right next to the railroad track that was under five dollars a night (after looking at 10 different motels). I swear it's true; I mean, it was nineteen seventy-four, but you still couldn't find a motel room for under five dollars, at least not most places. The room was gross; it had no phone or TV, the furniture was sparse and tacky, and it had stains all over the mattress. It was down a dark hall, and there was a bar on the corner. It was such a spooky place.

They let me keep the puppy with me; thank God, because I used her as a Kleenex because I cried into her coat all night long. I had no money or food, no phone or television; I just sat and listened to the noises outside of the room, and there were so many of them. There were people yelling at each other outside my door, and sometime during the middle of the night there was an actual fight outside my door. I just stayed huddled on the bed with my puppy, but I couldn't even take her outside, because I was too scared to go out of the room. The worst part was the bathroom was down the hall.

Eventually, the night ended and day came; I'd survived. Mom and Pat didn't come back to see me until almost eleven o'clock the next morning, but they brought good news. Pat was going to leave me there another night and had found a place for me to stay while they were in town.

Where fate takes us

Apparently, the relatives Pat had come to visit had just moved into this big, beautiful home, in a gated neighborhood called "Bow Mar." I had never even been inside a house like these people had, and this was where my family was staying while I was in the three dollar-a-night motel.

My stepfather's cousins still owned the house they'd just moved out of. It was on the market for sale, but it was empty (and I do mean empty). They were going to let me stay over at their recently vacated house. It was beautiful, too, with big white pillars out in front, a bay window in the living room, and big blue spruce trees in the yard. The house was two stories, with a finished basement. It was wonderful, except it had no furniture, but even so it was way better than that motel. Mom and Pat brought me a bright orange, not very thick swimming pool air mattress with a blanket, and that was about it.

They left me and the puppy there, and off they went to stay in the rich relative's house. Mom did bring me a plate of food from the new house eventually, but other than that, just a roll of toilet paper. Once it got dark, it was bedtime, because there was no electricity, no phone, and no food. I didn't even have a glass to drink out of that first day.

It was really boring; I would sit in the bay window and look out most of the time. I checked the house out, but that only took half an hour. Thank God I had the puppy. I took her out in the back yard and sat on the grass and played with her.

Even though the house was nice, I felt inadequate to be there. Since I had nothing to do, I sat and imagined what it must be like to grow up in a house like that; I had a lot of time to think. At night it was spooky, this big, empty house, but I did have the puppy.

The next day, Mom and Pat's cousin (the owner of the house) came to bring me some food. She seemed very nice and sincerely concerned about my predicament. Apparently, I could be around other people, as long as they didn't drink after me or use the toilet I used, stuff like that. It was my own fault; if I would have told them the truth about how I'd gotten hepatitis, then he would have known I had the kind of hepatitis that isn't contagious (except from blood exchange) and I could have stayed with them, or maybe he should have taken me to a doctor.

The woman who owned the house seemed appalled at my living conditions. She told me the next time my mom came over, she would send a book for me to read, and a glass, and a couple of dishes. I didn't have any food anyway, but it was nice to see some compassion. She apologized for there being no electricity, but I didn't have anything to plug in anyway. I sincerely thanked her for her kindness.

Someone came to bring me something to eat once each day; other than that, I didn't see anyone except the lady working in her yard next door.

The evening of the fifth day, I was feeling so sick. I had terrible pains in my stomach, and I was so bright yellow, it was almost pretty…"pretty weird."

I mentioned how sick I was to my mother when she brought me my food, but she said, "You're sick, I'm sure you don't feel good, April. I don't know what you want me to do about it. I'll be back tomorrow."

That night, I was in agony; I could hardly get up to go to the bathroom. It was all I could do to get up off my air mattress and let the dog out. I got worse as the night progressed. By the next morning, I was in really bad shape. I absolutely could not stand or walk; I was in so much pain, it's hard to describe. Every time I tried to stand up, I would be doubled over in pain. All I could do was just lie on the floor holding my stomach and cry. At this point, I was almost incoherent. I knew something was terribly wrong with me, and I figured it was the hepatitis. I didn't know what hepatitis was or what it did to you, but I knew I wanted it gone.

They never came to bring me my daily rations at any specific time; I didn't have a clock anyway. I'd waited as long as I could, then I was starting to pass out. I still had my nightgown on from the night before, but I was unable to do anything about that. I went outside in my nightgown and crawled to the house next door, where I'd seen the woman working in the yard. The last thing I remember is ringing her doorbell, and the next thing I remember, I was waking up in an ambulance.

The next memory I have is waking up again in the hospital, and this time my mother was standing over me. As soon as my eyes were open, she got down in my face with the look of Satan and screamed, "Do you know what's wrong with you? Do you know what you have? Do you? You have the worst case of VD this hospital has ever seen!"

I was still trying to wake up enough to figure out where I was. This must be a nightmare; I must still be sleeping. No such luck.

She again started in with the yelling. "Did you hear me, April? Do you know what gonorrhea is? Do you? They want to keep you in the hospital, and boy is Pat mad. We need to leave, we have things to do. I can't believe this, April. What were you doing, sleeping your way around Tucson? There's only one way to get what you've got." Blah blah blah.

I just closed my eyes and tried to pass out again. I did have a quick flashback to the afternoon Albert wasn't home and I'd gone to see my old school mate. Nothing I could do about it now. It had to be him, or else Albert, and I hadn't been with him for more than three months.

When I woke up again, I was in a semi-private room at the hospital and I had IVs in both of my arms, again.

The poor neighbor lady had called an ambulance and they'd taken me to Denver General Hospital, and there I lay. I had had so many IVs in my arms over the last few months, I was starting to feel like a pin cushion. This time I had one in each arm, but my stomach felt better, though.

A nurse came in and told me to roll over; I was getting a shot in the butt. She said, "You're a very sick young girl."

I asked her how long I would be in the hospital, and she just told me she didn't know for sure, but it would be a while.

\

That afternoon the doctor came to see me, and I was able to ask him a few questions. He told me I had a very bad case of gonorrhea, a very bad case of hepatitis, and I was way under weight. I now weighed ninety-three pounds and would lose more before this was over.

He told me that because of the gonorrhea, I would never have any more children. He didn't go into any details of why exactly. He just said I would never have another child. He did say I was young and would survive, but I was very sick. He also told me not to expect to get out any time soon.

Mom came to visit me in the hospital pretty regular. She was mad at me and let me know it every time I saw her. My stay in the hospital was so long, she and Pat had to make some business decisions. They'd decided he'd leave his position at Dow Chemical in South Dakota and practice law there in Denver. His cousin was an attorney in Denver, and he'd talked Pat into practicing law there at his firm. Remember, I told you he was an attorney also.

Mom and Pat had moved from Oklahoma to South Dakota, and he'd given up practicing medicine due to a malpractice suit or something like that back in Oklahoma. I never did know what he did at Dow, but apparently that was over and things were changing.

After I'd been in the hospital for about two weeks or so, I had a visit from my stepfather, the first one since I'd been in the hospital. When I looked up and saw him come into my room, at first I was pleasantly surprised; then I saw the look on his face and I got scared...he wasn't pleased. My doctor came into my room while he was there, and Pat immediately started in on him.

"I have things to do, and I can't stay here in Denver any longer because of her. I must leave and tend to my business."

The doctor said, "She isn't well enough to leave yet, and there's nothing I can do to speed up her recovery."

Pat abruptly said, "I'm a doctor; I can give her any treatment she needs. I'm going to take her, and that's all there is to it."

The doctor told my stepdad, "I won't release her!"

Pat said, "Then I'll take her without your release. I'll be back first thing in the morning to get her; that's all there is to it."

He turned and marched out of my room. He never even said hello to me. I think he freaked the doctor out, and I know he pissed him off. He asked me if I thought he would come and get me in the morning. I said it sounded like it. I told him I didn't really know the man. I explained how I'd just met him. He told me if I was to leave in the morning, he was going to have to be very aggressive with my treatment, and he wasn't kidding.

As soon as he left the room, a nurse came in with another shot. She informed me I was to get a shot every hour, and she meant it. All that day, and all night long, I got a shot in my butt, every hour on the hour. They came in and woke me up all night long. By about 3 in the morning, I was begging them to give me a shot, to numb where they were going to give me the shot. My butt was so sore. I, of course, didn't sleep all night. I swear, I felt liquid coming out of the other needle holes when they gave me another shot. I felt like a pin cushion.

The next morning at seven o'clock (right after a shot), Pat and my mom came into my room. Pat told me to get up and get dressed. He went and got a nurse to take the IVs out of my arms, and that was all they would do for me. Other than that, they wouldn't touch me. They wouldn't even help me get up, or dressed, because of the legality of him taking me out AMA (Against Medical Advice). So, I got up and got dressed. I was so skinny and yellow, and I walked funny because my butt hurt so bad. I looked terrible and didn't feel any better than I looked.

So, we got together my very few belongings and I put the clothes on my mother had brought me, then we left the hospital. When we got downstairs, my two sisters and my puppy were waiting in the car. Even though I was very glad to see them, I felt so crummy. I got in the back seat, and boy did my butt hurt. I thought the car ride to Denver in the little Toyota was bad, but this was going to be a real joy. There wasn't even enough room for me to turn sideways and give my sore butt some peace. I was so uncomfortable, but at least my mom didn't make me trade seats with my sisters, so I didn't have to sit on the hump.

The puppy was so good; if she hadn't been, I'm sure he would have dumped her out. This man was unbelievable. He and my mom fought all the way to Rapid City, South Dakota. Again he refused to by us any food; it was absolutely ridiculous. Why had she married this man? I saw no love between them. Of course they fought over us, always us. I think if it hadn't been for us, they would have gotten along all right, but I saw no real improvement in her life. Mom had been on her own for so long, it shocked me to see her that submissive. She was so strong-willed and independent that to see her like this was almost sad.

They fought over stopping for any reason. She would tell him to stop, and he would say no. She told him we needed to eat, and he would say no. None of us girls had the guts to say we needed to go to the bathroom, because of all their bickering. After hours of this, she made him stop at a burger place. I'm not making this up; the man actually bought one hamburger and had them cut it five ways. That was all the food we'd have the entire trip. Mom got Pat to stop for gas, and we'd go to the bathroom then. Other than that, we didn't stop except for that one burger.

Needless to say, we got to Rapid City in record time; I was so looking forward to lying down somewhere. That was all I thought of: I had to get off my sore butt. Later that day, I'd be sorry I wished for that.

We finally pulled up to Mom and Pat's house, and I was shocked: it was absolutely beautiful. It was early evening, and it had been storming prior to our arrival. It was the first part of September, and the foliage was gorgeous. This house sat right up against the bottom of a magnificent mountain. The back yard went from the house to Rapid Creek. The back of Mount Rushmore was on the other side of the creek. It was beautiful. There were pine trees and big leaf trees everywhere. It was grassy, and yet like a forest at the same time, and the running water was soothing.

I think I need running water in my life, I love it.

The house itself was wonderful. I had certainly never lived in a house this nice before. It was rustic, but not old in its appearance. It was three or four bedrooms, and it had a giant fireplace in the family room. Good thing, because my new stepdad refused to pay to heat it; except for that fireplace, it had no heat. They didn't even have the gas turned on in the house. He was getting stranger the more I got to know him. The house was beautiful until you had to live in it. It was the strangest place.

Anyway, we pulled into the driveway, and there had been a hail storm preceding us in. They had a one acre garden planted, and it had been damaged by the hail. He immediately started yelling at my mom about saving the garden. He told her we needed to immediately start picking and canning, and we couldn't stop until it was all picked and as much of it saved as possible.

So, they made us get out of the car, immediately get down on the ground and pick vegetables. I don't think I went inside the house except to go to the bathroom until late that first night. It was unbelievable. I was so sick and tired, I couldn't walk, and I don't remember eating anything except one bologna sandwich all day…oh yeah, and the one-fifth of a hamburger. I mean, come on; I'd just spent the last two weeks and two months out of the last three in a hospital bed. I was in no shape to make it on a chain gang.

They did have a bed for me to sleep in, and I literally fell into it that night. Honestly, by now I was expecting a cot with bars around it. He had some real nice furniture, though, old antique stuff. I knew it had to be his, because I knew my mother didn't have anything like this. I didn't have time to admire it, though, because over the next week we picked and canned literally an acre of food.

The house had a very interesting past. The creek that ran behind the house, "Rapid Creek", was deadly. There had been a tragic flood about a year or so earlier, and a hundred or more people had died in it. It was to be one of the worst flood disasters to date. The whole area was devastated by it. You couldn't tell by driving by and looking at it, but all the houses down in this area had been flooded to their roofs. That was why they'd gotten this particular house, because it was really cheap. Most of these beautiful houses were abandoned. I mean, people had died in them, and some had never been found.

\

This particular house had been owned by Chet Huntley. Do you remember the Huntley Brinkley news report? David Brinkley is super model Christy Brinkley's father, and he and Chet Huntley had a news show on television together quite a few years earlier. Anyway, this used to be his house. I don't know if he lived there when the flood happened or not.

Because of the flood, the house didn't have any carpet on the floor. It had never been replaced from when it was flooded, so the house was very cold and definitely didn't have a warm feeling to it at all, but that wasn't just from the lack of heat and carpeting.

My little brother Billy, now thirteen, got home the day after we got to Rapid City. He had been to visit his dead daddy's family in Kansas while mom and Pat made this trip. It was so good to get to see him. He took me around through one or two of the abandoned houses and showed me stuff. A lot of stuff had been left behind. In one of the houses, they had dug up a grand piano out of a basement. All the basements in these once magnificent homes were full up to the main floor with dried mud and God knows what all. If you opened the door to the basement, there would be only a dirt floor. These were all finished and furnished basements when it flooded, so everything was down there, under the mud, like a time capsule. It was eerie.

Billy also told me of an incident that had happened with our stepfather before I got there. This man (our stepdad) was a real strange fellow, and he did things every day that amazed me, stuff like sucking a raw egg in front of us, just because my mom asked him not to. He had a weird sense of humor; it was sadistic. Once, according to the kids, a stray dog had followed them home from school here at the Rapid City house.

Pat had gotten very angry; he had taken the kids outside and had forced them to stand there while he shot this dog. It took five shots to kill it. He told them it was to teach them not to bring home stray dogs anymore. I mean, this was getting more and more bizarre. He kills animals in front of children; in some circles, that would be the warning sign of a serial killer.

I told my brother that was so sad, and he said, "Well, he got his because the dog rotted, then it rained and flooded the creek, and the dog's body floated up in the yard and Pat had to dispose of it."

I said, "Yeah, poor guy. I almost feel sorry for him."

I liked him less and less every day. My little sister Shelley slammed her fingers in the door of the car, and he took a paper clip, straightened it out and held her fingers down while he jabbed it through the tops of her fingernails. She screamed the whole time. Maybe he knew something I didn't; after all, he was a doctor. Even if it was kosher, he definitely needed some work on his bedside manner.

Overall, he was a strange man, and anyone who hurt my brothers and sisters, not to mention defenseless animals, didn't make a good impression on me. I just couldn't get a break here.

After we picked and canned all the food, we had to pack it up, literally (that and everything else in the house.) While I was in the hospital, they'd decided to sell the house in Rapid City and move to Denver.

Pat's cousins were all lawyers; in fact, one of them was the US Attorney General for Nixon or something like that. They'd talked Pat into practicing law with them in Denver. So, we had to pack this huge house, full of furniture and belongings, so they could move to Denver.

\

So, over the next week, Pat, my mom, Billy, a neighbor, my two little sisters and I loaded up a thirty-foot U-Haul, a big cattle truck, and their thirty-foot Air Stream travel trailer. We filled all three until they were busting at the seams. Between the two of them, they had a lot of stuff.

I had no rest the whole ten days we were there, and I looked bony and yellow. At least the itching had stopped, but I was tired all the time. I felt so out of place and unwanted. I wish I would have had an alternative, I was so miserable, I missed the baby, and I was having real regret about that. Plus, I'd been out from under my mother's thumb for so long; this was really hard to deal with. On top of that, I was so physically sick, and this (stepdad guy) was too much for my brain to deal with. They were working me to death. Sometimes this "life thing" was just too damn hard to deal with.

Finally, we were loaded and ready to go, and we were leaving the next morning. Mom or Pat in passing said, "You know how to drive, don't you, April?"

I don't know why I lied, but I said, "Sure, I can drive, why?"

My mom said, "Well, we thought you could drive the Toyota to Denver!"

Their neighbor was driving his cattle truck, Pat was driving the U-Haul and pulling something, and mom was driving the Bronco, pulling the Air Stream. They had no one else to drive the Toyota.

I immediately started saying, "Well, I haven't driven very much, and I don't know your car." I was calmly trying to get out of it.

They told me it would be no problem and I could drive it around the block a couple of times to get used to it before we left. My mind was reeling with regret for lying to them, but once I got behind the wheel, it wasn't hard at all. For one thing, it was an automatic. In fact, I really enjoyed it. I have to say, I did so well, they never knew I didn't know how to drive. The last time I'd driven was when Albert tried to make me drive in Tucson.

So, we all left the next morning; it was a huge convoy. Billy rode with the neighbor, Shelley rode with my mom, and Darla, my littlest sister, rode with me. I got lost before we got out of Rapid City, but other than that I didn't have any problems. We all made it to Denver safe and sound.

Mom and Pat had purchased the empty house in Denver I'd stayed in prior to going into the hospital. It was the one his cousins were selling, the one that was so nice and had the big blue spruce trees in the yard; how neat. This man did have money; he paid for the house with cash. He paid for everything with cash. I wouldn't fully understand just how much money he did have for a long time, because he was such a penny pincher. I couldn't have imagined.

We pulled up to the house and immediately started unloading. We had to unload the cattle truck first, so the man who owned it and drove it could get back to South Dakota. By the time we got that truck unloaded, Pat and the man with the truck had the beds set up in the house. The man left immediately; he didn't even spend the night.

Next we unloaded the U-Haul, which had the major appliances in it. I was so physically and emotionally exhausted; I couldn't take much more of this hard labor. The man wouldn't hire anyone to help us. It was unbelievable; I felt like I actually *was* on a chain gang.

We finally ate something and went to bed, but not for long. Mom and Pat had me up early the next morning; they were immediately going back to Rapid City. You guessed it: they were going to leave me there in Denver with the kids while they were gone. They took the U-Haul back to the U-Haul place. When they got back, they backed the Air Stream up in the driveway, then he unhooked the Bronco. The kids and I started unloading the Air Stream as soon as it was unhooked. Mom stayed inside and found a few boxes of stuff to unpack. Pat got the fridge working and hooked up the washer, then they were gone. Yep, that fast, I was standing in a three-story house, with enough furniture and boxes of stuff to fill it up, all still packed, with three kids looking at me saying, "I'm hungry."

Pat had the phone turned on prior to our arrival, and thankfully the power was on, too, so we had a phone and electricity. The food we had was all the canned food from the garden and any non-perishable food they'd brought with us. Pat had left me thirty dollars and the keys to the Bronco because they'd driven the Toyota back to Rapid City. The Bronco was a stick shift, and I didn't know how to drive a stick. In a new city, I didn't even know where a store was.

So here I am again, lost and alone, only seventeen, sick, and in a city I knew nothing about. Now I'm in charge of three little kids: Billy, 13, Shelley, 11, and Darla was 9. Mom had told me they may be gone for a week or two; it would actually be almost a month before they returned.

The first day or two, all I did was move stuff and unpack. I couldn't even fix the kids anything to eat until I found the dishes, pots and pans. Plus, I had to help the kids set up their rooms, find towels and linen. It was a nightmare; I didn't know even one person within a thousand miles.

In one way, it was neat not having Mom and Pat there, but I was overwhelmed. I did make amazing progress, and the kids helped. Within a day or two, we had a functioning house. It's a good thing, because Mom called and wanted me to enroll the kids in school.

By the third day, I had to get to a store and find the schools. So, I had a crash course teaching myself to drive the "beast", which was what we called the Bronco. We also lived on a hill, so that was interesting. I made the girls stay at the house, and I took my little brother Billy with me. I knew the basics of the clutch; remember, Albert had tried to make me drive a stick shift once. I got the Bronco out of the driveway and onto the street without a lot of trouble. I couldn't believe it when I realized we were on the street, but facing uphill! This was turning into a ridiculous nightmare. It took me an hour to get around the block, but I was persistent since I had no choice. I eventually conquered the beast. Of course it was a gas guzzler, which was why my mom and Pat had taken the Toyota, so I couldn't go too far.

I found the schools and somehow got all three of the kids enrolled. They would have to walk to school, but I couldn't help that. The two little girls would go together. My brother would go to a school a block from them. They each had to walk about a mile or so each way to get to school. We were at that distance where we weren't far enough for a bus, but really too far for them to walk.

With some searching, I found a grocery store; it was a little more than a mile from the house. It didn't do me much good, though, because thirty dollars wasn't going to go far, especially after I put gas in the beast. I did get milk and bread, but I was stumped at how to get the kids school lunches every day.

By the end of the first week, I had no money. I did somehow get the kids a sandwich to take every day, but they all needed stuff for school I couldn't provide. It was sad and frustrating. I don't remember talking to my mom, but I'm sure I did, at least once. They weren't going to help us if it cost money; he just wasn't going to do it. I eventually got up the nerve to call Pat's relatives. His cousin was very sympathetic; she brought us over some food, money, and a little black and white television. This was a real treat, because one thing Mom and Pat hadn't had was a television. That lady was really very nice.

It's a good thing she was there, because they wouldn't get home for almost three more weeks. I got pretty good at driving the beast. There was a big area where people four-wheeled and rode horses, and it was just up the road from the house. The kids and I would drive up there and mess around. There were some horses boarded there, and I loved horses. I met one or two young girls my age who had their horses boarded there. I loved going up to see them and their horses. I even got brave enough to drive the beast up the dirt path once or twice, but I couldn't do it very often because of having to buy gas for the beast; still, it was fun.

Every time I went out of the house, I got stares and fearful looks because my skin was still the color of a lemon. With the combination of all the red hair I had, it must have been a real eyesore; a color clash that was almost too hard to look at, at least it was for me. The girls I met were fascinated by it, but if their mothers would have seen me, they would have grabbed them and run. I never had trouble meeting people, though; I loved to talk, and I'd been the new person so many times in my life. It was a learned art, I fit into any situation. People would say things about a perfectly simple subject, and my reply would always lead to an intense explanation. Something as simple as "Where did you go to school?" would lead to my mentioning the "Home", and that would lead to questions, which would lead to awe and wonder, which in turn would lead to more questions. I knew at an early age I wasn't "normal." It always brought out questions when people found out I'd been married and divorced, had a two-year-old child, and hadn't been to real school since 8th grade. Of course, all the stuff about Albert was a real jaw dropper. Those finding out I was only seventeen always got a reaction; sometimes good, sometimes bad, but never indifferent.

I always had something to say (I couldn't help it), and it was never boring. I didn't know it then, but I suppose I was looking for help. In my way, I was reaching out to whomever would listen. God, I sound just like that lady in "On the Waterfront" with Marlon Brando, when she flatly states she'd always depended on the kindness of strangers. Maybe I was, but so far not too many had thrown me a lot of bones. Is that still begging?

I guess I would have found it fascinating, too, if it hadn't all happened to me. If only I'd known then what a truly neat person I was...

How sad that today the world is full of people just like me. I call them "Lost Americans", constantly in transition, unstable, ungrounded, no sense of home or family, and no sense of self-worth. It wasn't like that then, at least not among the people I met. It wasn't normal for a sixteen-year-old to have lived enough life to be able to write a book about it.

Never a dull moment

My color was changing from a bright yellow to getting a green tint to it. I hated looking in the mirror, because I'd lost even more weight and I looked like I was dying.

Except for the lack of money, we were doing fine on our own until Mom and Pat finally returned to Denver. When they got there, they were happy to see I'd gotten every box unpacked, every book put away, and I had the place looking pretty good. Pat gave me twenty dollars, and Mom bought me a new outfit at K-mart for staying with the kids. That was the hardest twenty dollars I ever earned.

Mom and Pat wanted me to get a job, but I had nothing to wear. Mom took me to a thrift store to buy me any other clothes I would need. I remember my mom and I were both in the fitting room when this woman who worked in the thrift store pulled back the curtain and told us to leave. She said it was because the other customers were afraid to stay in the store with me. My mom told the lady I wasn't contagious. All the lady could do was say she was sorry. Customers had already left the store, that's how yellow I was.

Another time, my mom took me to get my driver's license, but the driving instructor didn't want to get in the car with me. It took fifteen minutes to convince him I wasn't contagious. It was so embarrassing, and my mom was always so loud and persistent. I truly stuck out like a giraffe in a pack of wart hogs. I'd lost even more weight, getting down to 87 lbs. I looked so gaunt and yellow, I would have crossed the room, too, if I'd seen someone like that. It was also like a bruise; the change in time changed the shades of yellow. It took months to look normal again.

Pat told me if I was to live with them, I had to go to school. He made me go down and enroll at John F. Kennedy High School. Luckily, my color was getting better, but I still had to explain to everyone I spoke to why I looked like a banana, and I wasn't contagious. I still got a lot of weird looks.

So here I was, again the new kid in school. It was sometime in late October, and school was well underway. So here I was, the new, old (for the age of high school), divorced, diseased (yellow with red hair), only been to school in a barn, crammed into a top notch BIG city high school, already been married and divorced, lost a child. There's just too much to list.

This wasn't going to work. It was ridiculous. I hadn't gone to high school; well, at least a real high school. I was either at the Home (and I already knew nobody accepted Bible as a credit), or I was married. I didn't fit in to any grade, and I had very little in common with these kids. I was placed in the twelfth grade because, believe it or not, there had been a fire at my old school in Tucson and a lot of the records had

\

been lost, one of which was mine. As you know, this was before computers kept all records archived for us. I was seventeen, so they were just putting me where I would be, according to my age. I hated it, because it was now 1974 and the Denver Public School System had just started mandatory busing. There were fights at school constantly, and I'd been cornered by a group of five boys; it was a scary place. In the end, I would never catch up with everyone else. Unfortunately, I didn't realize the rewards of school back then.

At the time, I hated school, hated living with Pat and Mom, and I hated feeling so alone all the time. I was desperate to get out of their house. There were things I needed that they refused to give me, so I went and got a job doing phone sales. It didn't last long; I wasn't very good at trying to sell magazines to little old ladies. I would always end up listening to their problems instead of selling them a magazine.

I was excited when I got another job, not too far from the house, at a place called Wyatt's Cafeteria. I seemed to fit right in and actually enjoyed going to work every day. I got to wear a little gold uniform, so I didn't have to worry about if I had the clothes or not. The first day I started, I met a girl my age who was as crazy as I was, and we immediately became good friends. She had a car, which gave me more freedom.

There were a couple of people there my age, and the older people there seemed to like me. Older people always like me, because I love them and they can feel that. Wyatt's became my favorite place to be, and I felt comfortable there. One of the best things of all was I could eat for free, and that made the stepdad happy.

The friend I made was one year older than me, and she was funny. Her name was Elzaree. That in itself was funny, and she would turn out to be my lifelong friend.

The restaurant was in a mall, so it was the perfect place for a seventeen-year-old girl. I used to sit around the break room and talk to everyone. It was good therapy, because I needed someone to talk to. Elzaree and I started going out after work together. She took me to her house, and I met her mom, Pauline, her brother, Duncan, and her sister, Karen.

Elzaree was 18 and still living at home. Her mom and dad were divorced, but I met him, too. They were all nice people and made me feel welcome. It was nice to have a friend to talk to.

We went out a few times with a group of people from work. I had a bad case of "fist-o-phobia"; I screamed or jumped when anyone or anything came near me from out of my view. I also had a terrible case of the "I'm sorry's" you know, when the guy next to you spilled coffee on the person next to him, I'd jump up and say, "I'm sorry." Elzaree had almost as low self-esteem as I did, so we got along great.

I had a boss at Wyatt's Cafeteria, his name was Roger. He was an assistant manager, and about twenty four years old. Roger wasn't like us at all. He was very quiet, and he would sit with us but never say anything. Roger had dark hair and deep blue eyes, and he seemed very mysterious. He wore a long black leather coat and had lived in Milwaukee, Wisconsin. Roger was living with a girl roommate in an apartment complex close to the mall, but he'd gone out with me and Elzaree a couple of times.

\

One Halloween, we all went to a Denny's restaurant and sat and hung out for about three hours. Elzaree and I were dressed like cats for Halloween. Finally, it was time for us to leave, and Elzaree was going to drop me off at home. On the way home, we came to a stop sign in a residential neighborhood. It must have been two in the morning. All of us were laughing and joking with each other, when all of a sudden two dark figures with black capes and glowing faces ran out from the hedges next to the stop sign. They both jumped onto the hood of Elzaree's car and pressed their faces against the windshield. We both screamed in unison as Elzaree slammed her foot down on the accelerator. As we peeled out, one of the guys flew off the car, but the other one didn't; he was hanging on for dear life, and his face was more freaky and distorted by the fluorescent paint he had on. He finally flew off the windshield and never knew what had happened to him. Elzaree was in flight mode and didn't slow down for a mile or more. We laughed and cried all the way home. If they tried that today, they'd run the risk of the driver having a gun in the car and using it. Times were different back then.

Another night, a bunch of us from work were hanging out together. I was driving my mom's little Toyota, and I still can't believe I'd managed to talk her into letting me borrow it. This particular night, I accidentally backed up into this guy's car at a stoplight. It didn't do anything to my mom's car, but it broke one of the other guy's headlights. Roger got out of the car and threw forty dollars on the hood; he talked the guy into taking it and not calling the police. I was terrified the guy would call my mom and tell her, but he didn't. It was a nice thing for Roger to do. I wasn't used to people doing things for me like that.

\

I offered to try to pay him back, but he told me not to worry about it. Forty dollars was half a week's pay for me back then. It was strange earning money; it was the first time I had money of my own ever in my life. I'd never worked before, except at the poodle parlor when I was fourteen, and there I'd only been paid in poodle! So, that didn't count, and Albert had never even let me touch money at all. As soon as I got my first check, Pat told me he wanted me to pay rent. I don't remember how much, but I knew I'd never save any money living with them.

I hated going home. They were always fighting, and my stepdad let me know, in no uncertain terms, that my stay was temporary. He really resented me coming into their lives after he'd made the commitment to marry my mom. It was like this wasn't part of the deal. Other parts of Pat's personality eventually reared its ugly head. I observed that he would pout and leave a store or business after fighting with my mom in public about the price or necessity of something. Mom and Pat would argue about the weirdest things, and it almost always involved one of us kids or money. They demanded I be home by nine o'clock, which was hard to do when I would work past that at times. My parents didn't watch television or do anything the kids wanted to do, but he made sure he was able to listen to his Elvis and stuff like that.

One day when I came home, I could hear Pat and my little brother Billy arguing. The argument immediately turned bad when my stepdad picked Billy up by the throat and slammed him into the wall. Pat had a look on his face that scared me, and I could tell he was hurting Billy. I was terrified of him once I saw there would never be love, or even compassion, in his decision making. From then on, I tried to stay away from him as much as possible.

There was this feeling when you entered their house that was…uncomfortable. It's hard to describe what made him so different, but it was a cold feeling he emitted. My stepdad would sometimes get a glimmer in his eye when he had the opportunity to punish one of us. It wasn't always physical punishment; it was the joy of putting us in our place, making us feel beneath him or belittling us in some way. No matter what the punishment, he made sure there was something in the punishment, or his verbal delivery of it, that demeaned us. He enjoyed being able to deny us any time he could. It was oozing from him that he didn't want to have me in his life, but it wasn't just me; he was like that to everyone. He and my mother fought all the time. My stepdad seemed to like it, because he would egg her on purposely. It was a chore every time I had to go back to their house.

My mother and I argued every time we saw each other, too. I just couldn't understand how she could allow him to treat us that way. Mom defended him constantly, and this from a woman who had never let anyone tell her what to do her entire life.

Then there was always the issue of religion between us, but I won't bore you with that. Anyway, things escalated to the point where I just couldn't stay there anymore.

I voiced my woes to my friend Elzaree a lot. One day, we were sitting around in the break room at work, and Roger was sitting in there with us. He told me if I wanted to, I could stay with him; he had a sheepish grin on his face. He'd shown interest in me before by hanging around wherever I was. I just never knew what he was really thinking because, as I said, he was always quiet.

I guess you could say he wasn't my type. He didn't make me quiver when I got around him or anything like that. Roger was cute, but older than me, and different from me in a lot of ways. He was so totally different from anyone I'd ever hung out with. Roger dressed different, listened to different music, was older than all of us, and there was always that mystery about him.

My brother David was no longer living with our dad and somehow ended up back at my mom's house with the rest of us. Now the stepdad was really pissed; he didn't like David at all and let him know it openly. David was only fifteen and apparently had a falling out with our real father in Kansas. He had nowhere else to go, as I didn't, so he was back with my mom (and now Pat).

We kids had never had a male in our lives in a domestic capacity. Well, I'd been with Albert, but David had always been the oldest male in the house, and he was now fifteen and coming into his own. I don't think up to this point David and Pat had ever met more than once, but this newfound conflict between them was terrible. Mom had told me at her wedding that she'd devoted her life to us kids, and now it was her turn. Nothing was going to get in the way, and she meant it. I knew Mom wasn't going to side with us. She just wanted us to go away and let her have her life, and all we wanted was a place to go away to.

David had found out the hard way that his newfound relationship with our newfound real dad wasn't going to be what he'd dreamed all his life it would be. When you're without one of your parents, you fantasize what it would be like to be a part of their lives; when in reality, if you get the opportunity to meet them, it's very likely your fantasy will be crushed.

The American Dream shouldn't be a house for everyone and a chicken in every pot; it should be two-parent families in each of those houses eating those chickens with their kids. Without that, we've lost the American Dream. We need to start taking parenting more seriously, either that or start putting birth control in the water. Oops, didn't mean to get up on that soapbox.

The time finally came when I couldn't take the trouble at the house anymore. That day, I had a terrible fight with my mother because she'd let our stepdad throw my little brother David out of the house. I went to Roger's and asked him if his offer was still good, and of course he smiled and said yes. I didn't go home that night.

The next day when I went to pack my stuff to leave, my mom said, "When you get into trouble, April, and you will, don't come to me for help next time. I'm sick of dealing with you."

So, I moved in with Roger, and again I didn't have to deal with my mom. It seems like I spent my life trying to get away from my mother, but my problems didn't seem to go away, even when I did; they just changed. Of course, that knowledge wouldn't come for years.

I don't know why I made the decisions I made, but I wish I did. The fact is, I did make them. I was now with Roger, and I feel bad because I used him to get away from my mother, I admit that. I did actually like him; he was nice to me, and good looking. Of course, Albert was, too, at first, so I was still very wary. I wasn't going to let any man ever treat me like Albert had again.

\

I had no thought of marriage or commitment. I barely knew him, and we were pretty different. As I said, he was very quiet, but I was kind of talkative. He never talked about his family or past, and I constantly talked about mine. I was young and wiry, and he was five years older but acted older than that. We also dressed differently and listened to different music. Roger would always have an air of mystery about him, and he never talked about himself. He had a scar on his neck that was visible, depending on what he was wearing, and it was pretty big, too. It made everyone who saw it wonder what had caused it, but no one felt comfortable enough to ask him about it.

My time with a stranger

Once we were living together, people would ask me about the scar on Roger's neck, because they didn't want to ask him themselves. He told me he'd gotten it in a fight; a guy had tried to cut his throat with a beer bottle. Roger had also been stabbed in the chest with a knife, but people couldn't see that scar. Stuff like that was different about him.

So, now we were living together, and it was OK for a week or two. He wasn't overbearing and seemed very happy in the relationship. He allowed me to continue my friendship with Elzaree, and I had a sense of freedom. I had a place to stay, he had some furniture and an apartment, and he let it be mine. I had work to go to each day, and the apartment was only three blocks from the mall and a grocery store, so I was kind of happy. We didn't have a car, but we didn't need one. I was able to spend some of the money I earned on myself, and we went out with people from work. It was a much better relationship than I had being married to Albert. He didn't talk much, but he let me talk and seemed truly interested.

I was a lot better physically by now; my color just looked like a weird tan, and I was back up to a hundred and six pounds again. I had to bring a letter from a doctor (Pat obliged) saying I wasn't contagious when I first got my job, and now you couldn't even tell.

Roger didn't seem to overpower me, and yet he seemed to be in control. It wasn't where I wanted to be, but it was tolerable for a month or so, and there was no real lust on my part or anything like that. I never planned a future with him or even talked about the future with him. It was just the situation I was in at the time. That's exactly what it was: a situation.

My mom never tried to see me, and I didn't try to see her. When I left her house, she was so mad at me anyway, and I think ready for me to go.

By the time I'd lived with Roger for two months or so, things were getting a little uneasy. We had a couple of fights; not physical, just disagreements. I felt things were changing. In fact, I'd felt something else, and it freaked me out. I'd felt pain during sex, and my breasts were sore.

I told myself it couldn't be possible, because the doctor had told me I would never have kids again, hadn't he? I tried to tell myself it was something else, but there's nothing else that makes you feel like you're pregnant, except being pregnant.

I went to Roger and voiced my fear. He immediately said it couldn't be his because he was sterile. Oh, great! I was so upset, I left his apartment and walked around all evening. That night, I stayed at Elzaree's. The next day, Roger came looking for me and told me he was sorry, that I'd just freaked him out. It freaked me out, too. I couldn't be pregnant, I just couldn't be, but it sure felt like I was.

The next evening, we were all sitting around the table at our apartment, Roger, Elzaree and I, when Roger said something derogatory to Elzaree. For some reason only Elzaree knew, she stuck her tongue out at Roger.

He asked her what she was doing, and she sarcastically said, "I'm drying my tongue out."

I was laughing, but he wasn't. Roger calmly walked into the kitchen and grabbed a big knife from the kitchen counter, then came back, held the knife up to Elzaree's throat, and stood her up. I freaked out and immediately ran out of the apartment and down three flights of stairs, screaming. Back then I still jumped anytime someone's hand came by me, even if they were just reaching for something. I was still in "Albert Mode".

When I got down to the parking lot, I ran up to a car with a man and woman sitting in it. I opened the car door and begged them for help. They just sat there with their mouths open. All of a sudden, Roger was there, telling them not to listen to me, that I was drunk. He pulled me away from the car and dragged me back upstairs.

The first thing I noticed was that Elzaree wasn't there, and I didn't see a pool of blood anywhere. I asked Roger where she was, and he told me she'd left. He said he wasn't going to hurt her and asked me why I freaked out like that.

All I could say was, "Why did I freak out like that? Why did I freak out like that?"

All of a sudden, there was a knock on the door; it was the police. Roger told me to shut up and keep quiet, then he made me duck down next to the bed. He put his hand over my mouth and begged me not to scream. Roger had never hit me, and I'd had a few minutes to calm down, so I didn't scream. He just kept the light off and kept quiet until eventually, after a while, the police left.

The next day, he told me we needed to go back to where he was from and see his family. He didn't want to stay in Denver anymore. He was from Milwaukee, Wisconsin, and that's where he wanted us to go. I didn't want to go to Wisconsin, but what was I going to do? I was now pregnant with this guy's child (or thought I might be), and I had nowhere else to go.

So, we rented a small U-Haul, filled it up, and drove off to Milwaukee, Wisconsin. I didn't say goodbye to my mother, but I did say goodbye to Elzaree and my boss at work. He was a nice man and tried to talk me out of going, believe it or not. Unfortunately, I knew he wasn't going to rent me an apartment or let me live at his house, so I went with Roger.

Nothing ever happens to me without a twist. I can't just have bad or weird experiences; they have to be bad or weird experiences, with something else included.

We didn't leave until noon, and we drove through the night. Once we got outside of Milwaukee, Roger pulled the U-Haul over to the side of the highway, looked at me, and said, "I need to talk to you, April."

I looked at him and said, "About what?"

He looked seriously at me and said, "You can't call me Roger anymore!"

\

I said, "What do you mean I can't call you Roger anymore?" He was freaking me out.

He said, "My name isn't Roger."

I didn't know if he was joking or what. I said, "What do you mean your name isn't Roger? What is it?"

He kind of smiled and said, "It's Marvin."

I laughed and said, "Your name is Marvin? Yeah, right."

He, on the other hand, wasn't laughing; he was serious, and he told me so.

I finally quit laughing and said, "You aren't kidding? Your name isn't Roger? Your name is Marvin? It can't be. I've seen your driver's license, and I've seen you cash paychecks as Roger. Why would you say it was Roger if it wasn't? I don't understand."

For a while he didn't say anything, then he said, "Roger is my brother's name; I was in some trouble when I was in Wisconsin, so I had to use his name in Denver."

I cautiously said, "What kind of trouble?"

He said, "I was in prison, and I jumped parole."

I started freaking out. I said, "What were you in prison for?"

"It was for having a fight, and that's where I got the scar on my neck from. I'm serious, April; you can't call me Roger in front of my family. From now on, you're gonna have to call me Marvin."

I can't explain what my brain was doing at that moment. I was sitting in a U-Haul, one thousand miles from anyone I knew, with a guy I didn't know anything about (and now I didn't even know his name) who had escaped from prison or something like that, and I think I'm pregnant with his child, and I had another child getting farther away from me by the minute. I think I was in shock. I'm serious; I honestly think I went into some kind of protection zone. My brain went into automatic safe mode and just shut down for a while.

I just sat in silence. What was I supposed to say? "Hi there, Marvin, it's nice to meet you, my name's April. By the way, did you see a guy here a minute ago named Roger?" I was so freaked out, I can't even describe what my brain was doing, but the night was young, and it would have to buck up for more.

We drove through this city at four in the morning. Now, I don't mean to put Milwaukee down at all; I'm just voicing my first impressions of it. Good or bad, it's the way it was. There was a bar on every corner we drove past; I'd never seen so much beer advertising in one place, it was even in the residential neighborhoods. They had a bar on every corner.

We drove deeper into the city itself, to an area that reminded me of Archie Bunker's house; you know, real close together and all the same shape and color. Three-story brick houses three feet apart, and all of them looked the same. Everything in this town looked industrial; not a lot of green things, more brick and metal. It was kind of spooky.

Marvin told me we were going to his sister's house as we pulled up to one of the houses in this long row. He finally got out and went to the door of one of them. I was sitting in the truck, thinking if I should jump out and run somewhere, but where?

He knocked on the door, and more than one dog started barking. It took a minute, but finally the door opened and this little African-American boy was standing there. A minute or two later, there was a little African-American girl there beside him, then an older child came to the door. Next, an African-American man came to the door and talked to "Roger-Marvin."

I was sitting in the truck wondering if his sister was African-American, or even if he was now. Roger had dark hair, but he'd told me he was Italian. Of course, he'd also told me his name was Roger. It was just another surprise of the evening. Finally, his sister came to the door, and she was clearly not African-American. She'd just chosen one as her husband, and they had five kids who were all absolutely beautiful.

Marvin's sister let us come in; she didn't seem overwhelmed to have us there. She was kind of cold and a little bit sarcastic to "Roger-Marvin". I didn't say anything; I was still in shock and couldn't get my mind off my predicament.   She took us upstairs to the attic. It was a real attic, too; little, and full of stuff. It was a small area in an A-frame shape. There was a mattress on the floor, and one window. His sister said we could stay there for a couple of days, but no longer. It was spooky up there, and cold, too. This was a nightmare that was getting more and more nightmarish.

The next day when I woke up and realized I wasn't having a dream, I met his sister and her family. Her kids were sweet, and her husband seemed nice, but she definitely didn't want her brother to stay long. There seemed to be a conflict of some kind between them, besides the fact that he'd just shown up on her doorstep in the middle of the night with a pregnant teenager, wanting to live with her.

He came and told me we were going to buy a car so he could go get a job, so we did. It was a rusted out, big monster car, but it got us out of his sister's place sometimes.

He took me one hundred miles away to a little town called Madison, to meet his parents. I was very surprised by the area and his family. It was a beautiful town; so green, with a lot of farms all around it. His parents had a nice house and seemed very nice. They were older than my grandparents would have been. They must have been pretty old when they had him. I found out his parents had eight children, and Roger-Marvin was their next to youngest. The brother whose name he'd used was the one just older than him. They seemed like very nice people, but he didn't seem to be very close to them, though. He was like the black sheep of the family.

I messed up and called him Roger more than once, but it didn't seem to cause too much trouble. Back in Milwaukee, he took me around town; it was weird. He knew people at more than one of those little bars, and I got the impression he'd spent his time growing up in the heart of the city, instead of that little farm town. That's where the difference in him came from; I was more rural, and he was definitely more urban.

He took me bowling with his sister, and another sister and their families went, too. He also introduced me to two of his brothers. None of them knew what to think of me. Of course, I guess the same could be said from my side of it, too. I was just as uncertain of the situation as they were, and with good reason, and the reasons were still piling up.

On the third or fourth night of this ordeal, we were asleep on our mattress in the attic, when all of a sudden ten or more police officers burst in the attic door with flashlights and guns. It was like a movie; I sat up and pulled the covers up to my chin. I was freaking out; I didn't know if I was still asleep or this was real. Either way, it was a nightmare.

Before I could grasp what was happening, Roger-Marvin was out the window and gone, and so were about eight of the cops right behind him. The other two or three police officers stayed behind and looked around with flashlights, asked me where he would have gone, then left. I told them I had no idea. The police left me sitting on the mattress, shaking and huddled under the blanket. They didn't ask me much of anything else. In fact, they acted like I wasn't there. I guess I'm grateful for that, except I wouldn't have minded knowing what was happening.

I got up and went downstairs. Roger-Marvin's sister was making coffee, so I asked her what had happened. She told me Marvin had been hiding from the police for over a year and she'd turned him in because she didn't want him or his trouble at her house. He'd already told me he'd jumped parole, but I didn't know what that meant exactly. I didn't expect them to bust in in the middle of the night and take him. I didn't realize he was in that much trouble. I never thought about the future; therefore, I very seldom thought about the results of the past. I dealt in the immediate. Maybe tomorrow or next week, but that was it.

Here I was learning lessons the hard way, again. I was standing in the kitchen of a woman I hardly knew, sure I was pregnant and getting more pregnant every day – but not even really sure, because I still hadn't been to a doctor. I was in a state, and city, over one thousand miles from anyone I knew, and I'd just watched the father of the child I was carrying jump out of the window with the police on his heels – and I hadn't thought things could get any worse? Ha!

They caught him that same night and took him to jail, but he wasn't there long; within two days, they sent him two hundred miles away to the state prison. This was getting better and better. What was I going to do now? His sister said I could stay there in the attic for a while, but she wasn't real happy about having me there, and I wasn't any happier about it than she was. If I would have had somewhere else to go, I would have.

I made some phone calls, and with his sister's help, "even though she'd been the one to turn him in," I found out where he was and where I could go see him. So, I drove the ugly, blue rusted out beast he'd purchased the two hundred miles to the state prison.

God, it was a horrible place. I had to be searched and go through gate after gate to get in. I noticed I wasn't alone; there must have been fifty other people there to visit someone. We all went in this big room that had a bunch of tables and chairs in long rows. It was cold, and everything was made of metal. I was scared; I couldn't believe I was inside a prison.

There were bars all around us, like a big cage. All the doors were bars, and there were no walls, really, because they were bars also. I could see inmates all dressed alike, milling around on the other side of the bars, waiting to get in to see their visitors. They looked very intimidating.

After we were all inside the big room, a whistle blew and one of the doors opened, then they started filing in as their name was called. I saw Marvin come through the door. My feelings at seeing him were really ambivalent; I was relieved, yet dismayed at seeing him, maybe even unemotional or burdened. Relieved because he was the only person I knew for a thousand miles, and yet this guy had put me through some real ordeals over the last two weeks.

\

It was a horrible hour. He kept trying to touch me there in that dirty, metal place, with people everywhere. It made me mad, and I felt repulsed by him. He'd never acted like that in public before; it was weird. I couldn't wait to get out of there. This man was my boss at one time. It was so weird being in this awful predicament, especially because I put myself there in the first place and had no one else to blame.

He gave me the name of his parole officer in Milwaukee. He told me he wanted me to go see this parole officer when I got back to his sister's and there may be a chance I could get him out if I told him of my predicament.

So, the next day I did just that. I went and found this parole officer and told him I was pregnant, had nowhere to go, and Marvin had had a good job and been a responsible citizen in Denver. I begged him to let him out for my sake. The man called me two or three times over the next couple of days, and unbelievably, two weeks later they did; they let him out on parole again. He had to get and hold a job and report each week to the parole officer, but they did let him out. The parole officer felt sorry for me, and that was why they released him.

We went to his sister's again. He'd been gone for two or three weeks, and I'd stayed there with them during that time. I still hadn't been to a doctor. This time, we only stayed at his sister's for a day or two. He'd gotten a job through his brother or his brother's friend, and he started the night after he got out of prison. Marvin worked the graveyard shift at a bakery from midnight to eight in the morning. He got us a room in a terrible part of town, and for the first few days, at least, I thought it was better than the attic at his sister's. We had a buffet, one room with a kitchenette, and a bathroom. As I said, it was in a terrible part of town, and he was gone every night, all night. We didn't have a phone, so I just sat there all day while he slept and cowered there at night when he was gone. I hated it.

Many nights, I would sit and think of where else I could go. My mom's house was out, and I'd thought of my aunt and uncle's, but they had two kids of their own. I'd already run to them two or three times, trying to leave Albert, plus they kept in touch with my mom. I thought a lot about my dad and his family, but I hadn't seen him since I'd gone there to escape Albert more than a year earlier.

One night while I was sitting there, hating life, I got up the nerve and walked to a pay phone a block away and called my dad. It was a real ordeal just getting to the pay phone. I got wolf whistles and cheers all the way there, and coming back was even spookier. I can't believe I survived it.

Surprisingly, my dad sounded as if he'd be willing to help me and have me stay at his house. I didn't tell him I thought I was pregnant; I just told him I was in an uncomfortable situation and had nowhere else to go. He told me he'd send me a bus ticket and let me come to Kansas.

I was so relieved; I got off the phone and made my way back through the jungle, to the cave.

I was happy when Marvin got home, but it didn't last long, as he was immediately mad that I'd gone out and called anyone at all. I knew he wasn't going to let me go without a fight, so I lied to him. I told him my dad had offered to give us a car if I came and got it. My dad had told me that he had a little used car lot and he'd help me get a car, but I told Marvin I would come back with a car so he would let me go.

\

It took a week to get the bus ticket from my dad. Once it arrived in the mail, I was so happy. I made plans to leave the next day, because it was Marvin's day off. He asked me over and over not to go; he knew I wanted to leave and not come back, and he was right. After much arguing, he took me to the bus station, but he almost didn't let the bus leave. He couldn't leave town because of his parole, or he definitely would have come with me. After I was seated on the bus, he jumped on and told me to get off; he didn't want me to go. He started begging me and almost yanked me off, but when I wouldn't come willingly, the bus driver made him get off and I was going, no matter what. Finally, the bus pulled away from Milwaukee, with Marvin standing in the terminal yelling for me to come back.

I was so happy to be leaving that city. For the first couple of hours, I was afraid he would try to follow the bus and get me, but he didn't. As we left Wisconsin and got closer to Kansas, I felt this feeling of peace and serenity settle in. Again, I wasn't thinking of the future; just today and tomorrow, because tomorrow I would be in Kansas, not in Milwaukee. I fantasized on the trip about being wanted, loved and happy.

We drove through the night and pulled in to Baxter Springs, Kansas, around noon the next day. My dad and little brother David were there to meet me. I was so happy to see that David had gone back to dad's, too. It was good to see them waiting there with smiles on their faces.

My dad came up, hugged me, and said, "How you doing, kid?"

I smiled at him and said, "Better now that I'm here." I barely knew this man, yet I loved him with all my heart.

Once he quit hugging me, he patted my belly and said, "You're not pregnant, are you, kid?"

I truthfully said, "Not that I know of."

We got my suitcase and went to his car.

My brother was fifteen now, and he'd shot up about five inches since I'd seen him at mom's. He freaked me out by driving off in his own pickup truck. Remember, we were in rural southeastern Kansas, in nineteen seventy-four.

When we drove up to my dad's house, I was shocked and impressed; they'd moved up in the world. They'd moved over across the state line five miles away to Oklahoma, to the little town I'd grown up in. They had a brand new four-bedroom house, on three acres of property outside of town. Apparently, Dad had gone to school and was now an X-ray technician. He worked at a hospital ten miles away in Miami, Oklahoma, and still had that little used car lot, doing very well for back then.

The girls seemed glad to see me, especially Chris and Jamie Dawn. The oldest daughter, Carol, was still married and had a baby of her own now. She didn't live with them anymore. So, it was my dad, his wife Juanita, my brother David, and the girls, Terri, Chris, Jamie Dawn, and now me. It was a full house.

The property they had was beautiful; it sat right off the highway, back about two hundred yards from the road. The house was a brand new, ranch style house with four bedrooms. It was painted a pretty yellow, a very big difference from the little shack they'd lived in when I met them. They'd made a place for me with a couple of my new sisters, and I was so glad to be there.

Dad and Juanita sat me down that evening and asked me if I was pregnant. I told them I didn't know and that I hadn't been to a doctor. He told me he was going to take a urine sample with him to the hospital the next day when he went to work. He would have a doctor friend of his check it out.

I was really shocked the next day when he called me and told me it had come out negative. I wondered what else could cause the symptoms I was experiencing, like tender breasts, swollen stomach, and loss of my period. I was even feeling movement; could I have a bad case of gas? The next day he took another one, and we got the same results: negative. After the third one came back negative, my dad told me he would pay for me to go see someone. Dad made an appointment, but it was two days away. In the meantime, I'd gotten a job at a little taco place. They were all so good about helping me get to town when I needed to go. I'd even gotten to see my other aunts and relatives on my mom's side of the family who lived in the area.

I had learned my aunt Kari Jo had gotten married, to a boy she'd gone to high school with. I'd met him and his family a year earlier on one of my flights from Albert. I got to spend some time with the two of them, too. I was really enjoying being there with everyone. I fell in love with my two youngest sisters, Chris and Jamie. They were ten and fourteen, and I was seventeen now.

Marvin called every day, but most of the time I'd tell whoever answered the phone, "If it's Marvin, tell him I'm not here," and they did.

The day came for my appointment, so we headed out to see the doctor. I guess I wasn't surprised when he did a pelvic exam and

\

immediately said, "My dear, you're about four and a half months pregnant."

My heart sank, but not at the thought of having another baby; I would love to have a baby. I missed Michael so much, but I knew this tied me to Marvin; there would be no disappearing and starting a new life of my own. This really put a kink in trying to get Michael back, which was why my heart sank.

How was I going to take care of a baby? I already had one I couldn't take care of. I couldn't even take care of myself. I was still just a baby. I was growing old very fast and was dragging now more than one child through this aging life with me.

That night after I got home from work and seeing the doctor, Marvin called again. This time, Dad got on the phone.

He said, "She's pregnant. If you want to do something about it, great; get here and do something about it. If not, don't call back." He then hung up the phone.

When I got home from work the next evening, Marvin was there at my dad's. He'd driven the rusted beast from Milwaukee. I never asked him, but I'm sure he didn't have permission to leave the state. He had the trunk full of paraphernalia; you know, pipes and bongs and stuff out of a head shop. The trunk was full of the stuff. I can only guess where he got it. It was all new stuff, with price tags on it. I didn't want to know where he got it, and I didn't ask. He told me his brother had given it to him from a shop that had gone out of business; maybe he did.

I was really upset at my dad for handing me back over to Marvin. I guess my dad figured I was Marvin's problem, and if he was willing to

\

do something about it, then let him. At least I wasn't in Milwaukee anymore.

Marvin had a little bit of money on him, so he rented us a ratty little apartment. It had a hole in the floor you could see the ground through, but it was rural Oklahoma poverty, not inner city poverty. I found myself back with Marvin, but at least I was back in familiar surroundings. There, I felt safe and wanted.

One of the doctor friends of my dad's did some checking for me and found out I was still covered through the government, on Champa Insurance. This was through the Air Force benefits I'd used all my life, and because I was only eighteen, I was still eligible. The only problem was that there wasn't a military base for over one hundred and fifty miles, so they allowed me to go to a doctor there who accepted that insurance. Unfortunately, the only doctor anywhere in the area who took Champa was this old alcoholic doctor who had delivered one of my brothers fifteen years earlier. He did C-sections, too, which I would need since I'd had one before.

In nineteen seventy-five, they automatically gave you another cesarean section if you'd already had one. Seriously, they wouldn't give you a choice; it was automatic. Now you can have multiple natural births after having a cesarean section, but that was then.

So, I started going to this strange little old doctor. He was such an alcoholic that when I went to get some blood work done, he was shaking so bad, after five or six tries he had to go get the nurse to come in and do it. Unfortunately, I had no choice; it was either him or drive a hundred and fifty miles to an Army base.

\

Marvin got a job at the BF Goodrich plant there, and we soon moved to a little nicer apartment. It was the upstairs of a two story, little old wooden house. Things weren't too bad. I got to visit with family, my aunt Kari Jo, and my grandma's sister, Aunt Marie, and her family. I got to meet and get to know some of my dad's family, and he had a lot of them, too. He was one of eight children. None of them seemed too interested in having a new relative.

There was one uncle who did quite well. He owned a small chain of automotive parts stores and had a nice house with a swimming pool. He didn't associate too much with the others, including one of his sisters who had eight kids and lived in total poverty, but I loved them all.

I had fun at the hospital where my dad worked; I would go down and play with the stuff in the X-ray department, look at X-rays, help my dad make barium, develop films, and stuff like that. My sister Chris and I would have wheelchair races down the halls. I got to know all the doctors and nurses. It was fun. My dad had some weird X-rays of a man's head who had been shot, and it was completely separated at the crown, like it had been sawed in two. There was another one that was of a Coke bottle up a guy's anus; how it got there, nobody knows. Still another one was a film of car keys found in a man's stomach. Somehow, he'd managed to swallow the whole set; how or why? Your guess is as good as mine. They were neat to look at, though.

My dad also had this book of medical oddities that was really gross. It had a picture of this man who grew hair out of his tongue, just like it grows out of our heads. It also had a story in it about this girl and boy who were riding a horse together, back in the 1800s. They were shot with a gun that used ball and shot, and the bullet went into the boy, picked up sperm, and entered and impregnated the girl. They were supposed to be true stories. Anyway, I liked going down to the hospital and hanging out.

I was getting a pregnant belly fast. Since I was almost five months pregnant before I was sure I was pregnant, it popped out real big, real fast. The doctor told me I needed to pick a date to have the baby. Apparently, when you know you're going to have a C-section prior to birth, you get to pick a day, two weeks before your due date, and go into the hospital just like any scheduled surgery. He gave me the option of Friday, the 1st of August, or Monday, the 3rd, because he wasn't going to do it on a weekend. Being pregnant in August in Oklahoma was pretty miserable, so I took the sooner date.

As I waited for that date to arrive, Marvin and my dad decided to get a business together. They opened a little restaurant that was connected to a gas station truck stop out on the highway. All of us girls ended up working out there. Marvin seemed to like it, and Dad still worked at the hospital, so everyone seemed happy, Dad's house was only a mile from the restaurant. It was working out pretty good,

Marvin and I didn't have a bad relationship, but we didn't have a good one either; we just didn't have a relationship, really. He was so quiet and introverted, and I was talkative and bouncy. We just kind of survived together. I think he would have liked to have a better relationship with me but didn't know how, and I didn't know how, or really want one.

Once, he took me a hundred and fifty miles down to see my aunt Reta and uncle John, and he wasn't mean to me once! Although, there was that incident with the butcher knife and my friend Elzaree's throat, but he never did anything like that again. I'd already decided no man was ever going to brutalize me again, ever.

As I got closer to the time to have the baby, I thought a lot about Michael. It had been almost a year since I'd seen him. I was having nightmares about Albert standing over me with a butcher knife when I woke up, or jumping out from behind something, or just plain stalking me. I was still terrified of him, even though I had no contact with him for that entire time. I still couldn't believe Albert would let me walk away with my life, but I would never stop thinking of the baby he made me leave behind. I'm sure psychologically I was hoping to replace the loss I felt for him, but I thought about him every day. The thoughts of him were sad and brought on feelings of frustration, pain and anger at Albert, and of course at myself. The baggage I was loading up would break an elephant's back. It's hard to describe the excuses I made to myself and those around me about why I didn't have Michael with me. Oh, I had legitimate reasons, like no money, no one who really wanted to help me get him back, no stable environment. No judge would take Michael away from where he was and put him into a more dire place. I had no way to compete with the backing Albert had, and now I was an unmarried, pregnant eighteen-year-old. The truth was, I couldn't fight with Albert. I knew if I ever beat him in battle, I would pay with my life. Still, I often thought about Michael and wondered how he looked. Was he was talking, walking, and becoming his own person without me? I couldn't bear the memories I had of him screaming for me with outstretched arms every time I had to leave him with those people who didn't want me in his life. I was terrified of the hold this baby would give Marvin over me. At least when I had Michael, I went into it planning a future with Albert.

Now I was in a relationship with someone I didn't even know, and I wasn't in love with him, even though the situation at present was almost peaceful. I guess you could say I was living in a mild form of acceptance at the moment.

Don't get me wrong, I didn't hate Marvin; I just didn't love him. Our relationship was based on circumstance. He let me spend time with my aunt Kari Jo, and he got along great with my dad, but who didn't?

The day before I was to deliver the baby, my aunt Kari and I went swimming together. Her husband was a strange caricature. He was a typical Oklahoma male: he loved fast cars, CB radios, and guns, and he flaunted all three. Kari always had to ask him if she could go with me. Sometimes he didn't care, and sometimes he would argue with her about what she did. He wasn't brutal; just bullish. He'd gotten a small insurance policy when his mother died, and with it he purchased himself a brand new, bright red Firebird and a new motorcycle. He was a male chauvinist to the hilt.

The way his mother had died was very tragic. I'd met her on one of my escapes from Albert a year and a half earlier. She was a very little woman, and everyone called her Tiny. I had Tiny babysit Michael for me one night when I went to the movies with Kari Jo and Mike, Tiny's son. The two weren't married yet, just dating. Tiny was a nice lady who also had a daughter named Michelle. She was a big girl, but very nice.

Tiny worked at a little store in Quapaw, Oklahoma. This little store also had a post office in it, typical of a small town. She was the clerk at the store and the post office both. Everyone in town knew her and stopped into the store at one time or another.

One day, her daughter Michelle stopped into the store on her way home for lunch from school. They had a typical teenager-mother argument. Michelle went on home to lunch. A little while later, someone called the house, looking for Tiny. This lady was a customer and had stopped by the store for something or other. The store was still open, but Tiny was nowhere to be found. Michelle told the customer Tiny was at the store when she'd stopped by before lunch. Tiny definitely wasn't at home. The police were eventually called.

Mike, Kari Jo and the family were all notified that Tiny was missing. The police, neighbors and family all got together at the store to discuss what may have happened to her, or where she may be. During this time, these people moved freely and unchecked through the store, destroying any evidence of a crime. Even when evidence was found, like a few drops of blood behind the register and her purse that had been left behind, it had been walked on and touched by more than one person.

The damage was done at the store, and valuable evidence was already lost. The family, their friends and townspeople formed search parties, which were based out at Tiny's farm five miles from town. With so many people involved, food needed to be provided, so Kari and Mike drove to town to get stuff for sandwiches for everyone. On their way to town, they were hit by a drunken woman and they both ended up in the hospital (when it rains, it pours). They weren't seriously injured and were released the next day. Meanwhile, Tiny was still missing, and the search continued.

Now, in this part of the country, there are a million places to hide a body. There are abandoned mine shafts that go down more than a hundred feet and are so covered by undergrowth, you may never even know they're there unless you fall in one. Half of the countryside was pits and holes; the other half was abandoned buildings or lush, overgrown woods and waterways. A million places to hide a body.

On the second or third day of her disappearance, one of the search parties, which included some of Mike's closest friends, went to a place called blue hole pond. One of the boys walked around the edge of the water and exclaimed to the guys with him that he could see something in the water. He bent down and moved the water around, trying to get a better view of whatever it was. As the water swirled around, Tiny's hairpiece floated to the surface, followed by her body, looking them directly in the face.

Her throat had been cut from ear to ear, and she'd been weighed down in the water by something tied to her feet. So much time had elapsed, her arms were in rigor mortis and had floated to the top before her. There was a rumor that when Tiny had been strapped down on the gurney, her arms flew up, taking the sheet with them, practically scaring the coroner and everyone else to death. I don't know if that's true or not.

It was a horribly gruesome crime, and everyone was under suspicion and questioned. Eventually, there was a grand jury investigation. There was so much speculation, and even more rumors about what had happened to her. Her family was all eventually cleared, after close inspection of all their "dirty laundry." Things were brought out and brought up, until at one point or another it made them all look a bit guilty. Unfortunately, in the end no one was ever charged with her murder. This isn't out of the ordinary in this part of the country. There's one county some of my other relatives live in that's had forty murders in as many years, and not one conviction. Everyone is related to everyone else or knows everyone else. Somehow, this is the way things are there. I shouldn't even tell you about Tiny's murder, as I know so little about it, but that's the way I remember it all happening.

I didn't like to go out to Tiny's farm after that happened, just because it held an air of mystery. It never felt the same because of her death, even though she didn't die there (or at least I don't think so), but it was weird anyway. Her husband remarried soon, "very soon", after her death.

Now that Kari Jo and Mike, Tiny's son, were married, she went out there quite often to see her in-laws or get something for Mike. So, sometimes I would go with her, but I never felt comfortable out there after that.

What made me think of Tiny is, the day before I was going into the hospital, Kari and I were swimming, and we were talking about Tiny. Not a very pleasant topic, but always interesting. I've always been fascinated by strange and unusual things.

Anyway, the day finally came; it was August 1st, 1975. Kari Jo came and took me to the hospital. I think Marvin went to work; I know he wasn't at the hospital with me.

My dad was working at the hospital that day, so he was there, and I knew all the nurses. They put me in a room and prepped me for surgery, then they put me out. When I woke up, I was back in the same room I was in when I went to sleep, but boy, I felt different. Kari was standing over me, asking me if I was all right and telling me I had a little girl. I wasn't nice to Kari at all, because my stomach hurt so bad, I actually cussed at her. That drunken doctor had cut my stomach open all the way from my belly button to my crotch, and it looked terrible. The cut was so crooked and wide; it was unbelievable.

When I had Michael, the doctor had done a bikini cut and it was barely noticeable; not this. I looked – and felt – like I had open heart surgery. I found out later the doctor had cut and tied my tubes and taken out my appendix, all without asking me. He'd just cut me wide open and gone in with a pit helmet. Oh well, what's done is done. Nothing I could do about it now.

They finally brought the baby in for me to hold. It was such a special moment. She was perfect, and she had the longest fingers and fingernails. I named her Katrina Michelle. That night, I slept so deep and was so contented.

They kept me in the hospital for a week. This was still back when they would keep a woman in the hospital until she was well enough to go home.

Once I got out and went home, the house was trashed. I had to get down on my hands and knees to vacuum the carpet, because my vacuum didn't have an end on it. There were no clean dishes, and no clean clothes. I couldn't even take the baby out of the carrier until I'd worked for hours with more than fifty stitches in my stomach. It was things like that that made me feel unfulfilled in my relationship with Marvin. I really couldn't believe he would leave the house like that for me to clean up.

After the initial shock of coming home, I didn't have time to do much but take care of the baby, and that was fine with me. We never talked or exchanged ideas. He worked, and I took care of the baby. Anyway, life went on, and the baby grew.

After the baby was born, I finally talked to my mom on the phone. She came to Oklahoma for a few days and saw me and the baby, which was interesting. I hadn't seen her for over a year, and it was ridiculous how nervous I always was around her. It's because she disapproves of me in every way and lets me know it constantly.

My dad and Marvin still had the little restaurant going pretty good, but my dad wasn't programmed for stability; it wasn't in his nature, and it wasn't in his future.

The restaurant was a funny place. There was this one lady named Mona who was so big, she couldn't get through the restaurant door. She had a terrible body odor, I'm sure from being heavy, but it was awful. The guys who hung around there were so unkind as to tell Mona to let them spray her off with the hose if she wouldn't take a bath. I honestly don't know where she could have taken a bath. If she couldn't get through a big door like at the restaurant, how was she supposed to get in a bathroom, let alone a tub? She hung out at the gas station all the time. I felt very sorry for her; she wore a terrible wig. I believe they figured she weighed around five hundred and fifty or more pounds.

We hired a sixteen-year-old girl to waitress at the little restaurant. Dad was having some problems at the hospital. He and a doctor or two were pretty good buddies, and they were into doing prescription speed. This was the good stuff, and the results of that were showing in his everyday life. Besides, like I said, he couldn't allow stability to enter his life, because it was alien to him; running was the way he knew best, and he did it so well. He'd run from every problem he'd ever been faced with, including me and my brother.

One night, my stepmother caught my dad and this young waitress together out in the backseat of his car behind the restaurant. Needless to say, things got ugly. He was already having trouble at the hospital, and now the speed problem.

The hospital had somehow found out he had a felony record and had lied about it to them, or something to that nature. So, my dad felt trapped and confined. Plus, just two days before the waitress incident, he'd had his fortieth birthday. So, true to his nature, the next day he was gone.

Dad just left my stepmother, the four girls, my brother, me, the restaurant, and everything else. Once he was gone, we found out all kinds of things about money he left behind, none of them good. He even took the car.

Now the restaurant was no more, and his wife lost the house. Juanita ended up taking the kids and going somewhere else. After all that, Marvin wanted to go back to Denver, so we did. We again packed up a small U-Haul trailer and towed it behind the car we'd gotten from my dad, then headed back to Denver.

I'd broken down and called my mom and told her we were moving back. Actually, she was glad to get to see the baby, who by now was exactly one year old. She'd had her first birthday one week before we left for Denver. My mother had even told us we could stay at their house for a couple of days until we found a place of our own. I was really looking forward to that. It was nice of her to offer, but our past history of confrontations made me very nervous. Luckily, the house would be empty for the first two days we were going to be there.

\

The trip to Denver was horrible. The baby was sick the whole way there, and Marvin and I both felt terrible. Neither one of us could keep our eyes open. We noticed there was an odor in the car, so we drove with the windows down almost the entire way, even though it was fairly cold outside. The last two hundred miles or so, Marvin and the baby slept the whole time while I drove. I had such a headache, I almost didn't make it.

When we got to my mom's, we literally crawled inside and passed out on the living room floor. I swear, we didn't move for over eight hours. The baby was in her car seat the whole time, and she never cried. When we woke up, we were so sick and had such headaches, I thought I was going to die; it was horrible. I realized when we got up that we'd been poisoned by carbon monoxide. We were lucky we didn't die. So it went from the time we got there; nothing went right. Marvin's past was catching up to him, and he couldn't get a good job because of it, which of course was a problem in itself. The real problem was us. We weren't meant to be together, and I was so unhappy.

We got a cheap apartment in a not-so-good neighborhood. The baby was exactly one-year-old now and getting a real personality. She was a joy and a pleasure, but as I said, Marvin and I grew farther apart each day.

One night, my mom, stepdad, and my youngest sister Darla came to see us before Christmas. They were leaving the next day to go to the stepfather's parents' home in Oklahoma City. Darla was the only kid still at home at the time. David was living on his own in Oklahoma somewhere, and Billy was at his other relatives' in Kansas for Christmas. Mom had found it in her heart to send my sister Shelley to the Home.

Yep, after everything I'd been through there, she still sent Shelley to the "Rebecca Home for Girls" in Corpus Christi, Texas. Shelley had been at the Home for almost a year by this time.

The next day, Mom and Pat left on their trip to Pat's mother's for Christmas. A week later when they returned, I got a call from my mom telling me Darla was also at the Home. I freaked out and asked when and why. She told me that when they left to come back to Denver, they'd given Darla a sedative and knocked her out. They then put her on a plane to Corpus Christi, "asleep." I couldn't believe it. She'd drugged and lied to Darla, and now she was at the Home. Good grief; she was only twelve. She'd finally gotten rid of all of us, and she truly didn't see the wrong in it. She always found a way to justify her actions.

Things deteriorated between me and Marvin, even worse. One night, we had a terrible fight. Well, I had a fight; he just sat there and said nothing. He wouldn't argue with me, and he wouldn't say anything; he acted like I wasn't there. I can't justify my actions entirely, but I packed what little bit of stuff I had, took the baby, and left him. My mother helped me, because of the baby. She brought her station wagon over and helped me fill it up, then took me to her house and gave me a place to stay. They still lived in the house I'd stayed in, when it was empty and up for sale. It was a very nice house, and I would have loved to feel comfortable enough in it to stay, but that wasn't going to happen.

The stepdad wasn't happy with the situation at all. He didn't want me, or my problems, at his house, or in his life. He wouldn't accept financial instability – no way, no how – and I reeked of it. His opinion of me, or anyone, is completely based on your financial situation. He and his non-emotional personality are a book waiting to be written, but that's another story. The results of it are prevalent in my life.

It wasn't long before I wasn't comfortable staying in my mom and Pat's house. They wanted my baby, but not me. My mom told me she and Pat wanted to raise Katrina. Both of them wanted me out of her life, and they told me so. When I was pregnant with Katrina back in Oklahoma, my mom sent me a 9 page, typed letter. She told me they wanted the baby and would give me something for it. Mom went on to say a baby needs two emotionally stable parents, not one very unstable one.

"We could give her a life you never could."

All true, but that isn't the kind of support I wanted from my mother. Katrina was the only child I would ever have; I couldn't have any more, ever. Remember, the doctor cut and tied my tubes after I had Katrina, without even asking me. My mom had already ruined five of her own, and I guess the fact that I had my only other child beaten out of my arms was my fault. I swear, she offered to buy her.

I forgot to mention my mom was still going to school. In fact, my mom went to school all my life. Now her major was psychology, and she used it all the time. One day, my mom casually told me she'd gone to Tucson and seen Michael. I was in shock. I couldn't believe it. I asked her question after question: how did he look? Was he talking? What was he like? When did she go? Why hadn't she told me?

Her answer was, "April, Albert is remarried now, and I met his new wife. She's a godsend. I just fell in love with her. Michael couldn't be in better hands!"

My brain went crazy! Michael couldn't be in better hands? Was
this woman sitting there telling me – her daughter, and Michael's mother
– that he was better off with a stranger than with me? I couldn't believe
she said that to me, even if she truly believed that. How could she so
casually say that to me?

Mom went on about how Albert had joined the Navy and was out
on a ship while she was there. She'd taken Michael and his new mommy
to a pizza place and taken pictures of him. She showed them to me. She
and his new mommy had a good old time talking bad about me to each
other. If you don't believe me, then get this: while I was gone to
Oklahoma, my mom called these two friends of mine, Elzaree and Linda,
over to her house for dinner one night. She sat them down and told them
I had mental problems and was a habitual liar, and not to believe
anything I said. For two hours, she talked bad about me to them. When I
got back to Denver, they both told me of the night they had dinner with
my mother, like it had been a spooky movie. They couldn't get over my
mom. They thought she was weird. She and the stepdad did other strange
things, too, like passing out "religious tracks" for Halloween instead of
candy. All the kids in the neighborhood talked about it.

Anyway, I was sitting there only hearing half of everything she
was saying, because my brain was racking itself, trying to figure out why
this woman hated me so much; a question I'd never be able to answer.

The reasons I couldn't stay with Mom and Pat were endless. So,
Katrina and I moved in with my friend Elzaree's mother. Elzaree didn't
live there, but I knew her mom, brother and sister were friends of mine.
We were all about the same age.

My mom threw a fit, and it probably wasn't the best environment, but I absolutely could not continue living with those people. The second day I was there, Marvin came over, yelling and screaming that he was going to bomb the whole block if I didn't come back to him. That was all I needed. I was still so fresh from fearing for my life from Albert, it brought up all the old terrors. Everyone always said, "God, you're jumpy," or "Why are you so nervous?" They didn't understand. Hopefully, they never would.

We called the police after one of his drive-by threats, and after that I never saw him again. He left town. Poor Marvin, I didn't know how to have an adult relationship, or an adult split up, and he didn't either. He was so mad and hurt, he didn't try to deal with me in a rational manner. I didn't even know at the time that people could split up and still have a relationship or be civil to each other.

When he saw the police were going to get involved, it scared him. With his past problems with the law and his present situation of leaving the state of Wisconsin without permission, he didn't have a choice. He didn't have any reason to be in Denver if he wasn't with me, so he left. He knew what I'd been through with Albert and Michael, and gratefully he didn't put me through that again. I regret to this day the way I handled the situation. It wasn't fair to him. Anyway, he was gone, and I was on my own with Katrina. She was one-year-old now, and just walking and getting into everything. She was so smart, it was spooky.

The situation at the house I was staying at wasn't good for any of us. Pauline, Elzaree's mom, was a sweet lady, and she was very kind to let me invade her house like I did, but I wasn't the only invader she had. Her house was the house all the teenagers in the neighborhood hung out at. We were free there; she didn't have control of what went on at her house. She was a divorced mother of three teenagers, and she worked. We took advantage of her lack of control. She tried to control us when she was there, but to no avail. Her son Duncan and daughter Karen smoked pot, grew pot, and sold pot in the house. Loud music played all day, and kids came and went constantly. It was the house in the neighborhood all the parents hated, talked about and told their children to stay away from.

Pauline got an offer to accompany a male friend of hers to travel with him in his semi-truck across country, and she took it. She would go in the truck for a week or two at a time, and we'd party while she was gone (my mom watched Katrina when I was doing all this partying, by the way). Don't get me wrong; these were good kids, and they had good values. They just did what most kids were doing in 1976. Don't get me wrong about Pauline either. She was a good mom and tried as best she could; we were the ones who took advantage of her. She didn't know all the stuff we did when she wasn't there.

I idolized the kids from this neighborhood. They'd all known each other all their lives, and it was a large group. There were two rock bands formed from these neighbors, and all their lives were intertwined. All the kids from the area had some form of stability. They'd all had the same parents throughout their lives, or at least until late in life, or they still had contact with their parents. They'd all lived in the same houses since childhood and had the same friends since kindergarten. All their houses were nice, and some of them had some money. It was so foreign to me, so desirable. I was in awe of them. It was what I'd dreamed of all my life: a sense of stability.

\

Of course, they had their problems. too, but to my dysfunctional eye it was utopia. They talked about things they'd done together in their past, something I'd never known. To this day, I still couldn't tell you what school I went to in what state or in what year. Or even what one of my teachers' names had been.

Everything revolved around the bands; we would either go watch them practice, go to a party they were playing at, or just hang out with them. All of us smoked pot, drank, smoked cigarettes and listened to music. It was 1976, and I was going to be twenty years old.

One of the kids we hung out with was the bass player from one of the bands. His name was Kevin O'Brien. He was younger than me by almost four years, which doesn't sound bad until you realize I was twenty with two kids, and he was sixteen and in the tenth grade. He didn't look or act sixteen. He had a full beard and could walk into any liquor store or bar and not be carded. He lived three or four houses from Pauline's house and was over there all the time. He'd had a job since he was fourteen. His parents were divorced, but he went to his dad's house almost every weekend. He was liked the most by all the parents in the neighborhood, he was the kindest, most honest person I'd ever met, and he was good looking.

Actually, I'd met Kevin two years earlier, when he was 14. He'd come over to our apartment in Denver to buy something from Marvin. He even knew my little brother David. I noticed Kevin right away. Other guys in the same group of people would put the moves on me, but I tried to tell myself I didn't want to be with anyone, EVER. The reality was, I didn't know anything about myself. I'd never been on my own since I was old enough to be with anyone. Right or wrong, I needed to be wanted by a man. I didn't really want to be alone. I guess I wanted what all uneducated, low self-esteemed girls wanted: I wanted to be loved, protected, and desired, to belong to someone. I thought it was all going to come from a man, but what I really wanted was a mother, father and unconditional love from both of them. I wanted support, acceptance and a solid family structure to start life on my own from. I wanted someone to tell me I had worth, ability and value. Of course, I had none of these things, and I wouldn't know for years these were the things I needed. So, I looked for a man who had these qualities. I guess I saw them in Kevin right from the start. Sixteen years old or not, I was drawn to him immediately. The weirdest thing is, Kevin and I started out as friends, not as lovers. He was just so nice to everyone. He was so polite, kind, generous, self-assured, honest and a true friend to all. I truly don't believe you could find anyone who would have a bad word to say about Kevin, and he was wonderful with Katrina. Of all of the people who came and went from Pauline's house, Kevin was the one Katrina liked the best. Every time he'd come over, she would toddle up to him, smile and ask to be picked up by him. Never once was he put off by her need for his attention. He would pick her up, smile at her, and carry her around with him. If she needed her diaper changed, he didn't break stride as he grabbed one and helped do what had to be done. The same went for if she needed a bottle or anything else. When we all went places together, he never acted as if she was a burden to bring along; just the opposite: he really seemed to enjoy her. That in itself endeared him to me.

Of course, everyone who met Katrina couldn't help loving her. She was the sweetest little baby, and so smart. Katrina never talked baby talk. From 13 months old, she could say, "Mommy, can I have some water?", and by 14 months she was amazing people with her vocabulary, communication skills, and physical beauty.

One Saturday, Kevin and I ended up going to a Fleetwood Mac concert together, and we were together from then on. Kevin started hanging out at Pauline's house every free minute he had.

I was wearing out my welcome at Pauline's. I couldn't blame her; she had her hands full with her own kids and their problems. She couldn't take on me and a baby.

One day, Kevin and I walked in and Pauline was on the phone. She was talking to Kevin's mother and didn't see us.

I heard her say, "Well, April says she can't get pregnant again, but you can take everything April says with a grain of salt."

I couldn't believe it. I hadn't even met his mother yet, and she was already getting the local gossip about me...great. I can't blame them; I mean, I did have a pretty sordid past. At that time, Kevin was just having his seventeenth birthday. So, I understand why they were concerned, but I also realized I needed to move out of Pauline's.

I went to my mom and broke down and asked her to help me, and to my surprise she did. They got me into an apartment and offered to help me pay the rent for a few months. I went back to work at Wyatt's Cafeteria, the place I'd worked two and a half years earlier, and where I'd met Roger-Marvin.

Things were getting better for me. Kevin started staying over at the apartment at night, even though his mother would call at 3 o'clock in the morning and say, "Don't you think it's time for Kevin to come home now? He has school tomorrow." We were happy when we were together.

\

My mother never knew he lived at my apartment. If she came over, he would hide in the closet until she was gone. She never questioned how I was able to pay the rent on what I made at Wyatt's. I only took their financial help for the first two months. My mother's help, like her love, was always conditional. A few years later, I would tell her Kevin lived with me back then.

Mom got a shocked look on her face, thought about it for a minute or two, and then said, "I knew that!"

Believe me, she never knew, or I would have heard about it.

Can the color of spots really change?

Kevin stopped going home at night as soon as school was out

for the year. He got a job cooking at a nice restaurant, which was what

he'd been doing for 4 years already, and Katrina and I started depending

on him. He loved her, and he loved me. He started telling me so on a

regular basis. I couldn't make the same commitment to him, though. I

was still in the process of telling myself I would never remarry or commit

to another man, and I told him so.

Every time he told me he loved me, I would say, "Don't say that

so much," then he would say, " I can't help it, April, I do love you."

Kevin was the sweetest and most considerate guy I'd ever met,

but I was so skeptical of love, and I had a hard time believing in it. I just

knew I was happy when I was with him,

\

I was over at my mother's one day, and I told Kevin to come over so he could meet my mom and stepdad. When he rang the doorbell, my stepdad was the one who went to the door and opened it.

Kevin was standing there and said, "Hi, is April here?"

Pat, my stepdad, without saying a word slammed the door so hard in his face that the door came off its hinges. I got the baby and left with Kevin. I don't know why he was so mean to Kevin, but I do know his anger wasn't directed only at Kevin.

I never felt any physical pain from Pat, but I've felt the emotional pain he seems to enjoy dishing out. It's almost like psychological sadism. The truly sad thing is that I wanted and needed a father so badly, I could have loved him completely, but it wasn't to be. He must have had a terrible childhood, because it seemed like he wanted to get back at somebody – and it wasn't just me, it was my whole family.

Usually, Pat's anger took other forms. He had his doctor's office in the basement of their house. He treated people down there, and I remember a few times some weird things would take place down there; all I can say is, those things are their business, not mine. There were things that were my business, but they acted like they weren't.

I hated it down there. I swear, his instruments were filthy. All my brothers and sisters have told ghost stories about having to have him treat us down there.

One day, Katrina and I were over at their house. They had a little miniature Doberman Pincher. It had been rescued from some guy who had abused it, and it wasn't a people dog. Katrina was playing in the dining room, while we were talking in the kitchen. All of a sudden, I heard her scream, so I went running in there. She was under the dining room table, and when I pulled her out, I was horrified at what I saw. Her lip had been ripped open by the dog. It just hung there, bleeding profusely. I turned around screaming, and mom and Pat were standing there. Pat grabbed her out of my arms and rushed downstairs with her. Mom followed him, and she shut and locked the door on me! I stood outside the downstairs door, crying and pounding on it. Mom yelled up at me to stop it. She said I was only making her cry harder. She wasn't going to let me in. So, Pat took it upon himself to sew up her lip. If I'd been mean or really thought about it at the time, I could have sued him for that. They were so like that. CONTROL, CONTROL, always, in every situation! Katrina did heal, but she always bore a scar from that.

I do have to say, though, that Pat did seem to accept Katrina's innocence and unconditional love. He didn't seem to harbor the same dislike towards her that he did to the rest of us, but then no one who met her could help falling in love with her. She was fascinating. She could talk at one-year-old and read by herself at three, and that's not an exaggeration. She fascinated all the people who met her.

They used to tell me, "April, make her say something," because it was fascinating to see a one-year-old say "Molybdenum". She never said, "Mommy, give me a dink of wa-wa"; from the start, it was, "Mommy, give me a drink of water." I truly believe some of her intelligence came from the fact that she was a C-section baby; just my opinion.

At two years old, she could recite word for word the whole story of Peter Rabbit with such emotion and animation that she would astound people.

Some of the things I'll admit to you I'm ashamed of or regret, but fact is fact, and in the end I hope you remember more of the good than the bad.

On Kevin's seventeenth birthday, he had a shot glass almost full of Jack Daniels sitting on the coffee table over at Pauline's. Katrina toddled up to it, picked it up and swallowed it, then she set the shot glass down, burped, let out a big sigh, and toddled off like it was nothing. We all, of course, freaked out, but I promise you, that was the last time Kevin was ever irresponsible in front of Katrina. They bonded immediately, and he was wonderful to her.

One time, a whole bunch of us were sitting around in a circle up in Duncan's room, and Katrina walked in. We were all laughing about something. She stood in the middle of this circle of people, looked at all of us, held her belly, and started laughing so hard (she was always very animated). We all busted up, it was so cute. Then she walked out of the room. A minute later, she walked back in, looked at everybody and did it again, holding her belly and laughing loudly. We all busted up again. It was hilarious. Then she walked out of the room again. I told everybody after she left that if she back came in and did it again, not to laugh and see what she did. Sure enough, a minute later here she comes. She stood in the middle of the circle, looked at everyone, grabbed her belly, bent over and started laughing. Everyone in the room was spitting and sputtering, trying not to laugh. Behind her back, I motioned to everyone not to laugh. Katrina quit laughing and stood up straight, then looked at everyone again with her head cocked to the side. You could see the confusion on her sweet face. She grabbed her belly, bent in half and gave us an extremely hardy laugh. As she did, she looked at all of us with a bewildered look and stopped laughing. Then she put her hands on her hips and went, "Ha-Ha-Ha-Ha-Ha!" None of us could hold it in any longer. We all busted up, and she giggled for five minutes. She was special from the moment she was born.

Kevin got a job cooking at the "White Fence Farm" restaurant. He was seventeen, and he was supporting both me and Katrina. I worked, too, but it didn't support us. Over a two-year period, he asked me to marry him at least 200 times. I always said no, because I was afraid to get married again.

Finally, one day I shocked him and said, "Why not."

We'd been living together for two years now. Katrina loved him more than life itself, and he loved her as if she were his own. In his mind, she was his. Even though I was afraid of it not lasting, I was happy. I hadn't heard from Marvin, and I really didn't think of him very much, except to worry that he would step in and take her from me somehow, someday.

As you can imagine, Katrina was calling Kevin "Daddy" all the time. Happiness had eluded me for so long. How could I tell her at that tiny age that the sweet, nice man she loved and laughed with and was so happy to have in her life wasn't her daddy? Stupid? Maybe. Wrong? Probably. But I couldn't help it.

Why couldn't it have been him? Why can one act of sex create something so precious, yet mean nothing in the life of that creation? Not that Marvin hated me or Katrina, not at all. Unfortunately for him, I didn't love him. With that one lack of emotion, it can affect the life of someone else forever. Wrong or right, once I said yes to Kevin, I never looked back.

\

As I said before, Kevin and I had been living together for more than two years before we finally decided to marry. They had been wonderful years. He never wavered in his devotion to me, and he carried all the baggage I had with seemingly no effort. In fact, I think he needed to be able to do that for me, and he doted over our now three-year-old, long haired beauty. What a little lady Katrina was turning into. She had grace, even at that young age. Kevin was at least as proud of her as I was.

During this time, we'd both met and become a part of each other's families, even though the news of our legal union wasn't a cause for true celebration from either of our parents. His family thought of my past and his future; my mother, on the other hand, never had a good thought about me. She only saw faults, flaws and negativity. Oh, she loved Kevin; it was me she disapproved of. She even told me once that if we ever broke up, she would take Kevin's side, no matter what the reason.

I wouldn't understand her feelings towards me for many years to come, but the truth is, my mother was very envious of me. She truly resented me, because I was the cause of ruin in her life. I was the first; the rest were incidental. Mom didn't dislike me on purpose; she didn't even realize she didn't like me, and to this day she'll deny that those were her feelings towards me, but they were her feelings. A sad fact is, I don't think she does dislike me now, but the past is a hard thing to overcome or let go of, and even harder to forget. I love my mother; I always have.

Anyway, my brothers and sisters were overjoyed when they heard we were getting married. They loved Kevin; everyone who met him did.

His two sisters, Denice and Pam, on the other hand, didn't feel the same about me (not at first anyway). I remember one time at his mother's house, they took me into the bathroom and actually threatened me with bodily harm if I ever hurt Kevin. I still loved them. I loved being part of a real family. They spent every holiday together. His mother made me the neatest cakes for my birthdays, and like everyone who met her, they couldn't help loving Katrina. To my face, they acted like I was completely accepted by them; however, I'm sure they consistently questioned Kevin's choice in a wife. Their concerns were real, I suppose: the fact that I couldn't have children; I had a sordid past and other men's children, all the things that would send every caring parent into a rash of questions. Lucky for me, there was no deterring him (thank God). Kevin was in love, and I'd found something every woman in the world was looking for: true, unconditional love.

So, with no financial help from either of our families, we planned our little wedding on our own. Financially, we were never secure at that young age. That was the biggest concern of Kevin's father. True love wouldn't put food on the table, and he never let us forget it. Richard O'Brien (Kevin's dad) was a very successful man. His mom and dad were divorced, and Dick was remarried, but he remained a big part of his children's lives, or at least he thought he did. He saw them on Christmas Eve and approximately 4 or 5 times a year other than that one holiday. He had a nice home, horses, and stuff I'd only seen in movies prior to meeting him.

Pat (my stepdad) had way more money than Dick did, but he didn't spend it or live like it. Every time we went out to Dick's house, he had to bring up money and the fact that we didn't have any.

He even said to Kevin once, "Are you going to sling burgers for the rest of your life?"

Neither of these men could fathom happiness without money, and yes, it is nice to have, and yes, it makes life much easier, but it isn't the only thing in life. Of course, neither of them was going to offer up any of theirs. I'm not saying they should have, but I don't think it should have been the only thing to judge Kevin and me by. In my opinion, if his dad was so consumed by his financial future, maybe he should have offered to help with a college education, or maybe a job at his company. He gave his new wife's sons jobs there, but he never offered Kevin one…wow.

I just watched some bitterness flow from me. It didn't seem to bother Kevin, though. He went to work every day and came home with a smile on his face each night when he saw me and Katrina waiting for him. I did work, too, but not at anything that would save us financially.

As soon as I was 21, I started cocktailing. That really made the parents proud of us, but Kevin was as proud of me as if I were the First Lady, and Katrina didn't care if we plucked chickens for a living. All she knew was that we loved her, and she loved us. She was only three, but gosh she was smart.

Our Wedding

So, on May 29, 1979, Kevin Roy O'Brien (a whopping 2 months after his 19th birthday) and April Ma-Lynn Martin (22 years old) gathered (more friends than family) at an inn in Empire, Colorado, to exchange marriage vows. It was beautiful! Empire sits in the mountains, about 40 miles from Denver. We were married out on the skeet shoot deck overlooking a lake, with the mountains behind us. Katrina stood between us during our vows.

At one point, she tugged on my dress and said, "Mommy, I'm cold."

My mom grabbed her and sat her down by her. It was simple, but beautiful. After the legalities were over, our band played and Kevin sang.

I was kidnapped by Paul, Lee and Allen, and everyone had to give some money to get me back. I believe they came up with a little over two hundred dollars when it was done; that was a lot of money from our friends back then. Allen took all the pictures and later gave us our wedding album as a gift. Kevin's dad gave us a check for $500; that was a fortune to us at that time. I have a picture of me when I opened it, and my eyes were the size of dinner plates. It was a wonderful day. The band played, and everyone danced. Even our parents, who turned up their noses at every choice we made, had a good time.

Mom and Pat took Katrina home with them, and we were off on our own. We stayed the night in Estes Park and rented horses the next day; we got lost up in the national forest on those horses. It was great. We had four of the most wonderful days together.

When we got back, we learned one of our very good friends (one of the guys at the wedding) had run his car into a telephone pole and died. It was the first loss we shared together, but there would be so many more to come. Less than a year later, we would lose another of our good friends to a car accident: Allen, the guy who had taken our pictures at the wedding and had given us the photo album as a gift. A new Porsche and a mountain would be his fate, and unfortunately he would take another friend with him, leaving Heather, his 9-year-old daughter, without a father. In fact, we had way more than our share of losses from that whole area around Kevin's mom's house.

The more I think about it, I'm remembering just how many weird incidents did take place in that area. The guy next door to his mom (I believe) shot himself in the head. On the other side of her, a few houses away, a police officer came home from work one day to find a teenager from the neighborhood burgling his house. Somehow, he chased him out the upstairs window onto the sidewalk and shot him, and he died there. Then down the street, a girlfriend of ours was killed in a motorcycle wreck when she was 17, and another lady a couple houses from Pauline's cut her wrists and died. Then her son (our friend) and some other kids from the neighborhood were at the house right next door to Pauline's one evening; they were playing with a gun, and one of them was shot and killed. Another one of the kids from this same group, unfortunately, died of AIDS. Another very promising guy from the group went diving at Decker's, broke his neck, and is a quadriplegic now. These are just some of the tragedies that occurred in this neighborhood, and that's not counting any of the losses we endured in our own families.

So much more has happened in my life. Never a dull moment where I'm concerned, but that's another book. This one is done for the time being (or I'll never get it out), but the next one is as good as the first. So many things I want to tell you. Like the time the guy chased me down the interstate with a gun, or the time a Cadillac full of men followed the city bus I got on all the way to my stop and chased me into some people's apartment. Good times, bad times, but never boring. It's just not in my nature to live a boring life.

I won't make you wait for some answers I know you must be asking. Yes, I now know my son Michael. I wish I could tell you we have no problems between us, but that's not true. We have the past between us, and it brings its own problems. He's healthy and a wonderful person, and he's just as good looking as his father.

Kevin and I are still married. We just celebrated our 26th anniversary, and they've been wonderful years, to be sure. Even with all the things that seem to follow me, at least he's been there with me through all of them.

My mother is still married to the doctor, but we don't talk anymore. Our lives have led us down different paths that don't seem to cross anymore.

I've now written five books, this being one of them, and I feel I'm not only a survivor, but a success, too. Kevin, Katrina, and I have had three of the best restaurants in the Denver area. We've had numerous articles written about us and our restaurants, and we're proud of what we've accomplished together.

I also taught myself to paint, and I've painted many landscapes, one of which is on the cover of, *"It Doesn't Get Dark until Midnight"* Another of my paintings graces the cover of this book. I did not paint the cover of "ENTER (at your own risk)" but they are all great stories.

I try to overcome the hardships and enjoy the ride. I've been able to experience every emotion humanly possible, including many that hurt intensely.

To those of you who took the time to read this, I thank you. A burden shared is a burden halved! The one thing I know about myself is that I'm a walking contradiction. I've had some of the worst things in the world happen to me, and you've only read about the first 20 years of my life, but I've also experienced so many good things. I've lived a quarter of a century since the end of this book, so it will take at least one more book to catch you up – but believe me, it's not boring. In fact, my life has and always will be tumultuous. I've come to accept that fact. I don't know why my life has been like this, but I get up every morning with the wonder of a new day, and I try to prepare for what may come. I try not to dwell on the bad. Some days it works, and some days it doesn't.

One day after the ultimate loss a person can experience, the loss of a child, I said to Kevin, "Why is there so much loss in my life, why me?"

Kevin held my face in his hands, lifted my face to his and said, "April, some people are never lucky enough in their entire lives to have anything worth losing. We were so fortunate to have this child in our lives. Would we give up one moment we had, or one memory we shared? No. We would gladly relive each moment given us." **I**'ve come to realize Kevin is right. I wouldn't be who I am today if not for all the yesterdays. This life I've lived, with all its twists and curves, has also had beauty and wonder, serenity and peace. I've known true love, both given and accepted, which is another thing not everyone will know in their lives. I've survived each event in my life with the determination of learning something from it. There must be a reason for all of this. Kevin and I have been together almost 40 years now. I love him more today that the day I met him.

So, I live each day, always looking for the next adventure or change that's inevitable. Longing for those I've lost but trying to live this short, extraordinary life to the fullest, learning and growing. While I'm here, I leave my mark on all I touch, hoping in the end a few of those lives that brushed by mine were changed for the better by the faint breeze I left behind. That ever so often, someone may say fondly, "April was here."

Not quite the end!

Watch for part two

April O'Brien

+Something worth losing

Kevin, oh Kevin, look what we've lost,

more than all words can explain.

How do we survive it? How do we go on?

Can mere mortals survive this much pain?

If we had the power to know what would come, would we do it all over

again?

The answer is simple; of course we would, dear, great losses are lessons,

and without them we've nothing to gain.

If we hadn't known her, been part of her life, the emptiness would still be

the same.

Kissing her cheek and watching her smile gave us so many wonderful

years.

Remember that summer when she turned 16

and it hit us that she had grown up?

We knew then that she was on loan to us to love.

We saw her wings flutter and lift her above us, when she got in that car

all alone.

She drove off toward happiness, we couldn't deny her and oh, how her

happiness shone.

Her first taste of freedom, we relished it with her, we wouldn't have

missed that for sure.

Sweet memories she gave us, memories we keep, she's with us each

moment we're here.

And until were together, we'll mention her name, and dream of her each

night when we sleep.

Katrina my love

First thing every morning my mind flows to you.

Then reality hits me, your time here is through.

No changing the weather, no mountain to move.

What reason for living, if I'm not living for you?

The mail came today, a letter for you.

I wanted to run up the street yelling!

  "She was here! See, it's true"

Your pictures tell stories that I wish people knew.

I just can't accept that your time here is through.

One day I pretended, you were asleep in your bed.

I screamed out your name, "Katrina, get up sleepy head."

I wanted so badly for you to have said, "Ten more minutes mom",

 but I got silence instead.

The sun still rises each morning, but its glow is gone.

Colors have lost their vibrancy, and we don't know how to go on.

I must find completely new reasons to do almost everything,

when just a short time ago "you" were my reason for living.

I'm so thankful for Kevin, he strengthens my will,

but the emptiness I'm feeling, he just cannot fill.

Both of our hearts are broken, our lives are ever changed,

but if we could do it all over again, we would never complain.

You were not just my daughter, you were my best friend.

Twenty five years here is not long enough,

it was just the beginning; it should not be the end.

People say that you are in a better place; I hope that is true.

All that I'm sure of is that your time here is through.

43271638R00223

Made in the USA
Lexington, KY
27 June 2019